Astrology and the Modern Psyche

DANE RUDHYAR was born in Paris in 1895 and has lived in America since 1917. He has been called a modern "Renaissance Man" because of his ability to express himself with exceptional vigor in many fields — music, painting, poetry, philosophy, psychology, and astrology. He has been writing on astrology since the 1930's, at which time he began to reformulate astrological traditions into modern forms and to develop astrology as a symbolic language that has the potential to bring individuals in tune with cosmic cycles and to foster self-awareness. In his many books, from a modern psychological perspective, he has clarified the basic principles underlying a constructive use of birth-charts. Always decades ahead of his time in all his innovations, Rudhyar during the 1960's and 1970's has been widely recognized as one of the most creative men of his generation, as well as the foremost pioneer of a holistic, psychologically-oriented, person-centered astrology.

Astrology and the Modern Psyche

An Astrologer Looks at Depth Psychology

by Dane Rudhyar

CRCS PUBLICATIONS
Asbill Court Building
111 G Street, Suite 29
Davis, California 95616

FIRST EDITION
INTERNATIONAL STANDARD BOOK NUMBER: 0-916360-05-9
LIBRARY OF CONGRESS CATALOG CARD NUMBER: 76-21583

Published simultaneously in the United States and Canada by
CRCS Publications.

Distributed in the United States by
CRCS Publications

Distributed in the Commonwealth and Europe by
L. N. Fowler & Co., Ltd.

Cover Design: Collage by Stephen Kaltenbach
Text Design: Kathleen Arroyo & Joan Case

Contents

★   ★   ★   ★   ★

Foreword

My interest in depth-psychology began in the Spring, 1932, when I was given a copy of *The Secret of the Golden Flower,* a treatise on Chinese esoteric doctrines with a commentary by Richard Wilhelm and Carl Jung. I was deeply impressed and soon after, I wrote a circular entitled *Harmonic Psychology** marking the beginning of my work in astropsychology, or as I called it much later, Humanistic Astrology. I had been studying astrology since 1920 and had begun to take a more philosophical and creative approach to it after reading some of Mark Edmund Jones' early mimeographed courses. At about the same time, I became enthused by the work of Ian Smuts, *Holism and Evolution,* which provided me with a central concept which at the time was entirely new — the concept of holism.

In 1933, I had the opportunity to read three of the four books of Jung that had been translated into English, and I became further convinced of the possibility of integrating astrology and depth-psychology. In that year, the first magazine promoting a popular solar type of astrology, *American Astrology,* was launched by Paul Clancy who, on hearing of my idea, offered to publish anything I would write in a monthly section that would be devoted to Psychological Astrology.

When Grant Lewi became editor of *Horoscope* magazine, he asked me to write articles as well. After Clancy declined to renew the exclusive clause in our agreement, I began to write two articles monthly for *Horoscope,* one of a shorter and more inspirational character; and this went on for many years.

In 1942 in New York, I met the associate editor of a now long discontinued magazine, *World Astrology.* She was eager to have articles from me and for several years I also wrote two articles monthly for that magazine. One series, printed under the pen name Daniel Morison, dealt with personalities and events of the day. In the other series, under my own name, I sought to popularize the ideas of some of the leaders in depth-psychology with whose works I was well acquainted, and to show how the basic psychological doctrines these men were promoting could be related to the character of their birth-charts.

---

* Much of this original circular has been reprinted in the Epilogue of my book, *The Astrology of Personality.*

It is this second series on depth-psychology and astrology which forms the larger part of this present volume. In the last section, several articles published in *Horoscope* after World War II have been added, as they refer to significant and related psychological issues. All these articles have been carefully edited and revised under my supervision by my friend and assistant, Leyla Rael, whose mind warmly resonates to the ideas and the world-view I have tried to promote during so many years. I am extremely grateful to her for her efficient collaboration. My thanks go also to Stephen Arroyo of CRCS Publications, whose idea it was initially to gather this material in an up-dated form. I might add here that the charts in this book have been recalculated with Campanus houses, as this is the house system which I have used during the last years, for reasons explained in the first part of my book, *The Astrological Houses: The Spectrum of Individual Experience* (Doubleday, N. Y., 1973).

As it now stands, the material contained in this volume presents, I believe, many valuable and perhaps novel vistas to both the open-minded person interested in psychology and the astrological student eager to gain a more complete understanding of the various aspects of a complex subject which has come to dominate so much of our contemporary lives. I hope and trust that it will help to bring deeper psychological insights to many people now attracted to the fascinating field of astrology, and as well, to suggest in a more precise and formalized manner to students of psychology the importance of studying the basic aspects of the personality of a psychologist if one is to fully understand the essential character and quality of his or her teachings.

Palo Alto, California
April, 1976

Part I

Depth Psychology and its Pioneers

1   *Freud & Depth Psychology*

A few decades ago, the word *psychology* was hardly heard except in discussions between philosophers, moralists, and students of religious techniques devised to purify and sanctify the lives of a relatively few individuals. Psychology was a matter of University study. Medical science paid but little attention to it. Mental troubles, hysteria, insanity — once attributed to "occult" causes of demoniac "possessions" — were mainly considered incurable diseases, and the individuals afflicted by them were branded as outcasts, and at times, as criminals. Sanity and rationality were seen as marks of the divine in man and as the individual was believed to have "free will" and to "own" his mind and feelings, to lose mental balance and self-control meant to more or less deliberately forego one's divine nature, becoming prey to animal or devilish forces. In most cases the insane were treated accordingly.

During the last century, ideas as to the nature of man, which had been unchallenged for ages, began to be sharply questioned. The materialistic philosophers of the German school questioned them on general grounds, seeking to prove that all the activities of the human soul and mind can be reduced to and explained as the products of bio-chemical, material processes. More specifically, psychological phenomena came under the scrutiny of the men whose task it was to heal the sick. Diseases on the borderline between the purely physical and the psychological — and particularly all forms of "hysteria" — had attracted the attention of investigators since the time of Anton Mesmer at the end of the eighteenth century. The series of varied attempts to cure these diseases eventually led to psychoanalysis and Sigmund Freud.

Since then, modern psychology has become divided into several branches: most basically, the "experimental psychology" of college laboratories along the line of Behaviorism and the study of primary phenomena of attention, reflex-action, association of ideas, etc. — and the various types of "psychotherapies" seeking to cure the diseases of the mind and inner life of man. What we shall mainly discuss are the kinds of psychotherapy which are not specifically occupied with the cure of acute forms of insanity, but whose basic aim is rather to bring the men and women of our chaotic age to a greater sense of health and sanity (psychological, moral, and mental) and a more vibrant realization of their inner powers. The types of disturbances which these psychotherapies attempt to cure is essentially produced by the maladjustment of individuals to their surroundings – to family, school, friends, society. They deal with the basic conflict between the individual and the collective, between the ego and all that is not the ego, thus, the "outer world."

Such a conflict is absolutely basic in human nature, and in human nature only. It is man's privilege to become individualized out of the herd, the tribe, the social-religious community in which he has been born. It is man's privilege to feel himself "separate" as an "I," an ego having unique characteristics. It is his privilege, and it is his tragic burden or responsibility. It makes of him a god, or a devil.

All psychotherapists, from Freud on, are essentially occupied with the ego – with the way the ego develops, matures or fails to mature, crystallizes along social patterns of acquiescence or rebellion, transforms itself by overcoming its limitations, and, in rare cases, becomes part of a larger spiritual integration. Each school of psychotherapists, however, takes a particular approach to the problems of the ego, and ordinarily emphasizes one type of disturbance at the expense of the others. This is so largely because the psychologist fails to grasp the entire human being as an *organic whole,* and especially because he has no way to directly picture to himself the structure of this whole.

Astrology steps in here; for, in the birth chart, the astrologer has a means to study the over-all pattern of a person's functions, faculties, and drives. He can study the blueprint of the total personality, as well as the general schedule of its unfoldment from birth on. He can therefore deal with the *whole person,* rather than with only one or two of the fundamental urges and activities contributing to the growth of the consciousness and the ego – or to their malformation and eventual destruction. However, the type of psychology featured by most astrologers and astrological text-books is, as a rule, quite unable to live up to these possibilities. It is a type of psychology still based on the works of Ptolemy and Aristotle – a "classical" type steeped in ancient religious and ethical concepts, and as yet little touched by the ferment of ideas which Freud and his successors let loose upon the modern world.

Freud is not a unique phenomenon. A basic correlation exists between the attitudes to life which were promoted and popularized by Darwin and by Freud. For in these two pioneers, we find the expression of a profound rebellion against the "classical" reliance upon the intellectual and rational factors in human nature based upon the explanations given by religious theology and eighteenth century rationalism to account for biological and psychological phenomena, for the genesis of natural species and of the individual egos of human beings. Whereas classical and religious psychologists believed in a God-given soul, and biologists in the separate creation of each species of life-entities by God, Darwin and Freud gave up the concept of such a creation "in the heights," and sought to picture a progressive, evolutionary unfoldment of species and egos "from the depth." Thus was born "depth psychology" — a psychology which daringly plunges into the subconscious depths of the human soul, an *evolutionary psychology* of the ego.

What Darwin and Freud sought to destroy was the so-called Platonic concept of a "spiritual" world of Ideas or Archetypes *prior to* the "physical" world of material organisms. These Archetypes, being direct "Emanations" from the Universal Mind and its Divine Hierarchies, were not considered to be "evolving." They were said to have been created complete and perfect. Evolution was to be found only in the material world: a slow attempt by physical (and psychological) organisms to ever more closely approximate the ideal patterns which constitute "Reality."

On the other hand, "classical" psychology is based on the assumption that man is a "divine soul" operating in a more or less close association with a material body and an earth-conditioned "personality." Every person is a "child of God"; or, in more philosophical terms, he is, first of all, a spiritual entity, whose essential structure and function are established as an Archetype *before* birth, and will be perpetuated after the death of the body. This spiritual entity is the "real" self; and to it belong the spiritual attributes of will, character, discrimination between good and evil, morality and rationality, and mental creativeness. These attributes are in constant conflict with the desires and passions of the earth-bound body and psyche.

During the Victorian Age, mankind, having found itself suddenly in possession of tremendous material powers, faced a generalized increase in the virulence of the conflict between spiritual attributes and personal desires for self-aggrandizement and self-gratification — especially as the power of the religious and social restraints of the past also was vanishing under the blows of intellectual criticism. The results were obvious: moral statements and high-sounding ideals were contradicted at every step by the "facts of life." Human beings tried increasingly to lead two lives at once. Neuroses, psychoses and cases of split-personality multiplied. The danger was becoming social as well as personal.

Something *had* to occur. Just as osteopathy and surgery had to develop at a time when occupational malformations and accidents multiplied with the spread of the machine age and of artificially confining office-jobs, so psychotherapy (the healing of the personal, earth-conditioned soul or "psyche") had to discover techniques which could alleviate the generalized state of mild insanity featured by the civilized and mechanized city-dweller of the post-Victorian Era. When a person, as a result of some deep inner conflict and fear, finds himself compelled to repeatedly perform actions, not only against his so-called "will," but without knowing he is performing them, classical psychology ceases to have any practical meaning. If I do not know who I am or what I do — then, for all practical purposes, the term "I" has lost its significance. The person under hypnosis is in such a condition; but so also is the man with a "compulsion neurosis" — only to a lesser degree. Classical psychology settled the issue by declaring the man "insane," the spiritual entity within him having "left the body."

However, when the borderline between sanity and insanity becomes crowded by millions of outwardly normal citizens, the problem cannot be dismissed so summarily. The problem of sanity and rationality — nay more, the meaning of will, of personality, of ego — has to be re-formulated. The formulation cannot be a *black-and-white* judgment on the basis of consciousness-or-nothing. It must admit gradations of *greys*: unconscious, subconscious, semi-conscious, part-time conscious ... perhaps consciousness of varying degrees of brilliancy and pervasive power; in some cases, consciousness gaining access to realms beyond the normal range of even "white light" — could we say ultra-violet consciousness?

Such a "scale" of consciousness suggests the existence of an evolutionary process; a process of growth from the roots up, an emerging from the depths. The individual "I," instead of being seen as an *a priori*, archetypal Self — as some "pattern of perfection" transcendent to organic life on earth — begins to be understood as the end-result of human living, as a victory to be won, as the result of a slow effort at integration and individualization (or "individuation"). And this effort may be abortive, as may birth. The "I"-consciousness may be born healthy, or it may emerge from the dark, unconscious depth of instinct malformed and twisted by frustrations and pressures of all sorts.

The emergence of ego out of instinct occurs through the years of childhood — it may even be conditioned by prenatal causes! The diseases of the will and the mind, and the "predisposition" to psychological shocks and moral-pathological breakdowns, must therefore be traceable to what occurred during the very early years of life. The psychiatrist should therefore go back to these beginnings of individual selfhood, just as the

Darwinian naturalist particularly studies those remnants of the fossilized past which show new forms of life emerging from older species. The naturalist and paleontologist seek their clues from fossils deeply embedded in ancient rocks brought to the surface of the earth by cataclysmic occurrences or by long ages of erosion. The depth-psychologist must also find his way down to the depths, to the earliest layers of childhood consciousness — or take advantage of psychological eruptions and cataclysmic crisis in the "soul's" growth which will bring to the surface long forgotten memories of shocks and frustrations.

Normally, however, *conscious* recollections of the mind already deformed by strain or fear can be of no real help to the psychologist eager to probe the contents of the area between unconscious instincts and the first glimmers of ego-consciousness. The ego resists this probing as much as a child would resist re-entering the womb that has conditioned its very structure. However, every morning as one awakens, he experiences anew this process of emergence of consciousness out of unconsciousness. At this "threshold phase" of mental activity, the type of conditions which prevailed in babyhood tend to be reproduced. We call these conditions "dreams." As we dream every morning, we are again babies struggling to emerge from the womb of instincts into the problems of ego-consciousness and ego-adaptation to our complex environment. Thus by learning to understand the world of dreams, we also become acquainted with the attempts which consciousness has made and is constantly making to assert itself and to deal with the power of instincts.

The instincts have power. They are life in action. Their power is what the psychologists call *libido* or psychic energy. As the ego finds its way in the world of family and society, it encounters conditions which challenge the expression of the libido. It tries to become adapted to these conditions, and in so doing, it often has to repress instinctual energy. As a result, conflicts are generated. Repeated conflicts and repressions cause tenseness, rigidity, and congestion in the growing structures of the consciousness. These are what the psychologists call "complexes," and these in turn condition the future adaptation of the ego to new experiences during adolescence and through youth. As it loses its spontaneity and flexibility, the ego becomes set, crystallized, and encumbered with defense-mechanisms — like a turtle with a shell — or develops one-sided aggressive attack mechanisms — like a tiger or rattlesnake. If confronted by a strong shock, the ego becomes the victim of its own unyielding mechanisms. Neuroses and psychoses develop, leading to pathological conditions and diseases.

In order to cure these disorders, the psychotherapist must find their original causes. He must "reduce" the ego crystallizations or "complexes" and set free the psychic energy which they have deviated and dammed. This is a kind of "soul surgery" or psycho-osteopathy; and this is what Freud attempted. Freudian psychoanalysis is essentially a *psycho-surgical technique*. It uses dream-analysis as a means to uncover hidden symptoms. It forces the ego back into the threshold state of emergent consciousness (child consciousness) and helps the person do what he failed to do in childhood.

Space here is not sufficient for a detailed study of the Freudian technique. I have only isolated some of the basic features of it, features most strikingly symbolized in Freud's birth-chart.* The chart graphically illustrates Freud's descent into the depths of the psyche — scalpel in hand! The scalpel is, of course, Mars, symbol of steel and cutting tools — Mars which is found at the very root of Freud's chart, and "moving backward." Generally speaking, such a retrograde planet represents a life-function which is turned inward. In the same way the surgeon cuts inward, Freud seeks to reach the deepest layer of the organism to free what has become twisted or congested, crystallized or festered.

When caught in the grip of a "complex," the libido turns destructive. When normal desires are frustrated, they become psychic abcesses causing auto-intoxication. Freud's retrograde Mars is at Libra 4°, at the point of the chart which represents the mother (and in some cases, the father). This Mars typifies the mother-complex, or Oedipus-complex, which is so basic in psycho-analysis. Libra is the Sign of emergent social consciousness — just as Aries symbolizes the emergent personal consciousness. And Mars alone in the lower hemisphere of the chart — pitting its power against that of all the other planets which surround the zenith — reveals a terrific strain within Freud's soul. Graphically, the planetary pattern is that of a down-pointing triangle — almost a drill!

The planets above the horizon are all within the square formed by Neptune-Jupiter in Pisces and Moon-Saturn in Gemini. And the Sun, at the center of the grouping, forms semi-squares to Jupiter and Saturn — quite a potentially stressful pattern. Saturn, in the house referring to introspection, confinement, retribution, or *karma* suggests that Freud indeed assumed a heavy burden. On the other hand, however, Saturn is on a degree symbolized by "bankruptcy" and the start of a new life of

---

* Another chart in use in Europe has recently been reproduced in America giving Scorpio rising. It remains to be conclusively seen which chart is correct.

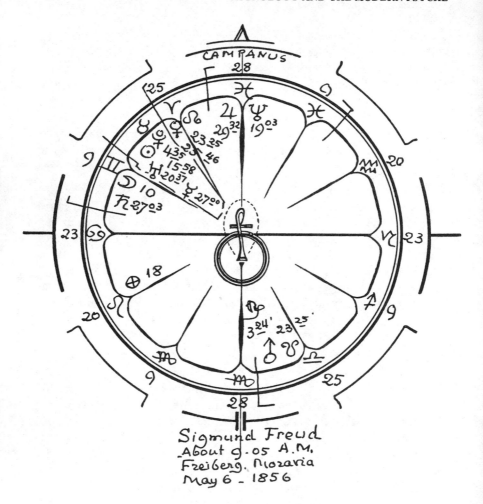

Sigmund Freud
About 9.05 A.M.
Freiberg, Moravia
May 6 - 1856

opportunity. Freud was of Jewish ancestry, and in a peculiar way, his birth-chart contains more than a hint of the deep pessimism and will to expiation of self-sacrifice which characterizes the Jewish spiritual tradition. His explorations into the depths of the human soul started a movement of thought which has yet to find its complete fulfillment. But his ideas also stirred a great deal of poisonous thought-substance, released many psychic "toxins," led to many abuses; and all this arousal of the depths became Freud's spiritual responsibility. Every great teacher must bear the burden of the misuse of his teachings by ignorant, unwise or greedy followers!

Freud opened a door. His disciples Carl Jung and Alfred Adler each gave to psychoanalysis a different direction. Adler — also of Jewish ancestry — represents essentially a tendency opposite to that of Freud (thus, complementing it). Jung, heir to the deepest spiritual tradition of Germanic Europe from Paracelsus to Goethe and to the free and integrative life of the Swiss people, presents a basic transformation of the implications and purposes of psycho-analysis.

Freud dealt with soul-surgery, Adler with the social welfare of maladjusted individuals. Jung is a modern type of "spiritual Guide"; his goal, the ever more inclusive integration of the personality — of the evolving human psyche.

2 *Alfred Adler & the Psychology of Individual Overcoming*

As I stated in the last chapter, modern psychology – or rather psychotherapy – has been deeply influenced in its beginnings by the concept of evolution developed by Darwin. Darwin's main preoccupation was to disprove the traditional idea that every species of life was an entirely distinct biological entity produced by a separate act of divine creation, and to show that the characteristics of these species were instead the results of a continuous process of evolution determined by the main principles of chance adaptation to environment and a survival of the fittest, or "natural selection." Darwin's method was to dig into the past, to study primitive men and fossils, to look for those forgotten periods of biological transition when the power of evolutionary adaptation introduced new organic departures in answer to external changes in the conditions of life on our globe.

Darwin essentially *looked back*. His method was analytical and "reductive" – that is, he sought to reduce present circumstances to prior causes, to show that what is today developed during some far distant yesterday. Sigmund Freud proceeded in the same way. He dug into the repressed and forgotten contents of the unconscious of his neurotic clients like a paleontologist or geologist digging into old rock strata. He analyzed the causes of neurosis by showing how the basic life-urge – the *libido* – had become challenged by adverse environmental conditions and had become destructive to the inner psychic evolution of the growing person. By "reducing" the destructive symptoms of the neurosis to their causes, the *now mature* consciousness is given a new chance to face the condition which produced the neurosis. The individual involved gains the opportunity to realize the fallacy or inappropriateness of the type of reaction he had in childhood, and he may thus eventually release the energy of the libido, which had given power to the neurotic emotions or behavior, into more constructive channels.

However, the Darwinian and Freudian approaches to the materials of their respective studies do not consider – or at least certainly do not feature – any *goal* to the evolutionary process. For Freud, there is a blind and fateful conflict between the instincts of the human individual and the traditional restraints or taboos of society, and there is really very little that can be done about it. His outlook, and that of Darwin as well, is indeed pessimistic and somber. All evolutionists, however, had not seen evolution in such a purposeless way; Lamarck, who antedated Darwin, had given a great importance to the creative drive within every life-species — and the realization that the entire evolutionary process is energized by the *pull* toward some more or less clearly definable goal or purpose became particularly evident in the thinking of some English philosophers of the last century, leading to the concept of "holism" featured by Ian Smuts, philosopher and statesman, in his great work *Holism and Evolution.*

In the psychological field, Alfred Adler was among those who came to participate in the discussions of the group reverently gathered around Freud; and Adler soon began to challenge the attitude of the "master" in a very basic way. Differences of opinion and temperament led to a violent clash. Adler had met Freud in 1906, and finally left his circle in 1911, emerging as a teacher in his own right and as the propounder of a psychological system which he named "Individual Psychology."

Adler brought several new concepts to the psychological interpretation of neuroses and related disturbances. These new concepts, or life attitudes, directly oppose those which were fundamental to Freud. Where Freud speaks insistently of "sexuality," Adler refers to the ego and its "will to power"; where Freud conceives everything as related to past causes and seeks to probe hidden depths, Adler sees everything as a plan conditioned by purpose, as an expression of "the goal of the human soul [which] is conquest, perfection, security, superiority" (Adler, *Social Interest,* p. 145); where Freud analyzes the psyche into partials, complexes, and the like, Adler stresses "the unity of the personality" — which he identifies with the ego.

His identification of the unity of the personality is most significant. Traditional psychology has taken for granted that a person saying "I" knows exactly what he (or she) is talking about and to what he is referring; it assumes that what is called "I" is an essentially permanent entity with a consistent character — indeed, a God-created "soul." Freud showed that the "I" was a compound of all kinds of factors, known and unknown, conscious and unconscious; that it could split into "partials"; that its unity was constantly a possible prey to instinctive energy, etc. Adler strenuously refused to have the unity of his personality *analyzed away.* He clung to his "I" with stubborn intensity, yet he had been confronted with the unchallengeable facts revealed by psychiatric research and dream-analysis. He had, then, to somehow reconcile these facts and his ego-centric protest against psycho-analysis. His "Individual Psychology" was built around such an attempt at reconciliation — though he was perhaps not at all aware of it!

Adler, a scientist and a man of the 20th century, did not suggest that human beings are born with God-created, indissoluble souls, but, taking for granted the individual as a distinct expression of the evolutionary impulse running through mankind, he saw personality as an organism continuing as a basic and consistent whole until dissolved by death. He saw what appear to be symptoms of psychic disintegration as the efforts of the personality-whole (viz. the ego) to solve its problems along ineffective lines. In reading Adler, however, one feels his *implied* condemnation of the man who chooses thus a wrong "style of life" — not unlike the contempt of the religious moralist for the person who "allows" himself to become insane, or that of the European well-to-do burgeois for the person who lets himself go bankrupt (an unforgivable social sin!).

Adler wrote in his book, *Social Interest: A Challenge to Mankind:*

> Each individual adopts for himself at the beginning of his life, *a law of movement*, with comparative freedom to utilize for this his innate capacities and defects, as well as the first impressions of his environment. This law of movement is for each individual different in tempo, rhythm, and direction. The individual, perpetually comparing himself with the unattainable ideal of perfection, is always possessed and spurred on by a feeling of inferiority. . . . (p. 37.)

> The fundamental law of life is that of overcoming. . . . (p. 71.)

> To be a human being means the possession of a feeling of inferiority that is constantly pressing on toward its own conquest. The paths to victory are as different in a thousand ways as the chosen goals of perfection. The stronger the feeling of inferiority that has been experienced, the more powerful is the urge to conquest, and the more violent the emotional agitation . . . . (p. 72.)

> Neurosis is a creative act and not a reversion to infantile and atavistic forms . . . . (p. 131)

> Neurosis is the patient's automatic, unknowing exploitation of the symptoms resulting from the effects of a shock . . . . The cure can only be effected by intellectual means, by the patient's growing insight into his mistake, by the development of his social feeling . . . (pp. 180-181.)

> Organic inferiority and, still more, a pampering regime in childhood, have misled the child into forming this particular style of life and have cramped the development of an adequate amount of social feeling . . . . (p. 133.)

According to Adler, a child is hindered in developing an adequate "style of life" (which includes a correct amount of social interest and social feeling) by *pampering, neglect,* and the *possession of inferior organs.* These three basic "handicaps of childhood" have to be met and overcome by "the creative power of the child." His success or failure depends on his "style of life," which in turn depends on the way in which the child "utilizes heredity and the influence of its environment" with "comparative freedom."

Exactly what causes the child to have "comparative freedom" in establishing his all-determining "style of life," Adler does not tell us clearly; but presumably he sees it as a distinct and individual expression of the creative tide of human evolution (Bergon's *Elan Vital*) seeking its ultimate goal of perfection. For Adler, every person must be met and treated as an individual case. Indeed, Adler's world is a world of individuals whose function as individuals is considered unquestionable and final.

However, in order to balance his extreme individualism and his emphasis upon the ego and the "will to power," Adler has also stressed social feeling and the individual's fitness to participate in humanity's evolutionary ascent. The value of a human being is determined, for Adler, by his ability to contribute to "the higher development of the whole of humanity." Those individuals "who have contributed nothing to the general welfare . . . have disappeared completely. Nothing remains of them . . . It has happened with them as it did with animal species that have become extinct because they were unable to get into harmony with cosmic facts . . ." because they had "not grasped the meaning of life."

The problem for the psychologist, as Adler sees it, is to help the individual to adjust his own urge to superior achievement and his own "goal of perfection" to the collective and "final goal of human evolution." The neurotic, drunkard, or criminal also has his "goal of superiority; but it leads in a direction so opposed to reason that we are unable to recognize in it a proper goal of perfection." Man's destiny is a "victorious assimilation with the external world," "the mastery of all the advantages and disadvantages ordained by the cosmos."

Who was this man who exalted thus the "will to power" and identified the ego with the basic rhythm of the totality of the personality? Alfred Adler was born February 7, 1870, near Vienna, Austria. His family was Jewish, but his father had been converted to Protestanism. He contracted pneumonia at the age of 5 and decided, as a child, to become a doctor. He acknowledges that his inferiority complex theory had its source in an early organic inferiority which he struggled to overcome – adding that: "just as nature affords compensation to injured organs, so the spirit of man can also be trained to compensate him for all psychic disturbances produced by defective organs."

He received a medical degree in Vienna in 1895, began a general practice as an eye specialist in 1897, and met Freud in 1906. As his progressed Sun reached Aries, Adler broke with Freud, formed his school of "Free Psychoanalysts" and published the journal *Internationale Zeitschrift fur Individual Psychologie.* He came to America in 1927, lectured at Columbia University, and in 1932 had the first chair of medical psychology established in an American college (Long Island College of Medicine). He died in 1937 of a heart attack while in Aberdeen, Scotland. He had married a Russian student in Vienna, with whom he had three daughters and a son – thus his home was a real laboratory for experimental child psychology, and an important factor in the development of his ideas.

I have been unable to find mention of his exact birth-hour and several possible rising Signs come to mind in view of his bio-psychological type and the pattern of his life. But the most likely Ascendant, considering Adler's features, is Cancer, with Uranus retrograde rising – the chart-pattern printed here. According to his biographers, he was "at once the easiest of men to know and the most difficult, the frankest and the most subtle, the most conciliatory and the most ruthless." He was a "short stocky man with fine eyes, a beautiful tenor voice" (*cf.* his Moon-Jupiter in Taurus); he had a "fiery temper (Mars-Sun square Jupiter-Pluto) under excellent control and a sympathetic manner with his patients" (a dominant Venus retrograde in creative quintile to Saturn).

If the birth-time selected is correct, the most interesting feature of the chart, from the point of view of pattern-analysis (or *Gestalt*) is the fact that Uranus and Saturn both stand below the horizon, respectively in the first and sixth houses, while all the other planets are included within the square of Mercury retrograde in Aquarius to Jupiter-Pluto in Taurus, on either side of the Piscean midheaven and Venus. The above-the-horizon planets – especially those in Aquarius and Taurus – refer to Adler's emotional tensions and his organic troubles; also to his problems of social adjustment (*cf.* Neptune square the rising Uranus), which may have been partly related to a religious-social conflict of which he may not have been aware. On the other hand, Uranus and Saturn symbolize his individual efforts toward the solution of his problems — and the exalted and elevated Venus retrograde, the publicly externalized and proclaimed end-results of these efforts.

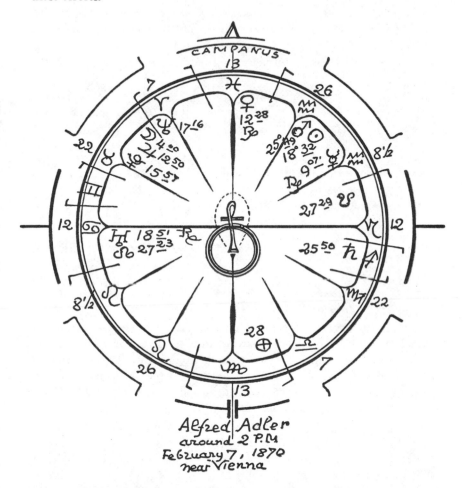

Saturn in the sixth house could represent the "inferiority complex" produced by physical weakness, as well as the trend toward establishing rigid self-discipline and mental prophylaxis. Uranus, rising in Cancer, would correlate with Adler's insistence on the creative power of the individual, ceaselessly seeking to overcome his inferiority and reach the pinnacle of human evolution. The Uranus degree-symbol (Sabian system) shows "an aristocratic and frail girl wedding a proletarian youth," and from it we derive an idea of a blending of past with future, of form with forward emotional drive. Also indicated is a trend toward the assimilation of unconscious contents ("the proletarian youth") by a cultured consciousness.

Adler placed no real value upon the unconscious, whether as described by Freud or as understood by Jung. He did not give much value to dreams either:

> A dream tells us nothing new — nothing we cannot find just as well in the patient's behavior. By the use of properly understood methods and by a selection from the contents of the dream one can recognize how the dreamer, guided by his law of movement, is at pains to carry out his style of life in opposition to common sense by artificially stimulating his emotions. (*Social Interest*, p. 179).

The only unconscious acceptable to him was the vast evolutionary drive toward a goal of perfection stirring the individual to overcome his weaknesses and reach power. This drive is *unavoidable*. Man is fated to "strive upward from below," from *minus* to *plus* values; and, according to Adler,

> . . . this does not only fix a fundamental category of thought, the structure of our reason, but what is more, it yields the *fundamental fact of our life*. The origin of humanity and the ever repeated beginning of infant life rubs it in with every psychic act: "Achieve! Arise! Conquer!" This feeling is never absent. (*Psychologies of 1930*. A paper written by Alfred Adler).

This "striving for conquest, surety, increase which lies at the root of all solutions of life's problems and is manifested in the way in which we meet these problems" can be seen, astrologically, in Adler's natal conjunction of Mars and Sun in Aquarius. Even the Sun's degree-symbol adds the meaning of "ascendancy" to this position. It pictures "a forest fire being subdued," and indicates an exaggeration of life-problems revealing to a person his real stature, testing him and challenging him to a total mobilization of his energies. Furthermore, Mars is placed on a degree symbolizing the testing of power and the capacity to deliver it. In zodiacal symbolism, Aquarius correlates with the release of power through human will and imagination in order to dynamize the search for new goals. Jupiter conjunct Pluto indicates a possible creative outlet for this dynamic release of power, for the square of Sun-Mars to the Jupiter-Pluto conjunction suggests a state of tension against conservative ideals of human destiny.

We might also add that the square of the Taurean Moon to the Aquarian Mercury retrograde implies a basic mental conflict with the "mother image," an inner rebelliousness which probably was transferred and transformed, later on, into conjugal tension. The mind of Adler was, as Jung pointed out, functioning along the line of introversion: To him, the inner reality — the ego — was far more important than the world of outer objects or persons. True, he developed a strong emphasis upon "social feelings" — but this was a purely compensatory attitude (*cf.* Jupiter, its placement and aspects). The ego was for him not only the center of consciousness (as it is in Jung's psychology); it absorbed the whole of the unified personality — and this implies that Adler reduced the field of personality to the *conscious level.*

What Freud had sought awkwardly to do in a clinical and reductive way, what Jung aimed at establishing on a far more comprehensive and wholesome basis, was to show that what the individual calls "himself" — his unified "I" — is not his total being, but only a surface-being. While Freud strove to reveal the depths of the human psyche, Adler, reacting sharply against such a revelation, focused all his attention, all meaning and value upon the *surface self.* He glorified the evolutionary drive from depth to surface, but the real self, for him, was the unified, one-pointed top of human evolution manifesting as the individual person with a unique "style of life" and "law of movement." Adler saw only integrated tops; he was not seeking to build human beings who are more total, more inclusive, with deeper roots and a more profound reach into the submerged sphere of instincts and basic energies. He only wanted to develop more *victorious personalities;* and it did not seem to matter to him at what cost came the victory.

Victory — he claimed — can only be proven by efficient social functioning. The goal of mastery is directed, *wrongly,* toward an oppressive superiority over one's fellowmen, or *rightly,* toward fullest cooperation with others and participation in the creative upbuilding of "the ideal community," of a perfect humanity. Lack of the "social feeling" leads to the wrong way; cooperation is the key to the constructive solution of the three "major problems" to which "all the questions of life can be subordinated — the problems of communal life, of work, and of love" (*Social Interest,* p. 42). How can the neurotic or socially maladjusted person be helped to change from the wrong to the right attitude toward society, his work and his love-activities? Adler answered as follows:

> Whoever has not acquired in childhood the necessary degree of social sense, will not have it later in life ... unless perchance some harmful errors of construction are recognized by the subject and corrected. No amount of bitter experience can change his style of life, *as long as he has not gained understanding.* The

whole work of education, cure and human progress can be
furthered only along lines of better comprehension (*Psychologies
of 1930*. p. 403). (*cf.* Sun and Mars dominating the ninth house,
which is essentially the house of understanding.)

Individual psychology considers the essense of therapy to lie
in making the patient aware of his lack of cooperative power, and
to convince him of the origin of this lack in early childhood
maladjustments. What passes during this process is no small
matter; his power of cooperation is enhanced by collaboration
with the doctor. His "inferiority complex" is revealed as
erroneous. Courage and optimism are awakened. And the
"meaning of life" dawns upon him as the fact that proper
meaning must be given to life. This sort of treatment may be
begun at any point in the spiritual life. (*Psychologies of 1930*. p.
404.)

Adler, especially in his later years, essentially became an educator and
a social moralist. His psychology was a psychology of individual success.
And he understood psychological success as a monolithic advance of the
rational individual, well-adjusted to society and a spearhead of human
evolution. Questions arise however: Will not this victorious individual be
superficial? Will not his successful personal and social integration hide a
poverty of inner contents and of roots?

Adler compensates for Freud's scavenging into the unwholesome and
subconscious "depths" of contemporary man's psyche by exalting the
"heights" and the will to victory of the conscious individual. But in
reading Adler, one soon realizes that his ideas and techniques can only
lead, in most cases, to shallow triumphs of the all-too-conscious (because
exclusively conscious) ego. For this reason he attained his greatest success
in an America which had passed through the flamboyant optimism of New
Thought, itself a freer version of evil-repudiating Christian Science. It
became Jung's task to take the best features of "depth" and "height"
psychology and to develop a psychological approach that sought to
achieve the integration of the total human being on the basis of a
never-ending quest for an ever more inclusive "assimilation" of the
contents of life, society, and the universe.

3   *Carl G. Jung & the*
Positive Approach to the Unconscious

In the preceding chapters, we have seen psychotherapy developing into a method for dealing with the aberrations of personal behavior which were considered as manifestations of neuroses. The analysis of neurotic phenomena (in behavior, thought, and feeling), revealed to the early investigators the fact that these phenomena were neutralized if — by means of hypnosis, dream-analysis, or other methods — the neurotic person could be made to clearly recollect certain types of painful occurrences in early childhood or adolescence, occurrences which had caused a deep impression or an emotional shock, yet which the person had forgotten.

This fact, and others related to it, led philosophers like Pierre Janet and psychiatrists like Sigmund Freud to realize that man's inner nature — the "psyche" — was not only constituted by an aggregation of *conscious* ideas, feelings, realizations, etc., but included also a vast amount of *unconscious* material. Beyond what a person knew himself to be — beyond the thoughts, feelings, moods, aspirations, desires, and memories which he knew as "his own" — there were also within him many unwelcome, strange, ugly, immoral, and perhaps even criminal impulses and yearnings, which his conscious ego could not accept and thus repressed in fear, disgust, or horror. Thus repressed, these unwelcome contents of the psyche were seen to fall back into the shadowy depths of the "subconscious," *i.e.,* below the threshold of consciousness. They were the outcastes and *pariahs* of the psyche. The psyche, like our modern cities, had "dark slums"; and if these psychic slums became overcrowded or aroused in one way or another, their haggard, uncouth, and criminal denizens spilled over, as it were, into the conscious part of the psyche — comparable to the "best society" — and caused havoc, manifesting as neurotic symptoms.

Various explanations as to the reasons for the existence of these "psychic slums" and their undesirable inhabitants were given early in this century, particularly by Pierre Janet, Freud, and Adler. Virtually all these explanations stressed the *negative* character of the unconscious factors within the psyche. In Freud's view, the unwelcome and repressed desires, feelings, and thoughts originated in the dark instincts of animal life and particularly in the first manifestations of sexuality; indeed, they were seen

as the result of a basic conflict between "life" and "social order." For
Adler, the unconscious contents of the psyche had hardly any meaning at
all, save as the result of a wrong method used by the individual in his
effort to gain superiority and assert his will to survival against physiological or social handicaps. The unconscious contents were refuse, toxic
materials to be eliminated by the healthy individual self-driven toward his
goal and the ultimate goal of human society.

Then came Carl Jung. In his books and his methods of healing, he
outlined – with a wealth of detail, analogy, and imaginative understanding
– an entirely different picture of the unconscious. We recognize some of
the traits mentioned by Freud in this picture; but Jung shows that Freud's
interpretation of the nature and origin of the psychic factors responsible
for neurosis, hysteria, and the like, is one-sided and incomplete. Above all,
Jung differentiates between a "personal" unconscious (Freud's subconscious) and a "collective" unconscious. And this distinction at once
removes Jung's method from the strictly clinical field of the cure of
neuroses, and brings it into the sphere of psychological education or
religious guidance. Jung's ideas thus become a matter of concern to all
individuals eager to live fuller and more balanced, richer and more
integrated lives.

Jung's psychology goes to the roots of the problem of human life and
heralds a new era of psychological and philosophical understanding. His
scientific caution and his desire to keep pace with the development of
20th century thinking have – I believe – limited the scope of his spiritual
vision, at least as we find it formulated in his public writings; nevertheless,
he has done for psychology what Einstein and his colleagues have
accomplished in the realm of physics. He has established a "new" frame of
reference for psychological thinking; and, as psychology is destined to
assume an ever-increasing function in the evolution of human thought, a
new civilization – now struggling toward adequate formulations and
concrete manifestations in the fabric of social and personal living – is and
will be profoundly indebted to Carl Jung.

It may be possible to trace Jung's interest in myths and religious
symbolism to the fact that his father was not only a liberal clergyman, but
also a man who had given much time to the study of Oriental thought. At
any rate, while in his late thirties and still associated with Freud, he
published his book *The Psychology of the Unconscious* (1912), which
was devoted to the interpretation of some basic themes found in ancient
mythologies and in the inspirational writings of modern poets and
visionaries as well. The publication of this work brought his differences of

opinion with Freud to a sharp climax. Freud (at least at that time) insisted on limiting himself to the field of personal conflicts having recognizable causes in the objective events of an individual's early life. Jung, on the other hand, began to probe into the common humanity of all human beings, that is, into the psychic heritage the past ages of human evolution have bequeathed to every new born individual.

In other words, Jung sought to establish the existence of a collective cultural and biological foundation in the human psyche — a foundation upon which every person builds or may build, in a more or less creative and original way, the structure of his individuality. This foundation is the product of inherited experience, biologically, socially, culturally, or religiously. It exists within the depths of any person's inner life, but it is normally as unconscious as the organic functions of breathing or food-assimilation. The materials constituting this foundation of consciousness, however, may come to the surface, or the conscious ego may choose to explore their cryptic depths. These materials then appear to the consciousness as images with peculiar vitality and power. They are revealed in such form to the mystic or the great poet, to the creator of artistic, religious, or political symbols having power to influence a vast number of men. They have such power because they actually dwell *in a latent state* within every person in the collectivity. While every person does not *directly* experience these symbols in his own consciousness, each is moved and aroused to feeling or action when presented with such a symbol, for instance in literature or in a painting.

Jung speaks of these images as either "primordial images" or as "archetypes" of the collective unconscious. Among these images, we can mention the "great Mother," the "soul-image" (the *anima* or *animus* of a person), the "wise old man," the "solar Hero," the "shadow," the "great serpent" (the life-power), the "symbol of salvation" or the "redeeming Savior," etc. These images are more than mere concepts or fanciful myths, products of the imagination of exceptional men. Jung regards them as basic contents of the collective unconscious, or as essential "structures" of the human psyche. The ordinary person discovers these images in the social and religious traditions of his youth; and while *as an individual,* he is not really conscious of the nature and meaning of these "archetypes," he becomes familiar with their meaning in his tradition, and is able to tap their power in the same unconscious way in which he breathes.

However, there are persons who, for one reason or another, lose this unconscious touch with their basic tradition and with the collective attitudes of their society. They seek, peacefully or – more often than not – under strain and stress, to develop their own individual approach and their own foundations of meaning. Not satisfied to take for granted what their community or race has built upon for centuries, they rebel. Just as, at one time, they had to rebel against their mother and her enfolding love in order to ascertain and express their own individuality, these individuals also seek to emerge from that "collective womb" which is tradition, religion, culture, and morality. This emergence from the collective Mother is the basic phase of what Jung calls "the process of individuation" – the process which alone leads to psychological and spiritual maturity.

Birth and spiritual rebirth, freedom from the mother and liberation from the past, are eternal themes in human experience. They are manifestations of the eternal struggle between the individual and the collective: a struggle which vivifies the significance of these two polar opposites found in all life, and which must take individualized, conscious form and meaning in the experience of every man and woman who can truly claim the status of mature individual selfhood. This type of experience is brought about by problems of human relationship which reach a certain depth of value, either in joy or in anguish. When that depth is reached – below the level of the "personal unconscious" and its repressions or frustrations traceable to stressful childhood occurrences and emotional shocks – the individual is confronted with unusual situations and unusual dreams.

The problem he faces is no longer that of normalizing his emotional reactions and of erasing memories of shocks or personal failures; it is essentially the problem of establishing *a new relationship in depth* between his newly won individuality and the fundamental drives, functions, and structural compulsions of his race and his ancestral tradition. He, an individual person, faces humanity – its entire past ... and, I would add (though Jung is not very clear on this point), its whole future, including the cosmic or divine purpose of human evolution. Such a confrontation must be squarely met. It can only be resolved into spiritual success or failure. According to Jung, success leads to the "integration of the personality"; failure leads to a regressing crystallization or disintegration of the psyche, to the overwhelming of the conscious ego by the energies of the aroused unconscious.

In order to understand the full meaning of such occurrences, we have to study the growth, development, and collapse of human nations and societies – and particularly of the European civilization. The "process of individuation" is a process universal in its scope, working as it does at various levels and in relation to various types of individualized entities. It is universal because it is based on the cyclic interaction and the constant struggle between the two poles of universal life — individual and collective. The meaning of these two polarities were well understood by the ancient Chinese wise men, who named them *yang* and *yin*, and who based their entire philosophy of life, their ethics, arts, and social systems upon the periodic rhythm these polarities display in nature.

This periodic rhythm is expressed in astrology, first of all, in the Zodiac and its symbolism, based as it is on the yearly oscillatory motion of the Sun *in declination;* that is, in the northward and southward displacement of the setting places of the Sun throughout the year. I have discussed this at length in my book *The Pulse of Life.* But, in relation to the chart of an individual, the contrast between factors dealing with the individual structure of consciousness and factors referring to the collective unconscious is represented by the distinction between, on one hand, the planets of the solar system up to, and including, Saturn, and on the other hand, the newly discovered remote planets beyond Saturn — Uranus, Neptune, and Pluto. I have called the former "planets of the conscious," the latter "planets of the collective unconscious;"* and in a subsequent chapter we shall study the meaning of this distinction and its use in the psychological analysis of a birth-chart.

The reader should have by now a general idea of how far Jung has departed from the type of psychological approach taken by Freud. With Jung we see emerging quite a different conception of the unconscious. In contrast to Freud's picture of the unconscious as a purgatory or hell of repressed and poisonous psychic contents, Jung presents the unconscious as a vast realm of psychic energy from which the conscious ego emerges. This process of emergence, called by Jung "individuation," may be accomplished more or less successfully and creatively; and the psychic materials which the ego has managed to "differentiate" and individualize during his lifetime normally return to the collective unconscious after death. In a sense, this realm is the primordial ocean of human being — the universal matrix of all that becomes, in the living person, desire, feeling, thought, intuition, and aspiration. In another sense, it is the collective reservoir into which goes all that human beings have contributed and will ever contribute to civilization, *whether it be of positive or negative value.*

---

*   cf. *The Astrology of Personality.*
The author has also dealt with these "planets of the unconscious" in great depth in his book, *The Sun is Also a Star: The Galactic Dimension of Astrology* (Dutton, N.Y., 1975). — Ed.

At this point, I should probably stress the fact that Jung does not think of "the" conscious and "the" unconscious as two kinds of entities. Jung essentially bases his doctrine and technique on empirical data, that is, on what he and his clients have actually experienced in their inner lives. He is not primarily a philosopher; he is an investigator and an interpreter who seeks to establish his interpretation on the widest possible foundation — and not merely on a limited concept of human individuality. He sees man's psyche as something vast, constituted by many factors (or "contents"). Some of these contents are conscious (that is, related to a central point, an ego, or "I"); many are unconscious, yet they press against the circumference or the "threshold" of consciousness and under certain conditions seep or erupt into the field of this consciousness, over which the ego presides, or autocratically rules.

By definition, we do not know what the unconscious is — or else it would cease to be unconscious! We know that, consciously or semi-consciously, we *resist* the coming of certain thoughts, feelings, impulses, realizations, and intuitions into the field of our consciousness. But why do we resist these hidden contents of our psyche? It may be because they are destructive in themselves, toxic refuse of "our unlived life"; but it may also be that they constitute a call toward a greater, fuller, more spiritual life — and that our ego refuses to admit them into its realm out of fear and inertia.

In other words, the unconscious contents of our psyche are those which the ego refuses to recognize, or those which are a challenge of further growth to its power and to the entrenched interests of the conscious, rationalistic (and rationalizing!) portions of our inner nature. Thus the unconscious superficially appears to be antagonistic to the conscious. Yet — and this is the essential point — they are the two halves of the psyche. As Jung writes:

> "The psyche consists of two incongruous halves that should properly make a 'whole' together . . . (but) consciousness and the unconscious do not make a whole when either is suppressed or damaged by the other. If they must contend, let it be a fair fight with equal right on both sides. Both are aspects of life. Let consciousness defend its reason and its self-protective ways, and let the chaotic life of the unconscious be given a fair chance to have its own way, as much of it as we can stand. This means at once open conflict and open collaboration. Yet, paradoxically, this is presumably what human life should be. It is the old play of hammer and anvil: the suffering iron between them will in the end be shaped into an unbreakable whole, the individual. This experience is what is called, in the later sections of this book, the process of individuation." (*The Integration of the Personality* pp. 26-27.)

All this adds up to a conception of "personality" as an organized totality of human experience and psychic contents, both conscious and unconscious. The unconscious is never to be considered as a closed realm with determinable boundaries, but rather as a channel through which the entire universe – past, present, and future – is potentially flowing into the human psyche. Thus, personality is open to unceasing expansion and growth. Fundamental growth results from the "reciprocal interpenetration" of conscious and unconscious; the mixing of rational order with the irrational energies of life. These polar opposites must be reconciled in the experience of the individual; they must be integrated in a vibrant, pulsating wholeness of personality in which no function is repressed or underestimated, but in which every function fulfills its proper place in the economy of an ever-expanding whole. Expansion is from fulfillment to ever greater fulfillment, through crises of growth in which the individualized consciousness assimilates an ever larger share of universal being. In this process of growth the individual learns to recognize that he has ultimate meaning only through his participation in the activities of society and, eventually, through his participation in the universal whole. Instead of acting from his merely conscious center – the ego – he moves on, rhythmically and serenely, from the center of the integrated totality of his being, which Jung calls "the Self." As Jacobi writes in her remarkable book, *The Psychology of Jung* (Yale University Press, 1943), the Self is "that focal point of our psyche in which God's image shows itself most plainly and the experience of which gives us the knowledge, as nothing else does, of the significance and nature of our likeness to God. It is the early Christian ideal of the Kingdom of God that is 'within you.' It is the ultimate experienceable in and of the psyche " (p. 123).

4 Jung's Approach to Personality & the Astrological Way to Self-Realization

What is "personality"? The answers to this question differ widely, as widely as the psychological approaches which men have taken to the central problem of human life. According to some medieval philosophers, only God is endowed with the supreme attribute of personality, for He alone is a complete, self-sufficient, and self-sustained being. In recent theosophical or so-called occult literature, the term "personality" has been used in contrast with "individuality," the former defining the ever-changing and earth-conditioned nature of man, while the latter refers to the relatively permanent and spiritually conditioned entity thought to be the essential reality of man.

Personality, in classical psychology, is definitely connected with consciousness; but Freud sought to reduce the previously taken for granted unity of the personality into unstable components, subconscious energies, psychic mechanisms, complexes, and somewhat hopeless yearnings for unattainable perfection. Adler reacted against the Freudian approach by stressing the unity of the personality, identifying personality with ego, and brushing off unconscious factors in the psychic life of the individual as residual and toxic by-products of an ineffective and unwholesome type of adjustment to life and society — an adjustment controlled by man's everlasting will to power and superiority.

In studying Jung's psychology, we find that his concept of personality is a very broad and inclusive one: that personality is an evolving organism, the wholeness and integrated character of which should not be taken for granted, but instead should be considered as the essential (but hard to attain) goal of life for individual human beings. The integration of the personality is not only a complex and arduous process; it has no conceivable end, because personality is essentially the result of the reciprocal interpenetration, harmonization, and integration of two fundamentally distinct and apparently opposite (yet complementary) types of factors in the psychic life of man. These factors refer either to consciousness and the controlling center of consciousness, the ego, or they belong to the realm of the unconscious. As the realm of the unconscious has no knowable boundaries, but extends theoretically *ad infinitum* in the direction of an ever vaster experience of the universe, it follows that no set limits can be placed to the scope of personality. The field of consciousness may always encompass a more inclusive totality of previously unconscious contents. A few brief quotations from Jung will help to bring his idea of the relationship between conscious and unconscious to a still clearer perspective.

> Just as the human body shows a common anatomy over and above all racial differences, so too, does the psyche possess a common substratum. I have called the latter the collective unconscious. As a common human heritage, it transcends all differences of culture and consciousness and does not consist merely of contents capable of becoming conscious, but of latent dispositions toward identical reactions. Thus the fact of the collective unconscious is simply the psychic expression of identity of brain-structure irrespective of all racial differences. By its means can be explained the analogy, going even as far as identity, between various myth-themes and symbols, and the possibility of human understanding in general. The various lines of psychic development start from one common stock whose roots reach back into the past.

> Taken purely psychologically, it means that we have common instincts of ideation (imagination), and of action. All conscious imagination and action have grown out of these unconscious prototypes and remain bound up with them (p. 83).

> Without a doubt, consciousness is derived from the unconscious. This is something we remember too little, and therefore we are always attempting to identify the psyche with consciousness. (Commentary on *The Secret of the Golden Flower*, p. 119)

> The distinction between mind and body is an artificial dichotomy, a discrimination which is unquestionably based far more on the peculiarity of intellectual understanding than on the nature of things. In fact, so intimate is the intermingling of bodily and psychic traits that not only can we draw far-reaching inferences as to the constitution of the body, but we can also infer from psychic peculiarities the corresponding bodily characteristics. (*Modern Man in Search of a Soul*, p. 85)

> The "psyche" is both physical and mental. (Commentary on *The Secret of the Golden Flower*, p. 131)

> The psyche is a self-regulating system that maintains itself in equilibrium as the body does. Every process that goes too far, immediately and inevitably calls forth a compensatory activity. Without such adjustments a normal metabolism would not exist, nor would the normal psyche. We can take the idea of compensation, so understood, as a law of psychic happening. Too little on one side results in too much on the other. The relation between conscious and unconscious is compensatory. (*Modern Man in Search of a Soul*, p. 20)

> No personality is manifested without *definiteness, fullness,* and *maturity.* (p. 285)

> The development of personality means fidelity to the law of one's being. (p. 289)

When all is said and done, the hero, leader, and savior is also the one who discovers a new way to greater certainty. Everything could be left as it was if this new way did not absolutely demand to be discovered, and did not visit humanity with all the plagues of Egypt until it is found. The undiscovered way in us is like something of the psyche that is alive. The classic Chinese philosophy calls it "Tao," and compares it to a watercourse that resistlessly moves towards its goal. To be in Tao means fulfillment, wholeness, a vocation performed, beginning and end and complete realization of the meaning of existence innate in things. Personality is Tao. (*The Integration of the Personality*, p. 304-305)

These quotations, however fragmentary, outline for us the basic picture of personality which Jung develops with a great wealth of details through his various writings. They also bring to mind the reason why the techniques devised by the astrological tradition can be of extreme practical usefulness to the individual seeking to tread the arduous path of integration of the personality — *provided these astrological techniques are used in a new way, in a way consciously directed toward the attainment of a positive, definite, full, and mature personality.*

To so use astrology *is not easy* — let there be no mistake or misunderstanding about this point! It is not easy, because an astrology geared to the integral fulfillment of "the law of one's being" has first of all to be purged of all the attitudes, beliefs, and traditional expectations which frequently create, in the student as well as the consultant, fears, a sense of inferiority, or a false optimism. Worst of all, astrology in its popular state often promotes a psychologically unhealthy dependence upon the advice of highly fallible and insufficiently trained practitioners of this most exacting of the arts. This dependence would not be worse, in principle, than the client's dependence upon his psychotherapist or "analyst" *if* the astrologer were a trained psychologist, and were truly dedicated to the psychological welfare of his consultants; but this unfortunately is not often the case. It is not the case, *not* because astrologers are less honest persons than psychologists, but simply because the approach the astrological public *expects* of an astrologer is one which on the whole is *not* psychologically constructive.

If a person goes to consult a psychotherapist, his purpose is usually to reach a better condition of psychological development, and perhaps to be healed of some acute mental trouble. He expects healing or greater wholeness of being. But the average person seeking advice from an astrologer expects the kind of information which normally does not lead to a fuller, richer, more definite, and more mature personal life.

To "know the future" – even if it is understood that there can be knowledge *only of the potentiality* of future events – is not, of itself, conducive to personal integration. It is not, of itself, sound psychological knowledge. Even the knowledge of what course of action is more likely to be "successful" in a given circumstance is not, of itself, psychologically valuable. It can be unfortunate if, while producing external success – or even *because* it produces external success – this knowledge creates a state of dependence upon badly understood astrological procedures and a false sense of psychological security.

What then is the psychologically valid use of astrology from the point of view taken by Jung? *It can only be the clarification (the making more conscious and objectively real) of the "law of one's being."* Any astrological procedure or practice which does not have this purpose, and which the practitioner or consultant does not expect to have this purpose, is detrimental to psychological health and cannot contribute to the process of personality-integration. This does not mean that astrological applications which are not concerned primarily, or at all, with the psychological welfare of individuals should not be practiced. It simply indicates the one basic goal of any constructive application of astrological methods to individuals, whether the astrological techniques be birth-charts, progressions, transits, etc. If this is the case, the question for us to answer is: How can astrology help any individual to gain a clearer and more objective consciousness of the law of his being – and thus of his own real self?

All my writings in books and astrological magazines have been essentially occupied with the answer to this question. Astrology, I have shown, can be used as a means to "self-realization," as a powerful help in the "process of individuation"; that is, in the process of becoming, in actuality and in the fullness of conscious living, what one is, at birth, only in potentiality. Individuality (that is, structural uniqueness of being) is potential or latent in every new-born child. It becomes *a fact* only through the persistent and consistent efforts of young and old alike as they seek to reach inner maturity. What astrology can do to make these efforts more successful is to present to the would-be individual – or to the confused older person who carries the burden of too many failures – the *blue-print of the structure of his individuality.*

Astrology, in other words, presents to an evolving personality, perhaps groping in unconsciousness and psychological immaturity, the archetype of his potential selfhood – that which he will be, if he becomes what he potentially is. An archetype is like a seed: the potentiality of a particular structure of organic being. The seed may never grow into a fully developed plant. But, if it does grow, it will become in actuality what the seed contains in potentiality. No acorn will ever become an apple tree; but seeing an acorn falling into the soil does not indicate whether or not, in that place, an oak will ever grow to maturity. *Astrology deals only with potentialities; never with definite or fated events.*

Jung constantly uses the term "archetype," and the way in which he defines it is of great significance to the astrologer who seeks to evaluate the proper psychological meaning of a birth-chart — an "archetype" of a special kind. Archetypes are, in Jung's philosophy, focal points or fields of force in the collective unconscious; that is, they are images determining and controlling the most fundamental activities of what we have called "man's common humanity." They express the most primordial and most common responses of all human beings to a few basic situations; and they appear as symbolic images in our dreams, as well as in all myths or religious conceptions. These symbolic images have enormous power. They can sway vast collectivities, resulting in religious conversion or leading to rationally inexplicable crimes. They have a dark as well as a light side.

What is important to realize, however, is that only their *form* is determined, not their contents; that their "ultimate core of meaning may be delimited but never described." "The form of these archetypes," says Jung, "is perhaps comparable to the axial system of a crystal, which predetermines as it were the crystalline formation in the saturated solution, without itself possessing a material existence." This "axial system" determines only the *possibility* of a certain characteristic's concrete formation. Which of these possible formations will actually become substantially realized depends upon the nature of the "saturated solution" — that is, in the case of the archetypes, upon the common experience of humanity, or of a particular race and culture to which an individual belongs.

When the dreamer dreams about a mysterious mother-figure endowed with cosmic attributes — or when the inspired painter paints such a figure — the image aroused is not actually the creation of the dreamer, or artist, *as an individual.* The image is already latent in his unconscious — as the leaf pattern of the oak is latent in the acorn. The archetype has thus a kind of objective being in an unconscious realm of potentiality — a realm to which Goethe refers in the second part of *Faust* as the "realm of the Mothers." Indeed, Jung makes it plain that "the unconscious is the mother of the consciousness." Occultists have also spoken, with much the same meaning, of the realm of the "astral light" which is creative in its higher aspects, and reflective in its lower regions. They have also used the expressions "Anima Mundi" (the Soul of the World) and the "Virgins of Light," relating the latter to the signs of the Zodiac, considered as symbolical expressions of the great "Creative Hierarchies" that are builders of the universe — and of generic man. These Hierarchies are seen as collective agencies, or spiritual Hosts, through which the *Anima Mundi* operates; Jung also speaks of the archetypes of the unconscious as "organs of the soul."

These "organs of the soul," however, are concentrates of the common experience of myriads of generations of human beings. They are inherent in mankind as instincts are inherent in animals and indeed in men as well. Instincts and archetypes are of the same nature. And, if this be understood, we also see how, in esoteric or "gnostic" cosmologies, the above-mentioned creative Hosts are considered as concentrates of the spiritual experience of vast collectivities of beings who lived through, and achieved immortality in, previous universes or solar systems.

> [The number of archetypes is] relatively limited, for it corresponds to the "possibilities of typical fundamental experiences," such as human beings have had since the beginning of time ... [yet] the sum of these archetypes signifies for Jung the sum of all the latent potentialities of the human psyche — an enormous, inexhaustible store of ancient knowledge concerning the most profound relations between God, man, and the cosmos. To open this store to one's own psyche, to wake it to new life, and to integrate it with consciousness, means therefore nothing less than to take the individual out of his isolation *and to incorporate him in the eternal cosmic process* ... To remove this isolation and confusion of the modern [individual], to make it possible for him *to find his place in the great stream of life,* to assist him to a wholeness that knowingly and deliberately *binds his light conscious side to the dark one of the unconscious* — this is the meaning and aim of Jungian guidance. (J. Jacobi; *The Psychology of Jung,* pp. 45, 47, 48)

I have italicized some of the above sentences, because they clarify the link between Jung's psychology and astrology. The symbolic meaning of the birth-chart of an individual, erected for the exact moment and place of birth, is actually, and as far as its psychological value is concerned, an archetype in his unconscious. It is perhaps the most powerful of all archetypes, when it is brought up to the light of the consciousness, inasmuch as it can determine the entire conduct of the individual, his entire attitude toward himself and his life, and the quality of his expectancy with reference to future events and to his destiny as a whole. The birth-chart is a symbol of extraordinary power, and this symbol, because it is based upon mankind's primordial experience of the sky — a wondrous realization of transcendent order in the midst of a life of earthly chaos – opens the door to man's ability "to find his place in the great stream of life" in terms of an archetypal pattern of order. This pattern of order is actually presented to man by the pageant of ceaselessly moving points and discs of light in the sky. It is his to behold. For a person to study his birth-chart means to *discover the order of the sky at the root of his being.* It is to discover the particular phase of the *Anima Mundi* (the Soul of the world, the Great Mother) which became the *mould* into which generic and collective human nature was poured, as the individual emerged into the world of air and light as a breathing new-born infant.

The moment of the first breath is the great symbol of the individualizing act by which unborn human nature emerges from the "dark mother" (the womb of the earth) and begins to operate in the realm of the "celestial mother." In the womb, man is bound and utterly conditioned by generic human nature, but as he emerges from this womb and finds himself under the dome of the sky (the celestial "church" in which the zodiacal "Virgins of Light" officiate), he finds himself entering a realm of essential freedom. He *breathes;* and in this act of breathing, man is the symbol-archetype of his individualized state of being. He is free to alter his breathing, and through the power of the breath – which is also the power of the uttered Word – man can prove himself individual and master, or condemn himself to thwarted and abortive individual living.

Ancient Hindu *yoga* was based on this realization of the meaning and power of the breath; and so also, in another sense, was astrology. Astrology was the means to relate the first moment of the individualized freedom (the first breath) to the "eternal cosmic process." Astrology was therefore, and can be today, a method "to take the individual out of his isolation and to incorporate him in the eternal process" – a method thus aimed at the very same ultimate achievement which Jacobi describes as the goal of Jungian psychological guidance. The purposes of the two approaches are identical in essence; and the means present many characteristic analogies, with equally characteristic differences.

The first point to stress is that the main function of astrology, considered in the psychological sense described above, is to help (in Jung's words) "to acknowledge one's self for what one by nature *is,* in contrast to that which one would like to be" – and, as Jacobi adds, "probably nothing is more difficult for man that just this acknowledgment" (p. 123). The birth-chart, considered as a symbol of the individual's *root-participation* in the *universal process,* can reveal to the individual what he is by nature, and thus what he can achieve, if he lives according to this "law" of his individual being. Yet the birth-chart deals with symbolic relations, with formulae of functional interplay, all of which must be interpreted, as dreams must be interpreted, if they are to become psychologically significant and effective. And like a dream, the birth-chart can be interpreted in many ways. It can be seen as a dynamic and creative whole, a challenge to integration, or as an aggregation of fragmentary bits of information about the most common preoccupations of mankind (wealth, home, love-affairs, health, marriage, business, success, etc.).

The ordinary and traditional practice of astrology deals with the latter. As a rule, the astrologer seeks information concerning events, past or future, or the knowledge of disjointed characteristics of his or her client's personal temperament. Astrology has then no psychologically integrative purpose — largely because the client or the astrologer himself *does not expect it* to have such a purpose. Most people approach astrology today in the same way they generally approach the subject of dreams — in an unorganized, amateurish, fragmentary and, therefore, unwholesome manner.

Whoever expects the symbols of dreams or astrological charts to lead him to a fuller, more inclusive, more conscious, and more mature personality must take a much more serious and responsible attitude. He should realize that while contact with the archetype of the unconscious and with the celestial patterns of the birth-moment *may* bring an individual to a rich and serene state of personality fulfillment, such a contact can as well bring dire psychological results. The birth-chart is very different indeed from a mere scientific tabulation of factors. Once it is studied and given vital attention, the chart begins to act as *a dynamic power within the unconscious.* It "does things" to the astrologer. It forces tendencies into the consciousness (and thus produces events) which otherwise might have remained latent and hidden. Whoever believes in the significance of the chart and in the validity of the interpretation given to it (by himself or by a practicing astrologer) is no longer quite the same person. *His orientation to the unconscious has become altered,* however slightly. Not to realize this is to court real danger, for a person's orientation to his unconscious is the most dynamic factor in his personality.

The process of integration of the personality is, indeed, always fraught with real psychological dangers. No one recognized this more clearly than Jung; and he bluntly stated that no one could ever succeed fully in this process unless compelled from within by a true "vocation," by an inner necessity.* How astrologers should also realize this fact! There are, nevertheless, collective as well as individual necessities. We are living in an explosive age — a global crisis in humanity's development — which demands that we all assume new responsibilities and deliberately face new dangers for the sake of a collective purpose we can no longer ignore. This is an age of global integration — whether by "globe" we mean the planet Earth, or the sphere of our total psyche, body and mind. We must therefore seek a path of total integration, in personality as well as in society. And we must be willing to accept risks — or become less than human. For to be human is to be consciously whole; it is to be a microcosm, a focal point of meaning and power within the vast organism of the macrocosm — the universal Whole.

---

*   cf. the last chapter of Jung's *The Integration of the Personality*, p. 281, ff.

5   The Anima & Animus in Jungian Analysis & the Moon-Symbol in Astrology

In the preceding chapters, we have studied the meaning C. G. Jung attributed in his psychological system to the unconscious and to the primordial images (archetypes) which arise from it at the threshold of the individual's consciousness. The archetypes of the collective unconscious are based on primordial experiences so vital and universal that the normal responses to them have become deeply embedded in human nature as instincts, traditional attitudes, and compulsive behavior. Such common human responses to universal life-situations are inherited; indeed they are conditioned by, and are the psychological expressions of, the organic structures of the body, especially the brain. And the average individual is no more conscious of the contents of his psychic depths than he is of the functioning of his digestive or circulatory system.

If, however, an individual places himself (or is placed by the peculiar demands of modern civilization) in circumstances which challenge or preclude natural or ancestrally established responses to basic and traditional situations of human living, some disorders almost inevitably result. These disorders affect the normal organic functioning of either body or psyche, or both. If the body is affected, illness and physical pain occur. If the effect is primarily psychological, psychic disturbances are registered by the consciousness and affect the ego. The disturbances alter the normal state of balance between the conscious and the unconscious and thus challenge the stability of the structures which the ego has built.

The ego, as the controlling center of the consciousness, rules over a field of psychic activity which is constantly surrounded by the vast and mysterious domain of the unconscious. The ego operates like a king of a country beyond whose boundaries extend seas, mountains, and forests inhabited by unfamiliar races. These races may be barbarians, or they may be highly cultured peoples. In either case, their peculiar and alien ways of living may be met on the basis of fruitful trade, and a vitalizing exchange of values may occur. Times may come, however, when under the pressure of internal or external conditions, the normal rhythm of communication and exchange between the kingdom of the ego (the field of consciousness) and the vast regions of the unconscious is disturbed. The ego may decide (or be forced by the pressure of social demands) to act or seek self-expression in a way which runs counter to the generic and cultural patterns of behavior which are normal to human nature or to the deeper traditions of a particular religion or culture. Then, the psyche as a whole (which is part conscious and part unconscious) is disturbed. If the disturbance is persistent enough, a complex is created, or a neurosis develops. The conscious becomes rigid or war-like, isolationistic or aggressive; it ceases to trade peacefully with the unconscious which, its energies dammed or put in bondage to the will of the ego, turns explosive and seeks revenge.

In the first stages of the conflict, the unconscious seems to give in. Human nature seeks to adjust itself to the demands of the ego and its conscious will; and we all know how much adjusting can be done – for a while. However, if the pressure of the abnormal behavior of the ego upon the natural rhythms of man's common humanity is maintained or increased, "human nature" rebels, overtly or in the way of "underground" resistance. The rebellion may not noticeably affect the equilibrium of biological functions at first; but it is likely to manifest in psychic ways, for instance as strange and obsessive dreams filled with anxiety and dark, menacing drama. Every instinct, as a common root-expression of human nature, may manifest as an archetypal image in dreams, or can be released through day-time fantasies and artistic symbols whose deep meaning may or may not be known to the artist. However, these archetypes of the unconscious come into the field of the conscious only when and where there is a *need* for them – a need of the personality within which they take form, according to ancient and ancestral patterns.

According to Jung, consciousness adjusts to the environment with direction, purpose, and finality, and the unconscious acts in a way which *compensates* for whatever is one-sided in these conscious activities. Jung stresses this compensatory function of the unconscious, considering it as proof that the psyche is an organic whole. Just as the body as a whole always tends to readjust the organic equilibrium disturbed by the willful and strained actions in which civilized man constantly indulges, and as the loss of one organ of the body (or the destruction of one part of the brain) is compensated for by the corresponding over-development of some other organ or function, so too does the psyche balance itself. If a person deliberately forces his psyche to respond to outer experiences in a standardized and one-sided manner, this artificial or over-conscious attitude will arouse an equally exaggerated and opposite type of activity in the unconscious.

If a young person has idolized his father and this worship has unbalanced his natural reactions to society and to his own development, then he may have insistent dreams in which his father appears as a petty, insignificant, or even monstrous individual. If a person so identifies himself with his professional or social attitude that he constantly exhibits the mannerisms and typical characteristics of his social position or class, he develops a mask (or *"persona"*) which he becomes increasingly unable to shed. The unconscious will compensate by forcing him to act in unguarded moments in a way just opposite. The popular hero, who has become identified with the expectations of his public and acts his part day in and day out, may nevertheless be known to his wife and children as weak, nagging, and irritable. In these cases, the unconscious reacts to a one-sided and fixed attitude of the conscious ego with a compelling pressure, forcing the person to act in a manner which would be repulsive to his ego, if he were conscious of this phase of his behavior. Jung calls this portion of the unconscious the *anima,* and the *anima* always tends to balance the *persona,* the part of the psyche which, seeking to become well adjusted to the demands of the environment (or to some organic inferiority or childhood complex), over-does the adjustment and becomes a slave to social attitudes.

The anima is the unconscious function which seeks to adjust the personality to the demands of "human nature," that is, to the normal type of response which a human being should make to outer and inner experiences if he functions as a healthy, wholesome, and total personality. Human nature is conservative, and the collective or generic unconscious (another name for "human nature") reacts to the stress and strain of conscious, willful, and over-individualized attitudes in terms of ancestral and archaic molds which are as difficult to modify as animal instincts.

In many cases, however, the accumulated wisdom of the past proves far more sane and safe than the over-differentiated and over-rationalized plans for action of an ego forced to adjust itself to a hectic civilization. Jung emphasizes the fact that what emerges from the unconscious in dreams, inspirations, and creative fancy reveals treasures of wisdom and often prophetic intuitions which are essential components of any personality claiming to be healthy, rich with human significance, and truly creative. Nevertheless, these dreams and inspirations are usually cryptic and they must be interpreted. They appear as images and dramatized scenes or symbols, because the unconscious is neither rational, logical, nor bound by sequences of cause-and-effect. Therefore, the unconscious can only manifest to the conscious as a multitude of images or archetypes. These images – related as they are to either personal and recent, or universal and archaic, experiences – constitute the only means of communication possible to the unconscious. If unconscious contents, warnings, or judgments are at times registered by the consciousness as actual words in logical and clear sequence, it is because they are first worked upon and, as it were, translated by *an intermediary psychic function* which ever seeks to make the unconscious intelligible to the conscious ego. The anima in its deepest and most positive aspect fulfills such a function.

So, the anima is to be understood thus: first, as a compensatory reaction to a one-sided conscious attitude with which the ego identifies itself (the persona). Secondly, the anima is the mediating function which seeks to bridge the gap between the unconscious and the conscious, between "human nature" and the ego, between the collective, permanent wisdom of the race and the differentiated, sharpened, intellectualized, and ever-changing forms of knowledge of the ego. In a third aspect, Jung also describes the anima as the ideal image of womanhood which every man carries in his unconscious mind, both according to his personal needs and to archaic impersonal traditions establishing the essential meaning of woman for man.

The anima in a man becomes in a woman the "animus." In other words, anima and animus represent the respective contra-sexual element in each. Here we come to recognize an essential point in Jungian psychology, a point which has also been an integral factor in astrology ever since the early days of Chaldean and Chinese civilization. This point is that all psychic manifestations are endowed with polarity, the same as are all forms of energy in the universe. *The law of polarity is the law of life itself.* Wherever there is life, two forces of opposite polarity forever interact, interpenetrate, and balance one another. Every living organism demonstrates this dynamic polar rhythm; it manifests, in one sense, as the law of compensatory activity above mentioned, and in another sense, as sex.

Sex (considered in its broadest sense as the polarization of human life-energy) refers not only to physical organs. Those deal with the *external and outwardly active* manifestations of sex in the body; but in the psyche, we find corresponding manifestations of opposite polarity constituting the *internal and inwardly active phases of life-energy.* And it is these to which the psychological concepts of anima and animus refer. It is indeed a fact that both masculine and feminine elements are contained within the total personality of either a man or a woman. What makes a man "masculine" is the higher percentage of male energy his *physical* nature includes; but the complementary fact is that, at the same time, his psychic nature will include a lower percentage of female energy.

Biological sexuality, in other words, is merely the central phase of the *externalized* aspect of the bi-polar life-force operating through – and indeed responsible for the building of – the human person. The aspect of this creative life-force which is externalized or released as sex, builds, sustains, and reproduces the body, under the direction of the still more primordial principle of differentiation (*karma*) symbolized in astrology by Saturn. On the other hand, the *internalized* and unreleased part of the life-energy (anima or animus) – of opposite polarity to the sex of the organism – builds and sustains those psychological functions through which characteristic forms of inner activity (or we might say "soul activity") occur. The anima-animus function is responsible for the primary development of all the images, symbols, and creative fantasies through which the unconscious communicates with the conscious ego. It is also the controlling factor in the growth of aspirational and devotional attitudes, or occult techniques, which develop as a result of the inward reorientation (or "conversion") of the ego, away from individualization or differentiation and toward the spiritual or root-realities in which all people share.

Whenever we deal with life-energy, we deal with what, in astrology, is basically represented by the Sun and the Moon. The realm of "life" (using the term in its strict sense as the power which builds, sustains, and reproduces living organisms) is the realm of duality. And, as I have made clear in my book on the subject,* this realm of life and duality is expressed astrologically through the cyclic interplay of solar and lunar factors. A third factor, however, which must be considered in any truly fundamental analysis is the Earth. The Earth establishes the positions and relative importance of what human beings perceive as the Sun and Moon. The *need* of these human beings (and all creatures dwelling on the Earth's surface) is what compels the manifestation of soli-lunar energy, and particularly the circuits of the Moon. In esoteric tradition, the Moon, although the satellite of Earth, is represented as being older than the Earth. The Moon is the mother, who diligently serves the needs of her child – and thus hovers around it, surrounding its every move. In another sense, the orbit of the Moon around the Earth outlines the boundaries of a "cosmic-psychic womb" within which all life on the Earth operates and

---

* Originally published as *The Moon: The Cycles and Fortunes of Life* (McKay, 1946), it was revised and subsequently published in Holland (Servire, 1967) and in America (Shambhala Publications, 1971) as *The Lunation Cycle*. –Ed.

from which it gains sustenance. This "womb" constitutes the *sub-lunar realm* of medieval astrologers – the world in which the lunar god, Jehovah, was said (by the Christian Gnostics of the second century, A.D.) to rule.

This god was concerned with the building of the "astral man." He was a jealous, possessive god, yet one who produced life structures to fulfill the need of earth-creatures. Because these earth-creatures, collectively speaking, are unready to receive *directly* the steady and impersonal creative energy of the solar Spirit, this energy is *stepped down and adjusted to their needs* by the lunar god, the *Demiurgos*. Solar energy is released to the Moon at every New Moon, but only in an amount acceptable to the limited capacity of earth-creatures. Then the lunar god (or gods) build specialized structures (of body and psyche) through which the solar energy becomes utilizable by earthly organisms and personalities.

The amount and type of solar energy released at the beginning of each lunation cycle is fixed by Saturn; for, while the Sun represents the center of the individual personality system, Saturn represents the boundaries of this system – the limitations, the particular destiny or fate of the individual. Saturn symbolizes the operations of the law of individual differentiation (the *karma* of the individual). It defines the permanent organic structure of the body (the skeleton), and *also* the structure of the ego. As long as the ego rules as the center of personality, and as long as the remote planets Uranus and Neptune do not succeed in challenging and dissolving the Saturnian grip over the personality, Saturn controls the release of solar energy (or universal spirit) through the forms periodically built by the Moon (the physiological and the ego-ruled structures of the body and consciousness). The challenge of the collective unconscious to the ego-centered consciousness operates primarily under the power of Uranus. But while Uranus is the challenger, the energy liberated by the challenge is also released by the Moon. All life-energy comes essentially from the Sun, but is released in a differentiated form by the Moon.

The challenge of Uranus to the Saturn-conditioned rule of the ego means that some new and revolutionary contents of the unconscious have become active, and that, as a result, the personality is about to face a drastic process of metamorphosis. This process leads from the ego-centered stage (Saturn-controlled personality) to that in which the Self (in the Jungian sense, the Sun) is realized as the integrating core of a total personality (symbolized by the entire solar system). This metamorphosis is what Jung calls the "process of individuation." The average man is, however, still rather far from such a confrontation. In him, Uranus acts in a *reflected* manner, as a factor of disturbance caused by unsettled and disruptive social conditions. In him, the rule of Saturn is not really challenged *in an individual way.* Such a person should therefore be considered to operate strictly within Saturnian boundaries, according to his normal psychological rhythm.

This means that his consciousness is normally immune from contacts with the powerful archetypes of the collective unconscious which, in superior (or unbalanced!) individuals, operate through a sharply and individually focused Uranus and Neptune. The average man's psyche nevertheless contains unconscious activities; but these refer, either to the individual's *personal unconscious* (Freud's "subconscious"), or to his unindividualized and passive response to the social, cultural, and religious currents animating the community, the class, and the nation which are his by birth and ancestral tradition. It is with reference to these two types of unconscious factors that the animus-anima functions essentially operate.

These functions constitute one aspect of the Moon in astrological symbolism — the inwardly directed type of lunar activity. The other aspect deals with the outwardly directed type of lunar activity, which, as we saw above, is occupied with the building of biological structures and psychological faculties whose aim it is to create the best possible kind of adjustment to the outer world. In other words, in the average human being, the Moon represents two distinct types of activities of opposite polarity. Ancient traditions clearly recognized this fact when they gave to the Moon a dual gender, speaking of the planet as *Lunus-Luna* — the masculine and feminine Moon. In the German language the word Moon is masculine, and in ancient Hindu books we find constant references to the Moon under the name of "King Soma."

This Hindu name is most interesting, because the same word, *soma,* in Greek means "body," and from it are derived many modern scientific terms referring to the body. King Soma, or *Lunus,* is indeed the ruler of all the activities dealing with the begetting, maintaining, and reproducing of the body and all those elements of the psyche which are oriented toward the requirements of outer life. *He is the male power in men, and the female power in women.* He rules over the externalized aspect of the life-force. And, in astrology, he is the Moon *outside of the Earth's orbit,* the Full of the Moon from First to Last Quarter — thus the Moon pulled by the attraction of Mars, Jupiter, and Saturn, the "masculine" planets of an astrology created by a civilization in which the men rule over all outward human activities.

The other aspect of the Moon is *Luna,* the power behind the internalized manifestations of the life-force — the anima of men and the animus of women; thus, the "contra-sexual" factor. This factor leads to the inner life production of all the anima-animus images and symbols which Jung has studied and interpreted in great detail, and which come under the general name of "Soul-image." This Soul-image is essentially endowed with feminine attributes in males (thus, the Great Mother, the Muse, the Redeeming Woman, Beatrice — and also all their dark polarizations: the Spider-Woman, the "Femme Fatale," the Temptress, etc.). It has masculine characteristics, positive or negative, in women. It refers symbolically to the Moon *within* the orbit of the Earth — i.e., the Dark of the Moon, from Last to First Quarter.

Because of this *Lunus-Luna* polarization, it follows that in order to increase the inward flow of life-energy, the outward current (represented mainly by sex, subservience to social patterns, and ego-centeredness — thus by Mars, Jupiter, and Saturn) has to be curtailed or dammed. This is the basic purpose of many occult and religious practices involving isolation, asceticism, and self-surrender — from Hindu yoga to Christian monasticism. The soul-life is seen thus as a polar opposite to the sex-life and to the ego-centered (or *persona*-ruled) social-professional life. It is also considered to develop in opposition to the rational life of the intellect, for while the latter operates in a realm of Saturn-ruled logical forms, the soul-life has its roots in the irrational animus-anima functions — and later, in the activities of the collective unconscious represented by Uranus, Neptune, and Pluto.

Jung's conception of personality development, however, is one in which no function is to be repressed at the cost of another. The technique of "individuation" — the achievement of fullness of personality through a rounded (global) development of its many functions — implies a "reciprocal interpenetration" of all psychic opposites, especially of conscious and unconscious. In astrology, this means that all planetary factors in a birth-chart have to be developed and that the chart must be understood as an organic whole, as a symbol of the totality of the human personality. The total development of that personality may occur through relatively smooth interactions or sharp tensions between the various functions; but there is no sense in calling the former types of relationships (i.e., planetary aspects) "good" and the latter "bad," or even "fortunate" and "unfortunate."

The birth-chart gives us remarkable insight into the functional balance within which a personality operates. What it presents, however, is only an abstract picture of complex relations, a formula or blue-print. Nevertheless the possession of such an *objective pattern* allows one to bring psycho-therapeutic procedures to the realm of what Jung calls the "objective psyche." It reduces the infinite complexity of physio-psychological activities to a very few basic *functions* (the "planets," including Sun and Moon, and secondary factors), a few characteristic types of organic operation (the Signs of the Zodiac), and a few fundamental categories of individualizing experiences (the Houses).

These astrological data are all *symbolical.* They must be interpreted, just as dreams must be interpreted. They must be given meaning *in terms of the needs and the level of operation of each person.* Yet, because these are common human structures in all individuals, because the experience of the sky is fundamental in human experience and touches the very roots of human consciousness, and because all human beings strive, however varied the roads they follow, toward one single evolutionary purpose, which is both the central self and the Image of God in every individual, the symbols of astrology have a universal validity. Their significance increases with man's willingness to face the totality of his nature, and to live in his depths as well as in his heights, in his common humanity as well as in his most differentiated and most unique individuality.

6   *Carl Jung's Birth-Chart*

Before interpreting the birth-chart of a man who has perhaps done more than any other living person to establish a consistent and inclusive approach to the problem of individual integration, I need to state again that the truly valid use of astrology, psychologically speaking, is the *clarification* (the making more conscious and objectively real) of the law of the individual's being — thus of the structural foundation of the individual's self. Any sound astrological interpretation should become a guide to self-realization, a help in the "process of individuation." It should seek to transform psychological confusion into a lucid understanding of inherent potentialities, and of the most "logical" manner (in terms of the "law" of the individual's being) to develop these potentialities into fully expressed actualities.

With these aims in mind, the astrologer should first of all seek to determine from the birth-chart the typical nature of the relationship between conscious and unconscious factors, for this relationship sets the stage for the process of personality-integration and self-realization. Obviously, this relationship constantly changes in its actual and precise manifestations; but it is nevertheless established on some kind of structural foundation, which constitutes the "archetype" of the future self.

In every individual, the conscious ego tends to develop in a particular and different way; it emerges from the matrix of the unconscious impetuously or with diffidence, under great pressure or in a smooth, easy manner. The attitude of the ego toward the unconscious depends upon how this process unfolds. This attitude is essentially defined by the time the individual reaches the age of 28 — which I have elsewhere* called the age of a theoretical "second birth." This attitude may still change; but, if it seems to do so radically, it will be in an act of revulsion; that is, it will tend to become repolarized into its opposite, out of sheer dissatisfaction with itself. No single astrological factor can indicate the typical character of the ego's attitude toward the unconscious — no more than any single factor in the birth-chart is sufficient to determine whether a person can be classified as extrovert or introvert — one of the most difficult points to

---

*   cf. the author's *Astrology of Personality* (1936); *New Mansions For New Men* (1938) both in current editions and more recently, *Occult Preparations for a New Age* (Quest Books, 1975). —Ed.

determine from the birth-chart. Yet, by considering the overall pattern of the chart and the way in which planetary factors are individually related, a great deal can be ascertained concerning these basic elements of character.

The over-all pattern of a birth-chart has been shown by Marc Edmond Jones to fall into a few fundamental structural types.* Whether or not one considers his definitions and characterizations fully satisfactory, the principle underlying such a classification is entirely sound, especially wherever the chart's pattern comes close to one of the ideal types. In his book, Marc Jones presents Jung's chart as an illustration of what he calls the *splay* type of pattern – a pattern presenting, in its ideal form, "strong and sharp aggregations of the planets at irregular points" and suggesting "highly individual or purposeful emphases in the life, where the temperament juts out into experience according to its own very special tastes." By considering the over-all pattern of the birth-chart, the astrologer is able to ascertain the relative concentration or dispersion of the person's interests and lines of activity – thus, his particular way of making his experience serve the essential purpose of his being. Experience must be *used* by the ego if there is to be integration of the personality and self-realization. The ego's main function is to personalize the harvest produced by the many experiences of an individual life by referring it to a relatively permanent structure of consciousness and giving it an individual meaning.

Where the planets are evenly scattered throughout the chart, the ego's tendency is to use various and sundry types of experiences or acquired knowledge to universalize the person's interests. The individual then may become involved in many areas of life, finding relationships between a great many facets of being. If the ego has a strong enough sense of structural integrity and enough breadth of vision to integrate this diversified material, the individual's contribution to humankind can be invaluable in its universality or its power to expand the horizons and participation of all human beings in the multifarious activities of a wide world. The particular planets emphasized in the chart by their angular positions indicate the characteristic form the manifestation of the planetary pattern will take. For instance, in the case of Theodore Roosevelt (given by Marc Jones as one illustration of this scattered – a *splash* – type of planetary pattern), Mars rising indicates an aggressive

---

* cf. Marc Jones' *Guide to Horoscope Interpretation.* Also, the author's *Person-Centered Astrology* (C. S. A. Press, 1968) includes an essay entitled "First Steps in the Study of Birth Charts," in which he renames and reinterprets the characteristic planetary patterns.

approach to the problem of integration. Pluto at the nadir, the Moon at
the cusp of the seventh house, and Sun in Scorpio at the zenith, further
stress the imperialistic and willful character of this actional type of
American.

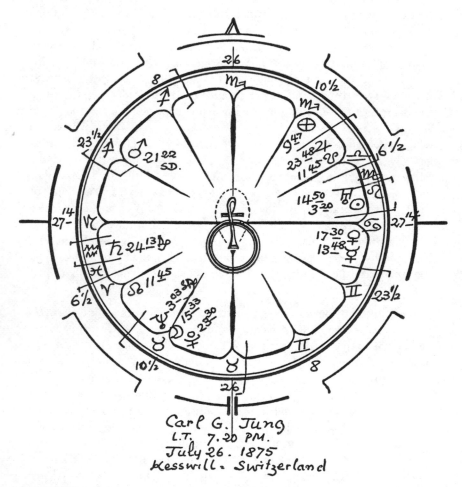

Carl G. Jung
L.T. 7.20 PM.
July 26. 1875
Kesswill. Switzerland

On the other hand, when many planets are bundled together or
divided into very definite groupings in space, the ego's tendency is to
depend upon definite types of experiences, stimulating emphases or
contrasts in order to organize the contents of consciousness and make
them significant. In studying some charts, we can sense the ego's ability to
control the stress induced by conflicting emphases or imbalance of

temperament. In other charts, the planets symbolizing the collective and transcendent elements of experience — or the pressure of the unconscious upon the conscious — have such predominant positions in the birth-chart that various types of danger to the ego may appear very great. These dangers range from fanaticism and irrational one-pointedness to actual splits in the personality — or any other kind of failure in the process of personal and spiritual integration.

Jung's chart displays a definite spreading of the planets; yet a remarkable symmetry as well. Nine planets are contained within two zones of about 90 degrees each — Saturn, Neptune, Moon, and Pluto in one; Jupiter, Uranus, Sun, Venus, and Mercury in the other. Midway between these zones stands Mars in Sagittarius in the hemisphere of the open sky — stationary, stubborn, and with great fiery intensity. Reduced to its essential elements, the pattern can be graphically schematized in the figure below:

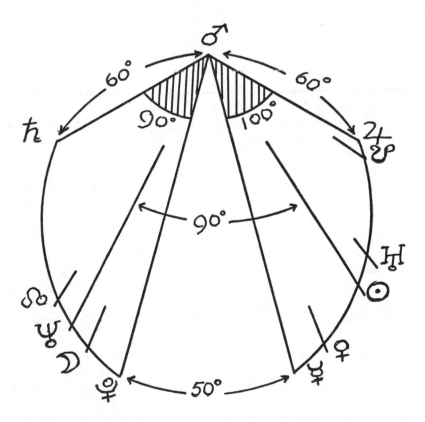

Several outstanding facts emerge as we study this significant pattern. First, we see a balancing of two groups of factors in the zones of the zodiac including the equinoctial points, each group containing planets of opposite polarity to the planets of the other (Saturn, Neptune, Moon in one group are of opposite polarity respectively to Jupiter, Uranus, Sun — and Pluto, in a sense, can also be said to be of opposite polarity to the "inner" planets, Mercury and Venus). Then, we find that these planetary groups are balanced in such a way that they seem to hang from the elevated Mars, somewhat like two loads hanging by ropes from a high peg. The added fact that Mars is in sextile to both the upper edges of the planetary groups (Saturn and Jupiter, which are therefore in trine to each other) adds a constructive and integrative undertone to the meaning of the over-all pattern. The Moon is likewise in sextile to Venus and Mercury, Uranus in sextile to Jupiter; and these several sextiles integrate and balance the strong squares of Saturn to Moon-Pluto, of Jupiter to Venus (and, distantly, to Mercury and the Sun), of Sun to Neptune, and of Moon to Uranus. Finally, the pivotal Mars strengthens the dynamic equilibrium of the power-laden configuration by being in sesqui-quadrate aspect to both Neptune and the Sun.

If all these aspects were considered one by one, as in the old astrological techniques, the result would be an extraordinary confusion of meanings. If, however, the entire planetary pattern is seen as an *engine operating for the integrated release of power,* the picture is both highly significant and inspiring. One rarely finds instances of such harmonic interweaving of stressful and power-releasing planetary factors. Jung's chart can thus be seen, almost at a glance, as a remarkable formula for personality-integration. If we now more closely examine the connected elements of this formula, we will also find a most interesting "balance of power" where the relationship between ego and collective unconscious is concerned. This relationship can also be interpreted as one between "form" and "energy," between "rational" and "irrational," between "meaning" and "life" — as can be seen from Jung's commentary on *The Secret of the Golden Flower,* a most significant linking of ancient Chinese mysticism and modern psychology. The realm of "life" is essentially that of the dualism of energies represented by the Sun and the Moon, while the principle of "form" is under the rulership of Saturn.

In Jung's birth-chart (according to the birth-data furnished by Jung himself to Mrs. Fleisher), we find that the last degrees of Capricorn are rising. Saturn, the ruler of the chart, is in the first house, retrograde in

Aquarius (which it co-rules with Uranus, opposing from Leo in the seventh house). This establishes the Saturnian element of form in strong predominance, even though the fact that Saturn is retrograde suggests that this predominance has to fight against internal enemies. In most cases, Saturn retrograde refers to an ego which has to turn its attention inward rather than outward in order to gain control of the energies of life; this, because the life-energies are not normally held in subservience to either the generic patterns of the human organism or the collective traditions and moulds of society.

Indeed, Jung's chart shows at once how difficult it would be for ordinary bio-social structures of themselves to hold in check his unusually aroused life-energies! Consider that Uranus is conjunct the Sun, that the Moon is surrounded by Neptune and Pluto, and that the two groups are in square to each other; and you will see how radically the "planets of the unconscious" challenge the very substance of Jung's physical and spiritual vitality. Bio-psychic energy is restless and explosive in Jung's being – and the fact that the Sun is powerful in Leo and the Moon exalted in Taurus adds to the intensity of a configuration which could easily lead to emotional explosions or a peculiar overwhelming of the conscious by the unconscious. On the other hand, the strength of this Sun and Moon indicates that, in his work of integration, Jung is able to depend upon a strong vitality, spiritual as well as biological.

Nevertheless, the need for Saturn is very great if the power of the remote trans-Saturnian planets is to be held in check. The metal of the engine of personality must be able to contain and purposefully release an enormous amount of unconscious, bio-psychic power, or "libido." If Saturn does the containing (with its attention "turned backward" toward the unconscious), Mars is in charge of the releasing; and this releasing is shown to operate in an extraordinarily balanced manner because Mars is the pivot of the entire planetary pattern. It is equidistant from Saturn and Jupiter (contraction and expansion), from Sun and Neptune (Selfhood, and its universalistic Vesture; Christ, and His "Robe of Glory") and from Pluto and Venus. It is in the house of social purposefulness and reform, in the sign of abstract knowledge and spiritual teaching.

Mars is the symbol of all directed releases of power, and, in a chart which reveals such a stress on controlled power, everything that relates to Mars is important. If that Mars-outlet should become clogged or distorted, a psychic explosion might indeed be inevitable – even in spite of Saturn's strength of resistance. The squares of Saturn *can* produce constructive power, yet if the dynamic balance were "unhinged" by something happening to the Mars-outlet, these squares would easily turn destructive – especially the ones in which Pluto and the Moon operate. Mars, however, shows outstanding strength – not because of its zodiacal position, but because it is stationary and occupies a focal position in the whole chart. It is strong because two masses of opposite polarities are balanced upon it, and almost neutralized; and, being stationary, it has a character of near immovability. The Sabian symbol for its zodiacal position (Sagittarius 22°) adds to the meaning of these Martian characteristics, for it reads thus: *"A perfect bit of the old world is found in the new: A Chinese laundry has its shutters up and is now itself* – This is the symbol of the reality of the interior world to which man usually shuts his eyes, the retreat of the soul where none but itself may enter. Positively, it is a degree of easy poise; negatively, the world at large in a fullness of enjoyment. The keyword is *Calmness."* (Marc Jones, *Symbolical Astrology.*)*

The literal accuracy of the symbol is quite amazing, for any deep student of Jung knows how he has found a metaphysical and alchemical basis for the interpretation of psychological processes in Chinese philosophy (the yang-yin cycle of compensatory changes, the principle of integration through a mediating function – the Emperor who "assimilates" the unconscious need of his people and projects the structural pattern of the Sky-self upon the State-ego). Besides, is not psychological practice a cleansing process and *catharsis,* which requires great poise, inner "calmness," and periodic withdrawal into one's own inner nature?

Mars, in Jung's chart, rules the ninth house (philosophy, wisdom, teaching) and is found in the ninth sign of the Zodiac; and teaching and psychological practice were for Jung a necessary release. As a psychologist, he had to stand, as it were, poised between *extroversion and introversion* – as the "stationary" Mars is poised between retrograde and direct motion, just going direct. In other words, this Mars is the point of release for a chart in which everything is in a state of balanced dynamism – and thus Mars is itself significantly balanced between two directions of motion. Its sextiles to Jupiter and Saturn establish a practical and smoothly constructive social foundation for the Martian release. Jung's revolutionary

---

* The Sabian symbols presented in this book are taken either from Marc Jones' *Symbolical Astrology* or from the condensed version of the symbols published in the author's *The Astrology of Personality.* cf. also, *An Astrological Mandala: The cycle of transformation and its 360 symbolic phases* (Random House, 1973) by Dane Rudhyar, an expanded reinterpretation of this most remarkable series of symbols. –Ed.

impulses operate within the framework of a mature attitude to society as well as to the conscious ego. The quality of vision and understanding signified by the trine aspect of Jupiter to Saturn is focused outwardly and imbued with idealism through Mars.

Mars' approximate 135° aspect to the Sun and Neptune reveals the deeper sources of Jung's public and educational activities. In any cycle of relationship, the sesquiquadrate aspect refers to the overcoming of actional crisis. It precedes the opposition aspect, which symbolizes (in its positive aspect) full consciousness and illumination, and it follows the trine which gives it a background of "vision" — thus a means to overcome the crisis. In Jung's chart the seventh house Leo Sun is a proud symbol of masculine power and self-development; Neptune, on the other hand, about to turn retrograde in Taurus, is a symbol of inner substance and wealth, of collective-racial evolution. The two planets are "masculine" and "feminine," spiritually speaking — and in square. The former is the center of the totality of being, the Self; the latter, the universal substance which this Self can shape into a "spiritual vehicle" for its manifestation. The shaper and the yet-to-be-shaped are in aspect of crisis — an exact square. Can the tension be resolved? It can only be resolved *if it is exteriorized.* Mars is the exteriorizer. By teaching others, by reforming psychological techniques, Jung *resolved his own crisis of spiritual formation;* and built himself a "body of immortality" — social, and presumably personal, immortality — the Diamond Body of Chinese esotericism, the Christ-Child within of the Christian mystics.

The extraordinary significance of this process of spiritual integration in Jung's life is revealed by the unusual fact that his natal Sun is 11½ degrees behind Uranus — his natal Moon, 12½ degrees ahead of Neptune. Uranus can be said to be in the "solar path" of relationship between the unconscious and the conscious; Neptune, the "lunar path." Again, we see these two approaches in crucial (or "cruciform") aspect to each other, with Neptune exactly squaring the Sun, and Uranus exactly squaring the Moon — a kind of flattened-out X-shaped configuration. Significant polarities are once more seen in a condition of interweaving.

In the last chapter, I stressed the meaning of the Moon in astro-psychological analysis as a mediatrix between the unconscious and the ego — and, in the case of a male individual, as the symbol of the "anima." Jung's anima is shown in an unusual light in his birth-chart, for, as I already said, his Moon is surrounded by Neptune and Pluto and squared by Uranus. In other words, it is entirely dominated by the planets of the collective unconscious. But the Moon is also squared by Saturn, and very strong *in a biological sense* because of its position in its sign of exaltation, the prolific earth-sign, Taurus. Moreover, it is in opposition to the Part of Fortune in Scorpio in the ninth house. In other words, the Moon receives the full pressure of a Cross in the fixed signs (power signs) of the zodiac, besides being universalized and expanded by Neptune and Pluto on either side. This Moon rules over Jung's seventh house (partnership, marriage). It is also in "mutual reception" to Venus in Cancer — a strengthening indication for both the Moon and Venus. This is a very intricate interweaving; and, as the Moon also represents the psychic energy focused through the woman-image in a man's life (another aspect of the *anima,* the mother-wife-daughter image), one may look for some very unusual part being performed by women in Jung's life.

Available biographical notes reveal nothing outwardly spectacular. In 1908 at the age of 28, Jung married a girl belonging to "a conservative Swiss family," with whom he had four daughters and one son. Marriage occurred as his progressed Sun was moving from Leo to Virgo — the mystical Sphynx point of the zodiac. By transit, Uranus may have been crossing progressed Mars at the time of the marriage, and Saturn opposed his natal sun; Pluto was opposing Uranus. The marriage presumably added stability to Jung's life. He had obtained his M.D. degree in 1902, was becoming acquainted with Freud's ideas (although he met him only in 1906), and had probably completed his studies in Paris with Pierre Janet. This was undoubtedly the formative period of his mature personality — but we do not know more than that. It seems, however, that his marriage must have been a polarizing factor at the concrete earth-level of biological-social fruitfulness. Venus has much to do with marriage, especially in Jung's chart; and the accent there is on concrete productivity. The essence of the Moon-function seems, on the contrary, to have operated at a more psychic level. The symbol for the Moon's degree may also be revealing — also the fact that the Moon is found in the third house.

The Moon symbol pictures *An old man attempting, with a degree of success unsuspected by him, to reveal the Mysteries to a motley group,* and it is said to symbolize "the conscious possession of greater knowledge and potentialities than it is possible to bring to immediate practical use." The "motley group" symbol is indeed interesting, for Jung's moon function may have been polarized in a universalistic sense (Neptune-Pluto influence) by the "motley group" of women who, as patients, demanded that he help establish in them a link with their own inner nature through some *spiritual* logos-fecundation. His Mars — the release point of his chart — is in biquintile aspect (144°) to his Moon (his Saturn also in quintile to his Neptune, and Pluto to his Sun), and the "quintile series" of aspects deals with creative activity (the five-pointed Star symbolizing man's victory over instinctual nature). Nevertheless, we can see Jung's Moon being forced into a focus of Saturnian activity through its participation in the square of Saturn to Pluto. However "mystical" his congenital adjustments to life and to the experiences of his environment — and one wonders what kind of person his mother was, or whether or not he had some unusual woman-relative — Jung's destiny (Saturn) compelled him to square these anima-adjustments to the realities of the outer world of society, to frame his undoubtedly most intense intuitional experiences within the logical moulds of a strong ego-consciousness. Without the latter (Saturn), and without the outlet provided by his activities as teacher and reformer, Jung's psychic energies would have become dissipated into an inexpressible "stratosphere" of transcendent vision.

The preceding discussion covers only some of the most essential points to be discovered through a thorough study of a remarkable birth-chart. What makes this chart so valuable for the psychologist is that it is an outstanding symbol of all Jung put into his life work. This, indeed, is always more or less the case when a great personality reaches the "creative" stage — that is, when an organic totality of living experience is brought to the condition of "seed," and thus gains the power to immortalize itself, reproducing its vision in the minds of the coming generations. We also saw the significance of Freud's birth-chart, with its drill-like shape and surgical emphasis, its cutting down to the roots of personality. And if we wish to realize what C. G. Jung brought to the psychoanalysis which Freud originated, we have only to study the birth-charts of these two men side by side. The story they tell is quite striking. To record it fully would take far too much space; but we can see at once that Freud's Sun stands on the same degree as Jung's Moon, and that a most significant relationship exists between the emphasized Taurus-groupings of planets in both charts. We can see that the birth-horizons of the two charts are *identical, but reversed;* the Ascendant of one being the Descendant of the other. And in both cases Mars (stationary in Jung's chart and nearly stationary in Freud's) occupies a position of structural stress or pivotal importance; but how different the implications of these two Mars! Freud's points to the deepest depths, ruthlessly uncovering the hidden remains of social frustrations; Jung's teaches the way to the heights, to a conscious grappling with the problem

of education and social reform or regeneration. Freud, the soul-surgeon —
Jung, the spiritual Guide, the modern Westernized *Guru* holding a most
receptive attitude to universals within the Saturnian focus of a clear
consciousness and a determined ego.

We can also compare these two charts with that of Adler, which
displays a brilliant panoply of self-confident and sanguine optimism, but
which is curiously anchored to the ground-level of consciousness by the
conflicting pulls of Uranus and Saturn — and without any bottom! Here,
too, we see Mars in a strong position in conjunction with the Sun; but it is
a direct, overforceful Mars (placed on Jung's natal Saturn) — and Venus is
retrograde. We have the same planetary emphasis on the sign Taurus —
Jupiter and Pluto on Jung's Moon, Adler's Moon on Jung's Neptune. One
wonders indeed if there is not a basic meaning in this triple recurrence of
Taurus 16° in the charts of the three most outstanding representatives of
the new psychology. Considering the Sabian symbol (above described) for
that degree, could it mean that these three men, in different ways and to
different degrees, tried to bring to the "motley group" of their followers a
knowledge which far exceeded the possibility of its being told to the
Western world at this time?

This chapter concludes our study of modern depth-psychology *per se.*
The next chapters will study a new generation of psychologists who, in
several different ways, have sought to bring to the new psychology some
of the religious or "spiritual" elements which Freudian materialism had
violently tried to discard.

Part II

Beyond Depth Psychology

When the psychoanalytical movement began with Freud, the main preoccupation of its pioneers was *clinical.* Freudian psychoanalysis started as a new approach to psychiatry, and an alternative to the "reduction" of neuroses by hypnosis. Psychiatry was then a very young science, hesitantly seeking its way by the side of neurology. It has developed greatly since 1900, but it deals essentially with the cure of diseased mentalities. It is properly bound to the study of disorders of the brain and the nervous systems. It concerns itself with definitely sick people, and with the removal of symptoms by specific treatments.

The abnormal stresses and the demands for sudden adjustments to unnatural conditions of living featured by modern civilization have, however, led to a state of affairs in which the borderland between acute mental sickness and relatively normal psychological health has become an extensive and thickly populated realm. Mentally or emotionally un-balanced people crowd our farm lands as well as our cities. They may not be really sick, in a patho-neurological sense; but they do not face life with a healthy or wholesome outlook. Their responses to experience are vitiated, deviated, or thwarted by mental-emotional pressures which blind them, or so weary them that they lack the power to adjust themselves vigorously and wholly to new situations. They meet life and people in a fragmentary, uncertain, frustrated, and meaningless or compulsive manner. We may call these persons "neurotics." It might be far better to consider them as individuals who have lost faith in themselves, in human beings, and in life; persons who have lost the power to give meaning to their experience; for they have lost their sense of security and the feeling that the universe is ordered, rich in values, and ensouled by divine intelligence and love.

Psychiatry usually has nothing constructive to offer to these people—no more than the modern type of clinical medicine can offer the millions of tired individuals who are neither diseased nor healthy. The medical profession today is primarily interested in curing diseases, not in giving people the power to live fuller, richer lives. Freud was typically a medical man; his method a reductive, analytical method — a surgical method. Whatever philosophy he had was a pessimistic one, which certainly could not stimulate faith in life, a sense of wonder, or a wholesome feeling of creative joy.

Adler's reaction against Freud's clinical, pessimistic attitude led him to a superficial optimism, and a straining of ego and will, somewhat less obviously paralleling the glorious "affirmations" of Coue and American New Thought. Success-psychology aims at the development of big, strong, positive egos with glowing "spiritual muscles." Social adjustments may be successfully made, but in most cases there is no possibility of real integration on an individual basis. The "success" obtained by such individuals leads, in the end, to a breakdown of the collectivity, because the shadows and frustrations of the "successful," artificially positive individuals may have to be absorbed by others, or by the community (and nation) as a whole.

Carl Jung understood this problem and sought a solution for it in the collective depths of the human psyche. The individual who, for some reason, cannot adjust in a wholesome manner to the challenge of human nature and social conventions becomes overly involved and lost in his difference from others — in the peculiar ways in which he feels separated from the norm. His salvation is possible only by his reorientation and readjustment to the norm. But this norm is not only — as Adler seems to have thought — a social norm, a matter of behavior and success. It is a living power. It is the profound source of the *common humanity of all men and women.* Jung interpreted this common foundation as a group of Primordial Images deep in every person's collective unconscious. The integration of the personality results essentially from the progressive "assimilation" of these collective-generic, bio-cultural images, which are presented by Jung as syntheses of ancestral experiences, the dynamic concentrates of mankind's past. The process of integration is pictured also as the "great work" of the individual person, not in isolation from society, but nevertheless as an essentially individual achievement. Jung, heir to the Swiss philosopher-alchemist tradition, was an individualist and a mystic. He met the universe and humanity *within his own collective depths.*

This approach is not possible for many persons. They would become lost on the way. They have neither the individual heroism nor the depth of mind required for this integration of the self by the self — even with the necessarily limited help of a psychologist-guide. They need something other than primordial images as centers of integration. They need not only an image of the "Self," or of divinity; they need a God who is real, who draws them, who is *with* them — as well as *in* them. They need to consider the "common root" of humanity, not only as a common foundation or source of power and substance, but as the creation of a universal Being who holds in His infinite Mind an "ideal" of them, and who, by His grace, is helping them to become like this ideal. The Jungian psychologist is called upon to be a modernized Hindu *guru,* with a lesser sense of responsibility and of psychic identification with his client-disciple. But most people today are not ready for a *guru.* They need a "religious teacher" who will not only "talk" religion, but practice psychology. Fritz Kunkel built his psychological approach in answer to this need.

Dr. Kunkel was born near Berlin on September 6, 1889; and when he shifted his attention from psychiatry proper to psychoanalysis, he was drawn at first to Adler. He eventually became President of the German branch of the International Society for Individual Psychology. Perhaps the determining factor in his attraction to Adler's viewpoint was the fact that during the first World War he was wounded at the firing line and lost his left arm. Adler's psychology gave much attention to the psychological results of organic disability, because, as we saw previously, it is a psychology of conscious overcoming. At the age of 28, the young Dr. Kunkel found himself facing a crucial readjustment. Twenty-eight is the time of the theoretical "second birth" − i.e., conscious emergence into individual selfhood. For Kunkel, this time of emergence was accompanied by a dire shock and his birth-chart reveals the complex workings of some compulsion of destiny at the time. In his natal chart, Mars and Saturn are conjunct in Leo in the 6th house (illness, army service, discipleship, etc.). When he was wounded (August 20, 1917), the Sun was passing over his natal Saturn, Neptune and Saturn over natal Venus (also in the 6th house and in exact opposition to the natal Moon), while the progressed Moon in the 12th house was coming to oppose the natal Mars. Thus, as Saturn completed its first transit cycle around his birth-chart, Fritz Kunkel was facing a new life.

A year later, he married − as Saturn crossed his 7th house cusp and Uranus crossed his Ascendant. It was not too happy a marriage, but children came, and, out of the experience of their growth, Dr. Kunkel undoubtedly gained the keen insight into the relationship of children to parents which not only brought him fame as a child-psychologist, but also developed into a foundation for his original contribution to psychology: the principle of the "We-experience."

I believe that Fritz Kunkel's life can be accurately divided into three periods, and that he was thus a very significant example of that three-fold rhythm of personality-growth which I discussed in my books, *The Astrology of Personality* and *New Mansions for New Men.* The first 28 years constitute the period of family and race expression. Kunkel was raised on large estates in Prussia; he attended universities in Berlin and

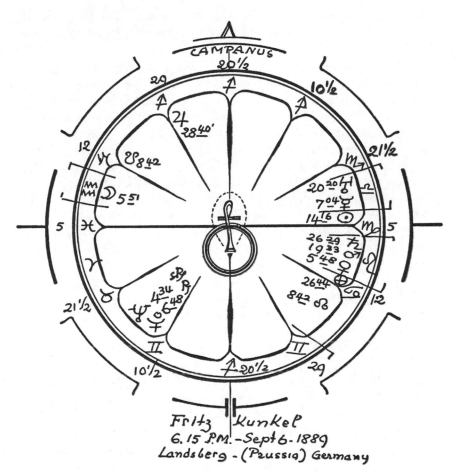

Fritz Kunkel
6.15 P.M. – Sept 6. 1889
Landsberg – (Prussia) Germany

Munich. He experienced the fullness of the upper-class intellectual German tradition. He was drawn into the war maelstrom, and freed from it — and potentially from much more, by "fate." The second period of Kunkel's life, between 28 and 42, divides itself into two halves; it involved the progressive arousal of his individual spirit *under stress and strain.* Kunkel won over fate by the power of his own creativity and faith. The result was the "We-psychology."

How can a growing person emerge harmoniously and happily from the matrix of the "primal We" — as a child, as an adolescent, later as a mature individual? How can psychology and education help to make this emergence successful? How can the ubiquitous crises of growth be met? How can the individual overcome the power of a collective past and any handicap of destiny? What faculties are needed? What psychological methods must be developed? These are the basic lietmotifs to be found in all of Kunkel's books.

During the first half of the second 28-year cycle, Kunkel had to seek answers, as it were, *against* society by overcoming resistances and pressures, unhappiness and the personal-emotional *karma* represented by his Venus, Mars, and Saturn in Leo (an intercepted sign in the 6th house) in opposition to the Moon in the 12th house. During the second half of the 28-year period (age 42-56) — after his second marriage in the winter of 1931-32 — Kunkel was able to give fuller form to his previous experiences, to demonstrate his wisdom and his dominant capacity as an educator and teacher. His books became famous and were published in America. He first came to America in the summer, 1936; then permanently in 1939. He settled in Los Angeles, where he died in 1955. He wrote, lectured, held seminars, and engaged in a private practice which he nevertheless limited in order to pursue his literary and creative work.*

The last phase of Kunkel's life really began when he landed in America (June 23, 1936). Neptune was then crossing his natal Sun, and Pluto his Part of Fortune; Uranus, entering his 2nd house, was in square to the one basic opposition (Moon-Venus) of his birth-chart. Saturn, in the first sector of the birth-chart since the preceding year, indicated a period of ego-reorientation. But Jupiter was nearing the zenith — opposed by a conjunction of Mars and Venus in the 4th house. The demand of his potential public destiny was opposing the rootedness of his personal life in the ancestral home. The stage was set for *a third level of overcoming.*

Kunkel's Jupiter holds the basic key to his destiny, just as the transits of Neptune mark the most significant turning-points in his life. This dominant Jupiter in Sagittarius, "lord" of the 9th and 10th houses (religion-philosophy and public professional life), is undoubtedly the "ruler" of the entire chart. It is the key to Kunkel's psychological doctrines — to the educational-religious emphasis in his teaching. Indeed the twin principles of *self-education* and *religious awareness* are the foundations of his thought.

At first, he stressed the passage from the primordial "We-experience" to the state of individual differentiation and isolation — he knew well the problems this passage produces as, crisis after crisis, the individual seeks to

---

*   His translated books are: *Let's be normal* (1929); *God helps those* (1931); *What it means to grow up* (1936); *Conquer yourself* (1936); *Character, growth, education* (1938); *How character develops* and *In search of maturity* (1943) were written in English — the last book is particularly remarkable.

reach his "true center," not only in the surface egohood born of social overcoming (Adler) but in the depths of unconscious ancestral roots (Jung). Having experienced this "unconscious of the past" in the depth of his being, Kunkel then attempted to become aware of its polar counterpart in the heights of consciousness, the "unconscious of the future." He realized that it is the "presence of God" that draws man futureward and is enthroned at the zenith of the psyche.

Kunkel became interested in religious mysticism, in the Quaker outlook, and in the living spirit of the Gospel. His book, *Creation Continues,* deals with St. Matthew's Gospel. At his 56th birthday, he began his last life-cycle under a near conjunction of Jupiter and Neptune on his natal Mercury, and with his progressed Moon about to cross his natal Pisces Ascendant (if the birth-time he himself gave is correct). The emphasis is indeed Neptunian-Jupiterian through a Piscean "focus of attention" (progressed Moon). Saturn is climbing the rising arc of the birth-chart; Uranus is close to entering the 4th house; Pluto, on the mid-point between Venus and Mars. A new period was beginning for the founder of the We-psychology, which was increasingly becoming a God-psychology.

> We-Psychology (as our trend in psychology is usually called) proceeds from the fact that every human being can only attain to self-experience insofar as he stands in relation to a group of persons. Even though he may actually live in complete isolation, he will yet be bound to some group (either in his thoughts or imagination) through desire or hatred, criticism or hope.
>
> The We-experience is never absent from the inner life of any single person. It is the factor which compels every one of us to share inwardly in the life of others and to intervene − by protestation or criticism, by advocation or contribution, or by the assumption of authority − in the destiny of groups, families, nations and civilizations. (*Character, Growth, Education* − Introduction)
>
> The more a person finds himself, the more he discovers that his personal interest is replaced by his responsibility for the whole. He is really himself only as far as he is a member of his group; and his group is alive only as it is related to mankind. The real Self therefore is not "I"; it is "We." Moreover, the human Self is not only human love and brotherhood; it is at the same time the creativity of the Creator, working through human individuals. He who really finds himself finds God. And he may say, as Saint Paul did, "It is no longer I who live; Christ lives in me" − in this sense our true Self is the final goal of our religious development. At first it is "I"; then it becomes "We"; and at last it will be "He." (*In Search of Maturity*, p. 76)
>
> We have to distinguish between the "unconscious of the past," our racial memory and inheritance, and the "unconscious of the future," containing the infinite pyramid of values,

possibilities, and tasks, which, as it were, are lying ahead of us. Exactly spoken of, these values are timeless, but they must be lived in the future. (*Ibid*, p. 42)

The power which moves us to love, to strive, to create, is not working through the past. It is not a blind force, pushing us from behind, as the exploding gasoline pushes the piston of a motor. It is the creative power of the ultimate end, the value ahead of us in the infinite future, drawing us like a magnet, training us, transforming us like a breeder who transforms flowers into more beautiful flowers. (*Ibid*, p. 49)

Kunkel's psychological approach stems directly from that of the Christian mystics; but he gave to this mystic approach a new formulation in terms of depth-psychology, and with reference to the profoundly changed background of society. Yet, however modified the method of spiritual development Kunkel advocates, it finds as its central core the basic process of interior metamorphosis which the mystics have described in terms of Christian imagery. Reduced to its simplest form this central event is a "crisis." Kunkel stresses this need for "crisis" if there is to be real personal maturity. With the dramatic intensity symbolized by his Leo planets, he wrote:

> The crisis then is the transition from an eccentric, less conscious and less powerful life – pivoting around the Ego-image or an idolized image – to a well-centered, more conscious and more powerful life – pivoting around the real Self. This Self proves to be the center both of the individual and of the group, and therefore transforms the individual into a servant of the group – that is love; and proves to be also our relation to God, and therefore transforms individuals and groups into servants of God – that is faith. The crisis, if it is complete, means conversion. (*In Search of Maturity*, pp. 221-222)

People are "forced into their crisis by the consequences of their deviations," and they usually, with great skill, "try to escape," postponing the inevitable. But there is no true spiritual development without a crisis; the purpose of "religious philosophy" is to find the better, smoother, more effective, less tragic and wasteful way of meeting the crisis.

In his teachings and practice, Kunkel greatly emphasized the value of crisis – even of nightmares! He was fond of saying to people he met in the evening – with a glint in his eyes – "May you have a good nightmare!" The reason for this attitude may be seen in his birth-chart. On the whole, one may consider it a smooth and easy chart with a basic grand trine and powerful sextiles, also a vibrant quintile (aspect of creativeness) of Venus to Uranus – a very different chart from the cruciform pattern of Jung's natal planets. The only square pattern is a very broad one, in which

Neptune and Pluto square the mid-point between Saturn and the Sun – about nine degrees distant from either. However, Kunkel's natal Sun is in Virgo, and, as indicated in my book *The Pulse of Life,* Virgo is a symbol of crisis. It represents the personal crisis; Pisces, social-collective crises.

Kunkel had Pisces rising. His individual destiny and his original life-purpose (Ascendant) were stamped by the social crisis of his era; and, as a German, he was particularly receptive to these values of crisis. But while his birth-land met the crisis of this era in a *regressive* (because neo-tribal) manner, he was able *to integrate himself out of it* through his inner revitalization of the Christ-Image. Thus, destiny led him to America just in time to make it impossible for him to be caught in the disintegration of World War II. He was thus, in a sense, an "archetype" of what his people *should have done.* He too had been maimed – as his nation had been in 1918. But he met his crisis and won. He can therefore be considered an Exemplar for the collectivity from which he emerged as a creative individual, as a Teacher. This was his spiritual destiny; but he had to win it, as everyone must. He won with the power of his elevated 10th-house Jupiter. He was a man with a "mission." He showed to modern humanity (and especially to Europeans) *a way of crisis-overcoming.* This way is the Christed Way – the way made more successful and glorious by the incorporation of the Christ-spirit *through* the crisis.

The center of crisis in Kunkel's chart is the conjunction of Mars and Saturn in Leo – with Saturn close to the "Christ-star" Regulus. Regulus, the "Heart of the Lion," is the Christ-star because it refers to the spiritual transformation of the center of the emotional personality into a Christ-center, the Heart of Man. When the "red lion" (of the Alchemists) becomes the "white Christ," Man is born within and through the individual human being. The "red lion" in the Germanic myth is Frederick Barbarossa (the Red Beard), whose caricatural and degenerate expression was Hitler, with the little mustache. Germans were taught to expect the reappearance of their great Emperor. But the Emperor can only reappear in spiritual value as the Christ – whose "kingdom is not of this world." The proud Mars-Saturn power must be broken, in the realm of the heart (left side of the body), before the heart can be purified and is able to welcome the "presence of God." This is the crisis, common to many – especially to all potential leaders, *including* religious leaders!

This crisis is further centered in Kunkel's chart at the Descendant, the cusp of the house of marriage and partnership, which falls between the Leo Saturn and the Virgo Sun. The Sun is also the mid-point of the arc between Venus and Uranus – a quintile aspect. The "partner" is then the center of crisis, receiving the full blow of the squaring Neptune and Pluto. These two planets stand alone, north of the exact line of opposition of Moon to Venus which links the 12th and 6th houses; thus they act as a focal point of stress, in the 3rd house and Gemini. Saturn is the *karma;* the Sun is the overcoming, in creativity; the Descendant is the field of overcoming. The challenger is the Neptune-Pluto conjunction — that is, the collective destiny and mentality of modern man. Jupiter is the message — and the Messiah within. It is the Light of Creative Meaning. Jupiter is also in near-quintile to Uranus and semi-quintile to Venus. Thus a creative chain of approximate quintiles and semi-quintiles relate the planets above the Venus-Moon line — which tends to be a line of deviated, or "karmic," consciousness.

Later on, I shall discuss the educative possibilities which astrological practice affords, along with the concept of religious self-education, one of the latest developments in Dr. Kunkel's psychological approach. But let me now point out that our present period constitutes a collective, global crisis — made particularly acute by the possibility of a nuclear catastrophy. Every responsive individual not tightly insulated by the structures of his ego is necessarily a participant in this crisis. The teaching of a method to solve the crisis — whether in its generalized social aspect, or as focalized through an individual — is thus the most important need of this day and age. The problem affects many more men and women that those who are ready for psychiatric care. It cannot be solved by an Adlerian glorification of the conscious "I," and the path of Jungian depth-psychology makes too many demands on both the psychologist and the client to be practical for the average individual.

Something more is obviously needed. What Freud took out of psychology must be reinstated, but in a new way. We may call it "the Soul," or "God," or "Faith," or "the Master." One thing seems certain: either human beings will very soon have to use some revitalized or new psychological method enabling them to transform themselves as creative persons, meeting and solving their crises freely and *on an individual basis* — or else, humanity will have to be swept by the compulsive fervor of a new world-religion oriented toward solving crises on *a collective basis.*

Perhaps both solutions can be integrated; but we must recall that in Christendom the individual salvation of the mystic was very much subservient to the collective salvation of the mass of the faithful. Even today, the value of an individualized solution to today's crisis must be powerfully stressed with utmost convincingness *if it is to be made acceptable to the many.*

8   *Jacob L. Moreno & Psychodrama*

A number of years ago, a few young people recently out of college became close friends of mine and talked very frankly about the problems of their youth. They had been to "progressive schools"; their parents were busy professional men and women in most cases; several had experienced homes broken by divorce; they had been left entirely free — free to express themselves, to experiment with almost every conceivable "fact of life." They had been so free, indeed, that I found, to my astonishment, that much of their later adolescence had been passed devising various kinds of regulations to *limit this freedom,* the responsibility and hazards of which they could not or did not dare to bear.

I was astonished because, born as I was in the Europe of the late nineties, I grew up in the very opposite atmosphere. My generation, and those before mine, passionately sought to break away from the bondage of family patterns, of social and religious traditions, even of European culture and Christianity. Our problem was how to achieve freedom; no cost — to ourselves as well as to those around us — seemed too great.

The difference in the psychological situation of youth, before and after the start of the World War era, is of the greatest significance. It provides a background for the discussion of a profound change that has been gradually taking place during the last decade in the field of psychotherapy — that is, with regard to the problem of curing the mental-emotional ills of human beings. Much of the responsibility for this change of approach rests upon the broad shoulders and dynamic mind of Dr. Jacob L. Moreno. Therefore, in this chapter, I will briefly outline some of the main aspects of the "creative revolution" he led in the fields of psychology and sociology and endeavor to relate them to some of the astrological characteristics of his birth-chart.

When Sigmund Freud publicized the concepts and techniques of psychoanalysis in Vienna, the Western world was still struggling out of the Victorian age and its hypocrisy, self-satisfied pomposity, and rationalistic, greedy materialism. When, in 1921, Jacob Moreno began to promote, also in Vienna, his actional-creative and socially oriented ideals and methods of psychotherapy (psycho-drama, sociodrama, group psychotherapy, etc.), he was addressing himself to a generation which had seen its past way of life shattered by World War I and which, in feverish excitement, was challenged to build a new world. This generation proved unable to meet the challenge effectively because its members, while set theoretically "free," did not dare to be truly "creative" *in a socially oriented and organic manner.* Whatever creativity there was — and there was much in the defeated Germanic nations — exploded primarily into anarchic self-glorification and irrational (rather than suprarational, spirit-illumined, and integrated) ways.

In 1900, Freud had to deal with individuals whose strenuous emotional attempts to become free from an obsolete and rigid social order produced in them psychological shocks, wounds, and malformations — neuroses or psychoses. These people were members of a society which had tried to dam up the root powers of life, frustrating as well the creative rhythm of the human spirit. Thus, man had only his middle-class ego left — that is, all that remained was the structure of his own adaptations to a society which was itself soulless and materialistic.

Freud was what I have called a "soul surgeon." His use of the "psychoanalytic couch" with the patient lying down as if ready for a surgical operation, his way of probing through associational materials as with a sharp knife, dextrous pincers, and blood-absorbent gauze (transference), his techniques and his reliance (after the psychoanalytic "operation") upon the patient's will-to-sanity (the circulatory system of the psyche) to somehow build up new soul tissues — all are typical of a surgical approach. Freudian psychoanalysis is clinical; it was born of the characteristically materialistic point of view of the century which produced Feuchner, Marx, and Darwin. His sociological approach was, in a sense, undeveloped; when he thought of group psychology, he thought of a person's relationships to other individuals primarily in terms of the trouble these relationships cause: "In the individual mental life, someone else is invariably involved, as a model, as an object, as an opponent" (*Group Psychology and the Analysis of the Ego*). In other words, Freud saw society as something *already made,* and the individual could only struggle against it, be hurt by it, and (after analysis) become adjusted to it — all for the sake of maximum comfort and happiness.

Dr. Moreno's view was an entirely different one. For him, society is *in the making;* we are all challenged to build its future form, and we can do so only as creative participants in a group activity which should be constant, ubiquitous, and protean (multi-formed). *Everyday, everywhere, and in myriads of ways, the individual must be co-creative with other individuals if he is to be psychosomatically healthy and if society is to be a wholesome and integrated interplay of group activities,* geared to the optimum development of creative, God-expressing freedom. This is the basic thread which runs through the many books and activities of the dynamic, challenging, outspoken, and revolutionary person, Dr. Jacob Moreno. He began life with his mind filled with religious ideals — and his earliest books are glowing attempts to reformulate traditional Western ideas of God. They sing of a God to be experienced as a central and omnipresent creative Reality, active in every moment, a God forever challenging to rebirth all those who cling to old social and cultural forms. Moreno's early writings reveal to us a God who not only creates as Father, Author, and Source of the creative potency in every movement, but who *re-creates* the world in a symbolical "turn-back" of imagination and enacted fantasy. In so doing, He frees Himself and His creation from the fate inherent in all complex group activity.

This glorification of the creative potency of every moment is not an entirely new idea in philosophy; but with Moreno, it took on a new meaning, for he translated it into terms of a practical and purposeful regeneration of a humanity which has left the archaic rituals of ancient society only to become bound, even more meaninglessly, to the modern rituals of mass-production and mass-distribution. Dr. Moreno's fertile mind was adept at devising new techniques and instrumentalities for the use of our technique-worshipping and science-haunted generations. The very complex and challenging methods of actional therapy covered by the broad term *psychodrama*, with all its physical and psychological devices, constitute a means for enabling individuals to re-enact, in a specialized and purposeful setting, those "moments" of their lives in which, because they failed to let the creative power within them act, they built their own chains, sealed their own fate, and set in motion their frustrations and illnesses.

A description of the psychodramatic process at work is obviously far beyond the scope of this chapter. The psychodrama is a world in itself; to operate successfully in and with it (whether as "director," "auxiliary ego," or "double") requires not only skill and training, but an intuitive faculty and a profound sense of human sympathy, not easily taught in college courses to self-consciously intellectual men and women. Briefly, however, a patient is made to re-experience familiar situations in actional awareness. Thus, he is given a chance to rebuild his world — not against his abnormal fantasies, but through them. The essential points are:

1. Action, on a circular stage with several levels, replaces the introspection fostered in many techniques by the patient's lying on a couch or sitting relaxed in a comfortable chair;

2. The doctor-patient relationship ("monovalent" relationship) is transformed into a multi-valent group relationship, in which the patient finds himself challenged not merely to "understand" himself, but to *release* what he, as it were, has *leased* to fate and to the automatic compulsions of complexes and the like; and

3. Verbal and largely symbolical communication (as in depth psychology) is broadened to become more total interaction between real persons. Through these enacted relationships, the personality comes to see itself less and less as a special product of circumstances, and more and more as a participant in a social process which, on the psychodramatic stage, constantly presents new opportunities to regain the lost touch with the creative power within.

It is because this touch was relatively or temporarily lost under some harsh confrontation that the person began to be emotionally and mentally ill. No "reduction" analysis of symptoms can ever guarantee that it will lead to the regaining of a renewed contact with the creative force. The analyzed patient may be able to function more happily and "normally," with less strain and a clearer sense of how to "adjust" to a society which he may learn to tolerate better; but is this *real sanity?*

I believe Dr. Moreno would agree with my often-repeated statement that unless a person who has passed through the crisis of temporary insanity *emerges from it a greater person than before,* the whole experience, including the so-called "cure," falls short of any spiritual purpose. It is all in vain — as many "victorious" wars are fought in vain and become spiritual defeats. What people and nations need most today is a way to emerge from crises, illness, and insanity with the experience of being greater, freer, more purposeful, more vibrant, more loving, more "human" *because of these crises.* This is what Dr. Moreno tried to teach after the war crisis and the revolution had led to no real creative rebirth of society. This is the deeper meaning of his action therapy, his stress upon the *conscious use, measurement, and creative arousal* of group relationship (sociometry).

Dr. J. L. Moreno was born (May 19, 1892, around 4 A.M.*), by a curious symbolism of destiny, on a boat on the Black Sea on its way to Rumania, where he lived for a few years. As a child, he was brought to Vienna, the city which was then witnessing the rise of Freud and the development of psychoanalysis. Beginning in early childhood, Moreno

---

*   The date given in official publications, May 20, is due to an error in translation in the Gregorian calendar of the original birth-date.

showed signs of a deeply religious temperament, as well as a passionate interest in acting out his fantasies. Before he was 20, he was gathering around him, in Vienna's parks, groups of children to whom he would tell and act out all kinds of imaginary tales. He opened a theatre for children, and, at the same time, he began his medical studies, graduating as a doctor of medicine in 1917. In 1919 he became superintendent of Mitterndorf State Hospital near Vienna.

It seems that he then decided that his religious and mystical experiences — which led him to a fresh and vivid approach to the nature and meaning of God — could best form the foundation of a new attitude toward the problem of healing human minds and souls. Led by his demand for *spontaneity and creativity* — the two pillars of his world-view — he developed the "Impromptu Theatre" in 1921, with the goal of establishing a stage on which individuals could act out their own and the world's problems in the absolute freedom of improvisation and in complete disregard for traditional plots, or what he called "cultural conserves." He built a circular stage that was raised above and surrounded by the spectators-participants. The performances were unique and striking, and many Viennese, yearning for a social and cultural renascence, attended. Soon, however, the theatrical gave way to the therapeutic, and the *psychodrama* was born. Thus was started the great psychotherapeutic revolution which has since changed most methods of psychiatry and psychology in America and throughout the world.

Dr. Moreno came to New York in 1925, and settled there in 1927 at the age of 35. He established his reputation as a challenger of the techniques of Freudian psychoanalysis. He strenuously opposed the Freudian interpretation of genius in terms of psychoanalysis and the "debunking" of great artists and religious leaders. He stressed the idea that where truly *creative* forces are active, the concepts of Freud became entirely inadequate and invalid. To Freud's essential pessimism and materialism, Moreno responded with a socially-oriented, spiritually healthy, "Promethean" attitude of creative optimism. He stood for *action-therapy* as opposed to the purely verbal, introspective approach of psychoanalysis. He insisted on transforming the couch into the stage — the psychodramatic stage on which individuals, defeated in the activities of everyday life, could regain faith in their own powers, their spontaneity and creativity, by *acting out* their problems, fears, dreams, and the frustrating experiences at the root of their maladjustments.

Moreno's methods removed psychotherapy from the realm of the isolated individual "confessing" to the more or less hidden and impersonal analyst, and transferred it to the open sphere of social and group activity. His approach indicates a realization that the maladjusted individual is a participant in a group-life (family, etc.) in which he has failed. The human relationships of this group life have confronted him with pressures, conflicts, attacks, or shocks that he could not withstand without fear, soul-paralysis, or collapse. The individual can therefore never really be well and healthy as a positive force in society until he learns to act freely and spontaneously as a member of a group — that is, from the creative center of his personality.

The complex techniques of the psychodrama — complex in spite of their apparent simplicity and seemingly improvisational character — were devised by Moreno to progressively lead the maladjusted or sick personality to actional participation in a group. First, the patient himself summons forth a group of specially trained helpers ("auxiliary egos" as Moreno called them); later, the group may be made up of his own relatives or associates who directly or indirectly participate in the healing process.

From the idea of healing individuals, Dr. Moreno was inevitably led to the concept of healing society. But here he refused to indulge in large-scale social schemes, reform programs, or ideological systems. Society, he realized, is in the making the very moment a few people act together and build (even unconsciously) a web of actional and feeling relationships — which he called a "social atom." Every individual is asked by life to be a builder of the future society, to improve upon its group-patterns of relationship, upon the *quality* of its group-communications and group-interchanges. Operating in many and varied ways, this act of being *co-creative with other individuals* is the very warp and woof of a psychosomatically healthy society. All social, political, and economic actions or programs succeed or fail, sooner or later, according to the extent group relationships are harmonious and creative interchanges or stress competitive conflicts, fear, or greed.

Moreno's contribution to this sociological problem is the new science "sociometry," the principles of which were formulated in his book, *Who Shall Survive? A New Approach to the Problem of Human Interrelations* (1934). Through the use of "sociograms" and numerous other tests, the structure of interpersonal relationships (attraction, repulsion, indifference) within the group is determined; whoever has to deal with the group can learn how to intelligently and effectively approach the group as a whole through its key individuals. This is highly important in a democratic society in which individuals and their ideas or personal decisions are (at least theoretically) the foundations of any group activity.

America, open to such psychological and sociological innovations, and eager for them, was to prove Moreno's initial field of achievement. He released into it his enormous vitality, his enthusiasm and one-pointedness, all the challenging power of a dominant planetary cross in fixed, energy-focusing zodiacal signs. At his birth, the Sun was at 28° Taurus, conjunct the Pleiades (stars of great mystic significance). The north node was close to the ascendant; Mercury was above it, in exact opposition to Uranus and square a tenth-house Mars in Aquarius. The Aquarian Moon in the house of social ideals and reform squared the Sun; the twelfth-house Jupiter squared Venus in Cancer, with the Sun in semi-square to both. In contrast, Mars was trine a nearly exact conjunction of Neptune and Pluto in the first house. The Sun was trine a sixth-house Saturn in Virgo. Several powerful quintiles, semi-quintiles, and bi-quintiles can be seen as clear

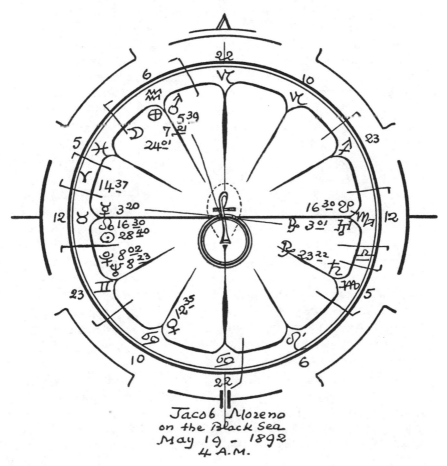

Jacob Moreno
on the Black Sea
May 19 - 1892
4 A.M.

indications of Moreno's potential "genius" and of his future emphasis upon creativity.

The chart, however, is not a peaceful one. Saturn and Uranus, both retrograde, are isolated in the sixth house, while all other planets are in the eastern hemisphere. This suggests deep inner conflicts and the possibility of psychosomatic disturbances. However, the exact opposition of Mercury and Uranus focalizes the conflict on a potentially creative mental-intuitive level, and the T-square of Mars to both Mercury and Uranus provides a dynamic release through the public life (tenth-house). The strength of the fixed-sign cross and the rising Sun is a token of stubborn vitality as well.

The twelfth-house Mercury and Jupiter indicate, therefore, that the pull toward psychiatry was deep — compulsive actually — as was the need to serve and work to fulfill a pattern of destiny. This compulsion of destiny is shown in the near coincidence of the natal horizon with the axis of the Moon's nodes (also near the Mercury nodes' axis), as well as in the 40-degree distance between the two retrograde sixth house planets. These planets, Saturn and Uranus, symbolize respectively the ego as a psychic structure and that which forever tends to shatter such a structure. Saturn in Virgo represents Moreno's insistent realization of the need for scientific methods and technical procedures, while Uranus in Scorpio (opposing Mercury and squared by Mars) stresses power conflicts and a fecundant intuition.

Interesting in the birth-chart of a man who is so much the "actor" is the lack of emphasis on Leo and the fifth house. Lack of emphasis on a house or sign means, however, lack of a *problem* in the corresponding field, *not* lack of function or *activity*. "Acting" for Dr. Moreno was not a problem because it was an irrepressible instinct! The problem in the chart is the twofold Saturn-Uranus emphasis in the house of work and service, personal crises, and illness. This house, and all that it implies, is stressed — and the stress can be, as always, interpreted either positively or negatively. Nevertheless, the tenth house Mars, acting as a dynamic focal release point for this sixth house-twelfth house stress, is a further indication of Moreno's innate and intuitive "acting out" — but, as clearly shown, an acting out quite different in quality from what one would expect from Leo or fifth house indications.

Moreno's great vitality and creativity (the quintile series of aspects refer to the "creative order" of experience) led to a positive statement of what, otherwise, could have made him change places with his patients! Indeed, genius is madness put to a creative use — and, in some cases, but not always — to the service of humanity and God. Moreno chose to serve, as well as to "create." He occupies a position of quite unique importance in the world of psychiatry, having made many bitter enemies among Freudians and various other analysts, especially as chief founder and leader of the movement for *group psychotherapy* (which should be sharply differentiated from the more Freudian type of "group psychology," with a strong attachment to the individualistic methods of depth psychology).* As the father of *sociometry,* Moreno also made a strong mark upon the field of sociology.

The remarkable thing about Dr. Moreno is that a man with his "radical" ideas and his revolutionary approach to psychology, sociology, therapy, and religion was able to establish himself in an official capacity in the psychiatric world and in the world of education. This obviously speaks well for his practical sense and realistic attitude. Among the centers and organizations offering educational programs and information about Dr. Moreno's work and ideas are The Moreno Institute and The American Society for Group Psychotherapy and Psychodrama. Dr. Moreno's devoted and efficient co-worker and wife, Zerka Moreno, continues training and group sessions at The Moreno Institute, Beacon,† founded by Dr. Moreno.

It may be too soon as yet to evaluate with sufficient historical objectivity Dr. Moreno's contribution to our civilization. His summons to spontaneity and creativity; his crusade against all stereotyped forms of culture and reliance upon memory and tradition; his daring attempt to

---

* Editor's note: Today, group psychotherapy and various forms of psychodrama are generally accepted and practiced by mental health professionals around the world. At the time this article was written and published (1951), Dr. Moreno was actively working in America, strenuously challenging the techniques of Freudian analysis, its pessimism, materialism, and its availability to those only of considerable financial means. The degree to which Dr. Moreno – and those who followed – succeeded in making a creative psychotherapy available to countless persons should be readily apparent to anyone interested in the field today. Indeed, group psychotherapies abound, and many of Moreno's psychodramatic techniques ave been adapted for, and incorporated into, current psychotherapeutic practice, such as Gestalt therapy and Transactional Analysis. In fact, Fritz Perls, founder of Gestalt therapy, admitted to the author of this work that he had taken most of his ideas directly from Moreno's work. It is unfortunate that in so adapting his techniques, many practitioners, teachers, and writers in the field have failed to acknowledge Dr. Moreno's innovations and contributions. It is perhaps even more unfortunate that in the popularization of these psychodramatic techniques, the profound and creative philosophy behind Dr. Moreno's work has rarely been considered.

† Most recently, the New Mexico Institute for Psychodrama has been founded (1976) under the direction of Eya Fechin Branham. Other centers in America which feature Dr. Moreno's ideas include Psychodrama Institutes in Boston, Phoenix, and Denver; the Psychodrama Section of St. Elizabeth's Hospital (Washington, D. C.); and the California Institute of Socioanalysis (Long Beach). In Europe, a Moreno Institute has been established in Uberlingen, West Germany.

take the neurotic (and who is not neurotic, these days!) out of the private "holy of holies" of the psychoanalytical confessional and make him act in the "real world" of human relationship (the psychodramatic session), while being safeguarded from the irrovacable results of actions and relations in a cruel and competitive society — these and many other departures which cannot be fully discussed here testify to his innovative genius. His techniques have proven successful, even though they are difficult to apply, except for psychologists and therapists who have somehow *experienced* in their own personal lives the validity of his spontaneous, creative, iconoclastic, and spirit-releasing approach.

Dr. Moreno spoke of "the Creative Revolution," whose beginnings are gradually becoming more apparent in the world — yes, even in spite of the seeming triumph of totalitarianism, mechanical standardization, and commercial materialism ... or, perhaps, *because* of them. We assuredly need such a revolution, and I, for one, have called for it through the last decades — in the arts, in philosophy, and religion ... and in astrology. We desperately need a new "descent" of the Creative Spirit. We need it in the hearts and minds of individuals — for the first and the last word always belong to individuals. Society must call for such creative individuals, such *avatars*. It must be healed enough to recognize them when they come, however strange their behavior or countenance. Society must *want* to be free, to be spontaneous, to be God-transfigured. I believe that creative individuals like Dr. Moreno are voices in the wilderness, stirring others to be free in the only way in which freedom matters — the freedom to act out their own inherent divinity, without which there can be no *real health.*

9 *Roberto Assagioli & Psychosynthesis*

The classical psychology taught in European and American universities until a very short time ago was based primarily on philosophical assumptions and religious revelations. It took the unity of the individual person for granted and viewed it as a transcendental reality. It understood consciousness, reason, will, morality, and definite classes of emotions — "good" and "bad" — as set attributes of this individual person, in whom spirit and matter, reason and passion, God and the devil, were forever waging a struggle for the control of an immortal soul. The individual, being endowed with "free will," could and had to choose which lead he was to follow. Left alone, he would be sure to gravitate toward matter and hell; but through the saving grace of God and His Son (or His Messengers, founders of religions and of all spiritual instrumentalities for regeneration), the individual could be "saved" and regain the divine heritage which somehow he had lost.

We may call this the Platonic-Christian basis of psychology; and it is against the spirit of such a psychology that Freud fought, as a representative of the pragmatic, empirical, and scientific approach to nature and human experience. Being a physician whose task it was to cure people with sick minds and disintegrating personalities, he determined to ignore all the *a priori*, taken for granted ideas concerning man-the-individual, and to observe afresh what he saw. He found that the study of acute cases of mental disequilibrium, and particularly of strong neuroses, revealed processes of psychological adjustment and inhibition which were actually duplicated, in less definite forms, in supposedly sane persons.

From this fact, he was led to investigate many traits of human behavior, experiences which did not fit into the clear-cut picture of individual man drawn by the Platonic-Christian psychology, or for which supernatural causes were claimed. His analytical probing went from dreams to mystical visions, from jokes to great artistic creations, from childhood attachments to the claims of Prophets. Ideals and idols toppled in his wake. Could their genesis not be explained on the basis of those psychological processes revealed by the insane? If a paranoic believes himself to be God, how different is this belief from that of the Prophets of old? If indisputably sick neurotics produce volumes of "automatic writing" ranging from chaotic statements to moral precepts, how are those different from the Koran, or "divinely inspired" books? If dreams can be

explained convincingly in terms of physiological or psychological disturbances, why not also the "visions" of the Saints?

Freud's "nothing but" interpretations of the experiences and activities
which brought to mankind the treasured products of its artistic and
religious cultures failed, however, to convince a vast number of thinkers
and psychologists. Without repudiating the facts uncovered by Freudian
analysis, Carl Jung sought to establish new interpretations of these facts by
associating them with other equally valid ones. Granted that certain
mental activities of the insane seem to duplicate or parallel activities and
experiences considered as profoundly spiritual in pre-Christian civilizations, the *results* of the two types are absolutely opposed. A madman
hears "voices" — and so does Joan of Arc. The former gets more insane,
the latter saves and integrates a people and becomes the foundation of a
nation.

In other words, the *observable process and psychological phenomenon*
may be the same in the two cases; yet, because the results are totally
different (indeed, opposite) we *must* conclude that the causes of the
abnormal conditions also are totally different. This leads to the problem
which Jung tried to solve: How can we discover the value and meaning of
psychological processes and experiences which are beyond the scope of the
individual person and beyond the norm of a particular culture or society?
How can we constructively interpret and deal with their first appearance in
a person's life so that this life (and the lives of others) may be enhanced
and integrated, rather than deviated and pushed to some tragic ending?

Jung consistently sought to remain at the level of observable facts of
human psychology. He has refused to take anything for granted, especially
any claim for the *real, concrete existence at a "higher" level* of
transcendental entities, such as "spirits," the Soul, or God — a claim made
by most religions, and by "occultism," modern or old. He interprets
human experiences — even the most puzzling and seemingly transcendental
— almost exclusively in terms of energies and processes. We face a world of
energies, neither good nor bad, neither constructive nor destructive. It is
our task to *use* them through the various processes of bio-personal
development. If, however, *for any reason* a person is afraid of them, if he
shrinks from making a positive, integrative use of them, or he opposes,
thwarts, or deviates the processes of growth within his total bio-psychic
organism — then, the energies turn destructive, and the integrative
processes of human nature reverse their polarities and lead to disintegration. The reason for this negative attitude may be collective or individual,
hereditary or environmental, seemingly accidental or linked with the

destiny of larger groups. Whatever it be, it should be uncovered by the psychologist and removed as far as is possible; then, under guidance, the processes of human nature will be restored in their positive direction, and the person's growth toward an ever greater state of integration will be resumed.

Jung's approach, like that of early Buddhism (in which man is left quite alone to face and overcome the eternal "Wheel of Change" and its illusory attractions) offers no supernatural agency for salvation; no Supreme Person to Whom one might pray, and no transcendent God-created Soul to pull spirit-ward its erring child, the "personality." As a result, it has seemed vague and not comforting enough to many people. In studying Dr. Kunkel's We-psychology, we have seen how this great psychologist with an eager, devotional-mystic feeling for God brought back to psychotherapy a sense of the reality — transcendent, yet "concrete" — of a Supreme Being, Who has an original purpose and plan for everyone and Whose "grace" sustains and draws the individual through and beyond his crises. Kunkel's psychology is an attempt to integrate depth-psychology with the essence of an undogmatized and individualized Christian mysticism. On the other hand, the Italian psychologist Roberto Assagioli, founder of the technique of Psychodsynthesis, sought to integrate depth-psychology with the modernized expression of the occult, Platonic-Hindu approach to man and God. The two efforts complement each other and are highly significant answers to the evident need of a confused and machine-haunted humanity.

Roberto Assagioli was born at noon, February 27, 1888, in Venice, Italy. He took his medical degree in neurology and psychiatry at the University of Florence. He had broad philosophical and cultural interests and participated in various groups of young Italian liberals and thinkers, such as the one led by Giovanni Papini and Guiseppe Prezzolini, whose organ was the review, *Leonardo.* In Florence, he directed the Philosophical Library founded by Julia H. Scott, an American woman, and from 1912 to 1915, edited the scientific periodical, *Psyche.* As a result of his varied clinical and educational experience, he evolved the technique of person-ality-reconstruction which he called "Psychosynthesis." In Rome, he founded his Instituto de Psicosintesi, which was presided over, until her death, by Countess Spalletti Raspoini, President of the National Council of Italian Women. He travelled and lectured widely in Europe and America. He died in 1974 after having published two important books, *Psychosynthesis* and *The Act of Will,* and having seen his ideas spreading widely in America and in Europe.

After the beginning of World War II, his work in Rome became
increasingly difficult because his humanitarian and international ideas and
attitude aroused more and more suspicions and hostility from the Fascist
government — until, in 1940, he was arrested and kept in solitary
confinement for about one month. Dr. Assagioli told his friends that this
prison episode was an interesting and valuable experience which gave him
an opportunity for undertaking special psycho-spiritual exercises. Later
on, he was able to lead a comparatively quiet life, secluded in the country.
In 1943, however, he was again actively persecuted and had to hide
himself in remote mountain hamlets. There he found companionship with
an English parachutist and several fugitive prisoners and had two narrow
escapes from the Nazi-Fascists who were after him personally and who
sacked and destroyed his family's country house near Florence. The arrival
of the Allied troops liberated him in August, 1944. After the end of the
War, he set himself to the task, which he had so long delayed, of putting in
writing the entire scope of his concept of psychosynthesis. I had been
staying with him in his lovely house in the hills above Florence in 1936
and seeing a good deal of him in Rome during that fall, and we renewed
our correspondence after the War. At that time, he wrote me that he was
working on an inclusive formulation of psychological ideas under the title
From Man to Humanity. He said that he was particularly interested in a
new definition of psychological types — more detailed than Jung's — in the
study of psychological disturbances attendant to the various phases of
spiritual development, and in a study of group-relationships of all types.
The following paragraphs, which he himself wrote, indicate at least the
general trend of his particular approach.

> The diagnosis of the trouble which is affecting psychology at
> present clearly indicates the necessary cure, or the ways to
> inaugurate a new and more fruitful phase of its development.
>
> This new phase, in contradistinction to that which has led up
> to the present crisis, will necessarily have an outstanding
> synthetic character. Such character and trend should express
> itself not only in one respect, but in several, which it is well to
> clearly realize:
>
> 1. The pooling of all available material which may be of value
> and usefulness without any exclusion of origin, time and place.
>
> 2. The starting point of the study of man should be his inner
> center of being, what he essentially is, and all other psychological
> facts, energies and outer manifestations should be studied in
> living relation to the center, which ever endeavors to co-ordinate
> and synthesize them into a living unity.
>
> 3. It should take into full consideration all the higher, the
> superconscious and the spiritual aspects of human nature which
> up to now psychology has mostly left to be dealt with by

philosophy and religion, thus creating an unfortunate separation, and often conflict, in the ways of considering and handling human nature.

4. The principle of synthesis should be extensively applied to group psychology, developing from that standpoint to a definite branch of inter-individual psychology in which the various kinds of group-psyche, from the couple on to the family group, to the various communities, up to the psyche of humanity as a whole, would be studied.

5. The use of the synthetic principle in the practical applications of psychology, developing thus the art and the techniques of psychosynthesis, aiming at a complete and harmonious development of human personality, with special emphasis on its higher and spiritual aspects.

What Dr. Assagioli means by "the higher, superconscious, and spiritual aspects" of man is made clear in an early article *Psychoanalysis and Psychosynthesis* published in 1934 in "The Hibbert Journal"; but before we come to this we should consider, at least briefly, the birth-chart of the psychologist himself — for the psychology is always an expression of the psychologist. Roberto Assagioli's chart is very different in general structure from that of Kunkel, or of Freud and Adler. While it is somewhat more similar to Jung's chart, it presents some very striking features; features which can indeed be seen to clearly symbolize his ideal of psychosynthesis.

The basis of Assagioli's chart is the configuration which I originally isolated and interpreted many years ago, calling it the "mystic rectangle." The term "mystic" was not particularly fortunate, and at times I have substituted for it the qualification "sacred" or "integrative." All these adjectives are attempts to characterize a configuration symbolizing a process of integrative synthesis of personality, to which is added an undertone of self-consecration to a super-individual purpose. In its simplest form, the rectangular configuration is one in which four planets are so related that they constitute two opposition aspects, two sextiles, and two trines. The oppositions form the diagonals of the rectangle, and in Assagioli's case they are those between Venus-Saturn and Pluto-Jupiter. The shorter sides of the rectangle are represented by the sextiles of Saturn to Pluto and Jupiter to Venus; the longer sides, by the trines of Venus to Pluto and Saturn to Jupiter.

Rectangles of such a shape can be considered as "altars" or "chambers of initiation," in terms of archaic symbolism. They define *a consecrated space within which a transcending process of integration and spiritualization takes place.* They are to be differentiated from the "Mandalas" (or magical squares), which Jung associated with the process of personality integration, in that they link only two zodiacal elements (in this case, air and fire) while a perfect planetary cross (or geometrical square) links the four elements. The perfect square has thus more finality, is more self-contained; while the rectangle configuration of planets emphasizes the resolution of two conflicting natures into a dynamic effort toward a transcendent or sacrificial goal.

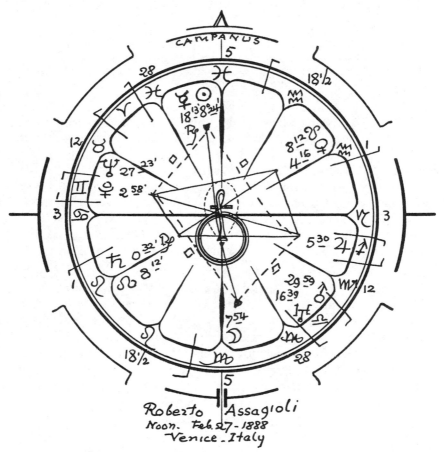

Roberto Assagioli
Noon. Feb. 27 - 1888
Venice - Italy

In Assagioli's chart, however, we see not only the above mentioned rectangle, but a far more complex pattern; there is also a Sun-Moon opposition (a full-Moon symbol of extreme awareness and illumination) which forms a perfect cross with the Pluto-Jupiter diagonal of the rectangle (and semi-sextiles with the Venus-Saturn diagonal). Moreover, Uranus is related to the Pluto-Jupiter diagonal through a sesquiquadrate and semi-square (aspects of stressful activity or response); while Mercury is also similarly related to the Venus-Saturn diagonal. As Neptune is only five degrees away from Pluto (and thus participates in Pluto's aspects), and as Mars also squares the Venus-Saturn diagonal, there exists an extremely complex pattern of oppositions, squares, semi-squares, and sesqui-quadrates held together by sextiles and trines.

What this means is that, in Assagioli's personality, a great variety of interests and foci of attention are represented, that his nature is widely open to the universe (Cancer rising, Sun and Mercury retrograde in Pisces) and contains many conflicting elements. These, however, are so disposed and interrelated as to make a very rich and complex type of personal integration *possible*. "Possible," of course — not certain. A birth-chart is a pattern of potentialities; it does not provide any proof that these potentialities will become fully actualized. But the very pressure of this unusually varied and inclusive potential upon Assagioli's consciousness, and the very challenge of a personality structure able to stand so many lines of stress and creative projection, is discernable in the ideal of psychosynthesis which he described.

I should stress again that a person's ideal creation is the exterior-ization of the goal to which his total personality reaches out. His ideal is exteriorized as a doctrine; his strivings are generalized into a method; the blueprints of the perfected type, which is himself as a perfected person, are projected as a "vision," or even "revelation" — even though the man himself is yet far from becoming in actual concreteness of living all these things which he teaches, visualizes, and strives toward. This applies to all of the psychologists whose charts we have studied so far. The chart reveals the character of the psychology, because the psychology is the projection of what the man *potentially* is, and what he seeks to become. He teaches himself — as he teaches others. The teaching is significant insofar as it is timely — that is, as it fills the needs of a group of individuals then living, or starting on their life-journey.

Dr. Assagioli's psychosynthesis is an answer to the chaos — but also the universalization of interests and strivings — which our generation has created. The multiplicity of energies and stresses, and the complexity of a global openness, are facts which must be met. Assagioli has had to meet them in his own person. And the solution has come out of the confrontation. How completely he has worked out the latter in his own life is beside the point here. The "pattern of solution" — the image of salvation, the principle of reconciliation of opposites — is obvious in his chart, and psychosynthesis is an interpretation of it. At the level of the personal life, *it corresponds to global planning in the new society now in the making.*

Space is lacking to adequately condense Dr. Assagioli's views on the constitution of the complete human being. This much, however, can be said. Man, he believes, includes: 1) the *lower unconscious* which "contains, or is the origin of" the elementary psychological activities which direct the life of the body instincts and lower passions, "complexes," dreams and imagination of an inferior kind, manifestations of lower "psychism" and medium-ship, etc.; 2) the *middle unconscious,* formed of psychological elements similar to those of our waking consciousness and easily accessible to it; 3) the *higher unconscious,* or *superconscious;* the region whence higher intuitions and inspirations come, the source of genius and mystical states; 4) the *waking consciousness,* the part of our personality of which we are directly aware; 5) the *normal conscious self,* the "I" which at once "is the *centre* of our consciousness and *contains,* so to speak, the changing contents of consciousness" (sensations, thoughts, feelings, etc.); 6) the *spiritual self,* "a permanent spiritual center, the true self ... fixed, unchanging, unaffected by the flow of the 'mind stream' or by bodily conditions," the personal conscious self being merely its reflection, its projection into the field of the personality.

This concept of the existence of a personal or lower self (which is a mere "reflection") and of a spiritual or "true" self (latent and unrealized by the conscious ego, in most cases) is typical of what we call the Platonic-Christian approach to psychology; it especially reflects the teachings of H. P. Blavatsky with which Dr. Assagioli was well acquainted. The entire structure of most religious beliefs — and also the claims of the "occultist," medieval alchemist, and modern theosophist — rests upon this dualism, which is nevertheless an "illusion," because there is, spiritually speaking, only one source of selfhood.

Freud (and the type of psychology based on "scientific materialism," empiricism, behaviorism, etc.) sought to prove that there was no validity in taking for granted the existence of such a transcendental and "true" self; that it could be very simply explained away. But Freudianism and psychological materialism do not offer a satisfactory or *healing* solution to the conflicts, insecurity, and generalized state of semi-neurosis of most people. In plumbing the subconscious depths and busying himself with "reducing" the complexes of the individual by mental surgery, did Freud not blind himself to the spiritual reality of the individual, the true self or spiritual soul?

While a psychologist like Dr. Kunkel seeks to reestablish this spiritual reality in human consciousness by the way of Christian *mysticism,* Dr. Assagioli pursues a similar end along the path of ancient and modern theosophy. In this sense, the Nordic-German approach complements the Mediterranean tradition, whose roots reach to the ancient foundations of Hindu transcendentalism and yoga techniques. According to Dr. Assagioli, his "conception of the structure of our being, while it includes, coordinates and arranges in an integral vision all the data obtained through various observations and experiences, permits of a wider and more comprehensive understanding of the human drama, of the conflicts and problems that confront each one of us; it indicates the means of their solution, the way of our liberation." The way to such a liberation, to a healing of the "fundamental inferiority of man," to "peace, harmony and power" is four-fold. The four stages on the path are defined by Assagioli as:

1. A complete knowledge of one's personality.

2. Control of its various elements.

3. Realization of one's true self, or at least the creation of a unifying center.

4. Psychosynthesis: the formation or reconstruction of the personality around the new center.

I cannot detail here the characteristics of each of these stages, but I shall say that the last one (the process of reconstruction) is divided into three essential phases:

a. The utilization of our energies, of the forces released by the preceding process of analysis and disintegration of the subconscious complexes and attachments, and of the powers, aptitudes and tendencies latent, and up to now neglected, which exist at the various inner levels (the application of psychodynamics).

b. The development of the elements which are deficient or inadequate for the purpose we desire to attain . . . by means of direct evocation, auto-suggestion, creative affirmation, or by methodical training of the weak or undeveloped faculties; a training very similar to that used in physical culture or in developing technical skill, as in singing or playing an instrument.

c. The coordination and subordination of the various psychological energies and faculties, in the creation of an inner hierarchy, a firm organization of the personality. This order and rule presents interesting and suggestive analogies with that of a modern state, with the various groupings of the citizens in towns, social classes, trades and professions, and the different categories of municipal, district, and state officials.

The criticism which will be levelled at such a doctrine by many psychologists is that it is too rational, too well-ordered, too formalistic, or that its "spiritual realities" are taken for granted, not based on direct experience, but rather on religious authority or "esoteric" interpretations. The more mystical and less formalistic approaches of Jung and Kunkel stress more the factor of "process," of flow. Psychosynthesis does not start the study of man with "his inner center of being, what he essentially is," for conscious human experience does not begin with this inner center. In Dr. Assagioli's system man is viewed as if from above, or outside of what he himself feels, knows, experiences. It can be said to be a theoretical or philosophical, more than a purely psychological view; a mental, rather than an experience-conditioned, approach. *Structural clarity* and a well-defined workable formula for psychosynthesis may be its fruits; yet there is danger in that a philosophical system tends to be superimposed upon the living substance of human search and human conflict – and sometimes *substituted* for the throbbing actuality of the experienced need of the moment. It is a danger inherent in all types of planning, and in all but the simplest kinds of classification. The most disputable point in Dr. Assagioli's approach is that which deals with his attitude to the "spiritual self"; and because the central key to any psychology is the psychologist's understanding of the nature of this self, I feel it is necessary to devote an entire chapter to this subject.

The central problem of psychology is the determination of the nature of the Self.* What do we mean when we say "myself?" And how far can we make a distinction between the expressions "myself" and "the Self within me?" What significance is there in speaking of a "universal Self" in contrast to the "individual Self?" The answers given to these basic questions differ greatly among the contemporary psychotherapists whose approaches we have discussed so far. The scale of opinion stretches from Freud, the materialist, to Assagioli, the transcendentalist. All these men observe the same phenomena and all seek to heal; yet each sees his task in a different light, because, to each, the Self also appears in a different light.

If we consult the dictionary, we find the word "Self" defined as "an individual known or considered as the subject of his own consciousness. Any thing, class, or attribute that, abstractly considered, maintains a distinct and characteristic individuality or identity." (*Funk and Wagnalls.*) But what is exactly meant by "subject" and by "consciousness?" The concept of "subject" cannot be discussed without considering its opposite, the concept of "object." Consciousness (as known to man) is a relation between subject and object, between the "I" and the world. Our experience, however, is not limited to the "outer world," that is, to the things which we see, touch, hear, bump against, sensually enjoy or are organically hurt by. We also experience an "inner world," an uninterrupted sequence of feelings and thoughts or mental images – even if we close all the gates of our senses and withdraw in undisturbed solitude and muscular inactivity. Solitary, silent, inactive as we may appear to be, we can nevertheless know emotional pain of the most acute type, or bliss – we can be haunted by mental images forever repeating themselves, or be illumined by inspiring realizations.

Whether experiences deal with this inner world, or with sensations

---

* Several different concepts of the "self," with or without a capital *S*, have been put forth and are logically acceptable if consistent with certain metaphysical premises. In *The Planetarization of Consciousness,* Rudhyar has used the term *self* (without a capital *S*), referring to the root-power which sustains the entire organism from birth to death. It is an unvarying vibration which is power, but not consciousness. The task is to bring this power to the condition of all-inclusive consciousness. When this is achieved, one can really speak of the *Self.* In the following two chapters, however, Rudhyar has followed the thinking of depth psychology, particularly as formulated by Jung and Assagioli. –Ed.

induced by external physical entities, they must be considered as referring to "objects" of which a "subject" becomes conscious. This subject is what we call "I." All experiences, however, are due to the fact that the subject notices *changes* in the nature, position, and activities of objects to which he is related — whether they be physical objects, or mental-psychic images of his inner world. But could the "I" actually notice changes in his world, if he himself kept also constantly changing? Briefly said, consciousness is the relation *between objects which are in a state of change, and a subject who does not change;* thus, who "maintains a distinct and characteristic individuality or identity." If the subject (or "I") is not able to maintain these, if he is caught in "the wheel of change" and loses his distinct and characteristic identity, then consciousness vanishes and is replaced by unconsciousness. The "I" is overwhelmed by the world; the (relatively) changeless is defeated by change.

In order that the world may not overwhelm the "I," it is obvious that this "I" has to be basically different in nature from the world. He has to be *"in* the world, but not *of* the world"; a rock of permanency in a sea of change. But what most persons call "I" is actually similar in nature to the world — that is, they themselves are "affected" (thus, changed) by violent or persistent changes in the society and the body of religious and cultural truths or values of which they are most definitely parts. The average person's Self does not maintain its characteristic identity in times of social convulsions, simply because it is *rooted in* a particular type of society and conditioned by particular social-cultural structures. Indeed, this Self is basically an expression of *the place and function the person occupies in his society.* Astrologically speaking, the character of this Self is determined by Saturn; and the nature of his participation in society, by Jupiter. These two planets are essentially representatives of social, collective functions — that is, a person's differentiation from and stable maintenance within a greater whole of which he feels himself a part.

If a person lives in a static kind of society which remains rooted in a stable economy, a steady religious and class outlook, and a set geographical environment, the unchanging character of this society reflects itself in the person's life as a Self. Whatever changes are experienced by this person (mainly on account of his organic development, capacity to work, and age) can be readily explained by his religion and the traditional wisdom of his culture and made to fit into broad patterns of cyclic order. He thus remains firmly established in his place, social function, and his relationship to other persons similarly stable and well-rooted. His "I" is steady, simply because it is a function of a steady social order. But if the person lives in a society which is in a state of wholesale upheaval and crisis — like ours today — and in the midst of disintegrating beliefs, morals, and social patterns, his "I" inevitably becomes involved in this frenzy of change, *as long as it is rooted in the soil of society.* As this happens, there is no longer in this person any permanent center or frame of reference to which the continual and unpredictable changes in his outer and inner worlds can be related. Consciousness slips away. Unconsciousness, and the dark, destructive powers it hides, overwhelm the "I." The "rock in the sea of change" is eroded away by the demented sea. It *can* be thus disintegrated, because rock and sea are both substantial entities. Then the person unconsciously performs actions which he cannot significantly relate to his "I," actions which dismay or revolt whatever is left of that Self and its "characteristic identity." Because of fright, the "I" freezes or splits and disintegrates, and neurosis, psychosis, and insanity follow in sequence.

When the "I" breaks down in such a manner during a steady social period, the event is exceptional; and it is attributed to "possession" by elemental or evil forces which the church attempts to ritually exorcise. But when the society and the religious tradition disintegrate, and the breakdown of "I" becomes a frequent occurrence, the need for a general and basic reconsideration of the nature of the Self becomes imperative. The psychologist has no way to rebuild or to stop the disintegration of society and culture. He can try to help the few individuals he can reach to rebuild the Self that has become rigid beyond the possibility of relationships which "make sense" to their inner and outer worlds. He may piece together the shaken rock of the Self and try to give it more strength to face the onslaught of the sea. This, however, cannot lead to very lasting, and certainly not to creative and radiant, results. The only other course is to admit that the shattered "I" is not the *real* subject, the dependable center of reference, that it is not, by nature, permanent and steady — but only so if all around it is ordered and static. A *real* subject or center must be discovered. The shatterable "I" is then called the "ego" in contradistinction to the real "I," named the "Self" or the "higher Self" (in contrast to the ego or "lower Self"). Psychotherapists such as Jung, Kunkel, Assagioli, et al., recognized this distinction and have at great length defined the two factors, thereby providing a basis for a new type of psychological healing.

According to Carl Jung, the ego is merely the subject or center of a person's field of consciousness. The Self is the subject or center of *the totality of the personality;* "it includes not only the conscious but also the unconscious portion of the psyche." For Jung, "the unconscious processes stand in a compensatory relation to consciousness," and these two parts of the psyche "complement each other in the Self." The Self, therefore, is to be regarded not only as the "center" of the total personality, but as the "circumference" encompassing both the conscious and unconscious activities which this total personality includes. The Self can never be *fully known* by the ego, for this would mean that a limited part (or aspect) would know and be able to describe the whole – an impossibility. To the ego, the Self can appear, however, as the ultimate goal of personal development; as an all-inclusive container of experiences which includes far more than those of the ego; as the permanent center of reference and ideal subject. The Self can also be seen as *our individual share in God,* that focal point of our psyche in which God's image shows itself most plainly, the experience of which gives us the knowledge, as nothing else does, of the significance and nature of our likeness to God.

Dr. Kunkel describes the distinction between the ego and the Self more in terms of their being respectively the "false" and the "true," or the "temporary" and the "essential," centers of the personality. He sees the ego also as "the sum total of what we know or what we think we know about ourselves ... a system of statements concerning our goals and means, gifts, capacities and limitations ... an inadequate portrait we make of our real Self." This ego tends to live a life of its own, as an independent, rigid "object," while the Self displays new qualities and growing maturity. In many cases the Self and the ego develop in opposite directions. Our behavior-pattern and decisions come "to serve the ego instead of the Self" – and this is *egocentricity* – whereas, when our actions "flow from the real center" (the Self) they show true creativity. The ego's influence is *always* unfavorable. Egocentricity begins in early childhood as a natural adjustment to the child's egocentric environment. Kunkel also writes that "The very essence of 'sin' is the substitution of a sham center, the ego, for our real center, the Self." This substitution results in loneliness and distrust of people in our group, isolation from and loss of knowledge of God, and then anxiety. "Our creative center, the Self, is our positive relationship to God." It is "the creativity of the Creator working through human individuals" – and "the more a person finds himself, the more he discovers that his personal interest is replaced by his responsibility for his group and humanity, the real Self is not I but We" (*In Search for Maturity,* Ch. II). Thus, for Kunkel, the ego is a "wrong," "ex-centric" factor hindering our creative life; while Jung thinks of it rather as the unavoidably incomplete first phase of the development of personality, in which conscious processes alone are recognized.

The Italian psychologist Roberto Assagioli presents a somewhat different picture, as he places the Self, in his diagrams of man's total constitution, *at the top* of an ovoid shape, at the center of which the ego is found; moreover, he does not use the term "ego," but contrasts the "normal conscious Self, or 'I' " with the "spiritual Self." In his view, the conscious Self is merely a projection of the spiritual Self with which it is linked by a magnetic "thread" or *descending ray*. These ideas of a "descending" projection of the true Self (the source of spirit and light) into the field of the personality, of a true Self which is transcendent to the field of personality (yet from which every "student of man should start"), of an opposition between "the lowlands of our ordinary consciousness and the shining peak of spiritual Self-realization," are all characteristic of the Platonic-Christian or "occult" approach to psychology. As the "lower Self" comes to be united with the "higher self," the individual, in whom this most arduous process reaches its consummation, "transcends altogether the human kingdom and becomes a true spiritual being." In this process the transcendent Self acts as a new "unifying center" around which a new and equally transcendent personality is built: the goal of psychosynthesis.

In studying the various definitions of the Self and of the ego offered by the modern psychotherapists, one is likely to be struck by the confusing use of the term "center." I believe that this confusion resides in an inability to differentiate between *structure* and *contents*. To say that both the ego and the Self are "centers" is, in my opinion, to ignore the fundamental differences between them. This difference should become clear if we return to our first stated definition of the "I" as that *permanent factor in reference to which the forever changing elements of human experience (in the psyche as well as in the outer world) become conscious and significant*.

Two types of things, however, can be considered as permanent factors of reference: a (relatively) set structure (the ego) — and a (relatively) unvarying quality, vibration, or tone (the Self). For instance, in a classical symphony, all that takes place musically can be referred to a particular scale; and the scale is a set structure — that is, a fixed pattern of relationships between a series of notes. These notes have meaning and function with reference to that pattern, in terms of the place they occupy in it. But this element of structure is not enough. The symphony is not only a written score, an abstract structure of "notes"; it is also a very complex combination of sounds or "tones" actually played on instruments and heard by human ears. There is something to which all these tones are referred, an unchanging factor in relation to which they acquire an absolute character or vibration — the diapason. The *notes* C and F have structural meaning as component parts of a scale; but the vibrating *tones* to which these names are given have significance in terms of an absolute pitch established by the diapason. If this diapason's pitch changed, C would represent a new tone, a new vibration, a new rhythm of being — though it would have the same function in the patterns seen in the score.

This illustration must not be taken too literally, as the facts of human existence are far more complicated than those mentioned in this musical metaphor. Yet the analogy should help us to realize that the ego is, like a musical scale, essentially a product of family and social conditions, or more accurately, a set of responses to heredity and environment. Every culture develops its own musical scales. *Every race and society produces a few basic types of ego-structures* (just as it produces a few basic types of bodily structures). A person belonging to a particular race and society is, as far as his ego is concerned, a melodic-harmonic variant of one of these basic ego-structures (or scales of response to the generic potentialities inherent in human nature — *i.e.,* in the common humanity of all human beings). When a society is steady and set in its collective patterns, the ego-structures of the members of such a society are also quiet, steady, secure, and permanent. When, on the other hand, the society is in a condition of crisis and disruption, then the ego — its differentiated product — is structurally insecure. Having no frame of reference within which they can be related, the responses of the ego to the environment and its chaotic events inevitably slide below the threshold of consciousness and meaning. The human person can no longer significantly say "I" — and he has forgotten how to instinctively feel "We" (cf. Kunkel and his "Primal We-experience").

Then, the only possible solutions for the individual, beside an insensitive freezing in sheer egocentricity within the congealed memories of an absolute tradition, are:

1. To participate in the building of a new society — which usually implies revolution and the coercive imposition, by strong persons and a dominant Group (Church or Party), of new social and mental patterns upon society, and fixed places and functions for every individual (cf. Soviet Russia).

2. To reach beyond subservience to ego-structures and social patterns toward the creative source of all livingness and all spiritual progress — viz. the Self.

The first alternative implies the rebuilding of a new ego, usually under the compulsion of a new society, a new religion, or a new leader or idol. The new ego-structure *may* be broader and more inclusive — but it may also be regressive, depending upon the type of group to which allegiance is made. The allegiance and the service given is an ego-restoring, structure-rebuilding act of salvation: a new operation of the Jupiter-Saturn function.

The second alternative means *going through the "crisis," as an individual; and a direct linking of the organism-as-a-whole to a source of creative emanation – the Self, the God-within.* This implies, astrologically speaking, an arousal of the functions of psychological metamorphosis represented by the transcendent planets, Uranus, Neptune, and Pluto.* These planets are linked in a mysterious way to that of which the visible Sun is but a focus of radiation – the radiant fullness of the space defined by the orbit of the earth and eventually by still vaster motions.

The *visible* Sun is the source of the cosmic and atomic energies which arouse all nature into being, which call forth and sustain all organic species in a generic, unconscious sense without regard to individuals. These cosmic energies are those that are locked within the atoms by the Saturnian "binding force." They are thus locked within the structure of the ego, within the patterns of a particular social structure and culture. The life that energizes the contents of these structures is that which streams, astrologically speaking, from the Moon, for Saturn and the Moon constitute a pair. Saturn builds the structures; the Moon energizes the contents – thus all the purely conscious Images, reactions, *and complexes* which fill our tradition-ruled, egocentric life. This Moon-energy is, however, but a *reflected* portion of the energy unceasingly pouring from the Sun. It is solar energy filtered through and colored by the limitations (*karma*) imposed by Saturn. The form-structure of the ego (and also the skeleton of the body) is thus signified in astrology by Saturn (its zodiacal and house positions and aspects); the life of the contents of this ego is represented by the Moon. The visible light and power of the Sun is the universal power that arouses, enfolds, and sustains all there is everywhere – all that vibrates at the core of every atom as well as in the activities and responses of every human being. Its power makes every experience possible and animates every experiencer at every level. It shines indifferently upon all things; it is both constructive and destructive. It is universal vitality and atomic power. It is the source of what the Hindus call *prana.*

The visible Sun, however, should *not* be considered as the Self. It is only the point of release of the energy of the Self. The Self can only be symbolized in its essential reality by space – space in *fullness* of being. We can only perceive and realize this space, however, as our own motion

---

*   cf. *The Sun is Also a Star* (Dutton, 1975) and *From Humanistic to Transpersonal Astrology* (Seed Center, 1975).

through it establishes a focus for the release of its universal power. We come to know that power as spirit, as light, as creative intelligence. But we know it at first only through the upheavals it causes (*via* Uranus, Neptune, Pluto) to our Saturnian security and our egocentric, culture-centric, church-centric rigidity. Indeed, we can only know the Self at first *through our crisis,* and in a negative manner. We know it by what it is not — as Kunkel has clearly pointed out, following the ancient Oriental wisdom of the Upanishads and of Tao.

Yet we can ultimately experience this Self, if we emerge — and as we emerge — successfully from our crises. We experience it *mystically,* as an intense expansion of awareness and an inexpressible feeling of identification with a universal Subject in the consciousness of Whom we are but one of many objects — a small orb within cosmic immensities. We experience the Self, in a more concrete *occult* manner, as a realization of "our place in God" (J. Jacobi), a realization of our innermost quality and tone of being, of our functional participation in a transcendent spiritual Communion that encompasses solar systems and stars.

11   *The Self: An Astrological Key to an Integral Psychology*

Consider the physical organism of a human being: it is made of skin and muscles, intricate circulatory and nervous systems, digestive organs and endocrine glands — and, keeping them all in consistent alignment and in their proper places, is a bony structure, the skeleton. The psyche of an individual person, even though one may not wish to describe it as an actual and substantial organism itself, is nevertheless to be regarded as having a basic structure. Within this structure are functional *systems of response* to experience which enable the psyche to "assimilate" this experience, to learn and grow from it, and to direct bodily activities. When Jung characterizes the psyche as "a self-regulating system" obeying "the law of complementariness, according to which the various psychic factors stand in complementary or compensatory relation to each other," he implies the functional nature of the psyche. And function presupposes structure, provided we give to the term "structure" a very broad meaning — the meaning of (at least relatively) a constant *pattern of operation.*

A "self-regulating system" is, in this sense, a structural system. The ego is the structural foundation of the psyche; and likewise, in the realm of mental activity, logic is the structural foundation of coherent and rigorous thought. In the modern theory of relativity, space-time is considered as the structural foundation of the universe of human experience. The ego-structure, however, is susceptible to profound modifications and differentiation. It must be understood to exist at several levels of evolutionary stages.

First, there is the *generic ego-structure,* which is merely "human" — the root of psychic processes, the sum-total of the basic laws which regulate the psychic (or "inner") life of human beings wherever born. This generic ego-structure differentiates into several "types." Some of these form the basis of a seven-fold classification outlined by Dr. Assagioli; the others are determined by racial and national, religious and cultural — even family — characteristics. Finally, as a result of a long historical process of social, religious, cultural, and economic evolution — and through the synchronous action of the spirit — the differentiation of *individual ego-structures* is made possible. While the more basic structures develop during the prenatal period, the individual ego presumably begins to be differentiated as soon as the shock of birth occurs and the environmental-social impacts of the extra-uterine world are experienced. The period of individual ego differentiation seems to be essentially ended around the time of the seventh birthday. The *contents* of this ego will constantly increase as the experience of the individual expands. They continually change in substance and orientation. But the *structure itself* can be considered formed at seven (perhaps before). The ego develops further for a number of years, yet its essential characteristics are quite set before adolescence, entirely so by the age of 28.

This individualized ego-structure is the *foundation* of our sense of "I," and it constitutes a permanent frame of reference to which personal experiences are related. Thus related, they become conscious. Consciousness is an expression of relatedness. The ego — the individuality of the person — is not, however, only a bare structure. It is a structure energized or vivified by what Jung calls "psychic energy" (or *libido*). Astrologically speaking, the structure is "ruled" by Saturn; the energy within this structure is symbolized by the Moon — the polar complement of Saturn. This energy does not remain at a steady level. It ebbs and flows, just as the Moon waxes and wanes. The ego is "I am" — "I" (the structure) and "am" (the energy within it).

But what an educated American person means today when he says "I am," and what the tribesman of olden days, or the Hindu of 2000 B.C. living in the steady and static society described by the *Laws of Manu*, meant by similar terms are very different things. In ancient times (and even today in many parts of the world) when a person says "I" he refers to his generic ego-structure and its social-cultural differentiations. These structures *are* his frame of reference — his ego — and he knows no other. His is a *collective* ego structured by biological instincts and social-religious traditions, desires, and "taboos." But it is nevertheless the person's ego; he is conscious by referring his experience to this permanent psychic "self-regulating system" — and in no other way (save for exceptional cases).

However, as the general process of structural differentiation proceeds in the vanguard of humankind and as *individualized* ego-structures appear in increasing numbers in societies whose *level of civilization* gradually rises, these newly differentiated ego-structures are thrust into the limelight. They become endowed with the highest value, and the individuals who can significantly and successfully refer their life-experience to them increasingly tend to forget the older and simpler frames of reference — the collective ego-types. Then these collective structures slide into the unconscious, simply because they are no longer valued as significant frames of reference for the development of consciousness out of the raw materials of everyday experience. However, they do not altogether disappear. They emerge above the threshold of consciousness in dreams and under conditions of great stress. They still constitute the foundations of psychic processes; but when individualized people become so concerned with erecting cupolas, manufacturing stained glass windows, or playing organ-music in the "upper regions" of their psyche, they no longer pay attention to these foundations — unless something goes wrong with the building or a social earthquake shakes the walls. These "upper regions" — in which everything recognized as being of value now happens — alone come to be called the "ego." The modern person's "I am" is identified with the highly differentiated structures of the psyche, for it is only through the use of these structures that he obtains consciousness. The "lower structures" — the crypt and the foundations — are frames of reference only for most unusual experiences which nothing "above the ground" can make significant, thus conscious. Whatever happens in relation to these "lower structures" is therefore normally unconscious. Yet these "lower structures" were once considered the ego.

The historical evolution of the ego in humanity somewhat repeats itself during the first years of babyhood — and first of all during the embryonic period of intra-uterine life. What Dr. Kunkel — with the keenest insight — called the transition from "the primal We" to the egocentric type of consciousness (cf. particularly his outstanding book *Character, Growth, Education*) is the change from the earlier foundational and instinctive frame of reference to a new and more differentiated one — which comes to be known exclusively as the ego, because consciousness depends more and more entirely upon its use. However, the ego is not (as Jung says) the "center" of the conscious. Rather it is a frame of reference in relation to which the raw data of experience becomes conscious. Neither should it be considered as a "sham center" (Kunkel), but as a psychic structure (within which energy ebbs and flows) conditioned and differentiated by a particular set of social-cultural, hereditary, and environmental pressures. These pressures constitute the "mould" (or *karma*) which gives form to the ego-structure. They are the totality of the experiences of humankind, and a particular race, culture, family — to which the new-born child adds its own set of experiences, as determinant of the more individualized portions of this ego-structure.

However, can one speak of experiences without implying an experiencer? Is there not more to the ego than structure and energy — a mysterious something which, for lack of a better term, one is almost compelled to call a "center?" Indeed, I believe that wherever there is a definite and relatively permanent structure with energy circulating through it, we can speak of some kind of dynamic center, or center of gravity. We should speak even more of a point of influx of energy, a fountainhead of power. But one cannot understand what this fountainhead is, or means, unless one realizes the nature and origin of the psychic energy which fills the ego-structure; and this leads us to consider a transcendent reality, the Self.

For reasons of psychological experience and philosophical understanding, I believe that it is necessary to assume the reality of a Self. Behind or beyond the "I" (which can be shattered by the pressure of social chaos because it develops as a function of collective experience or individual reactions to social conditions) there must be a more permanent factor which Oriental philosophers have called the Experiencer, the Watcher, the Admonisher, the Ingatherer of all the fruits of human activities, the Divine Witness. But we must be exceedingly careful in determining its character, meaning, and function. This Self — as we conceive it — is to be essentially regarded as *a universal factor, even though it can become more or less "individualized" in human personalities.* Because it is universal we should not give it a geometrical position. We should rather call it Space, or the wholeness of the Whole, or the Great Harmony — or with the Chinese, *Tao.*

In astrological symbolism, the Sun is usually made to signify the Self — Dr. Assagioli's "higher Self" — and the Moon, the "conscious (or personal) self." But these two celestial bodies should be considered as sources of energy-radiation rather than as "centers." The Sun — even in the modern heliocentric system — is not a true center. It is one of the two foci of the ellipses which constitute the planets' orbits. The Sun is the common focus of all these orbits, the focus which they all share — Dr. Kunkel would say the "We"-center. But each orbit has another focus which is strictly its own, which it does not share. It thus is far more significant to say that the Sun is the source or fountainhead of energy for the entire solar system. Indeed some occultists have called the Sun "a bundle of electromagnetic forces," a veil thrown over the "real Sun." This "real Sun," however, should best be understood as the space defined by the orbit of the planets. *The real Sun for the Earth is the space circumscribed by the Earth's orbit.* This space should not be considered, however, as an *empty* something; but, instead, as *fullness of being.* It is the true symbol of the Self. At a higher, because more inclusive, level of universality, the Self takes the symbolic appearance of the space of the galaxy, then of the entire universe. It is always "space." The energies streaming forth endlessly from suns and stars are inter-related in space and harmonized in a continuum of relationship which is the substance, or substratum, of universal being.

The stars, however, are simply *points of emanation* of energy. Indeed, energy streams *through* them, rather than from them. They are fountainheads. Likewise this "Self" which modern psychologists regard as "the center of the totality of the psyche" is not the reality of the Self, but rather the *point of emanation of light, spirit, intelligence, creative power, and tone.* "Through" it that essential *quality* of being which is an aspect of divinity, one of the "attributes" or "names" of God, radiates; it pervades the whole of our individual nature. We "live, move, and have our being" in this emanation of the Self. But this Self, being universal, cannot reach our consciousness or affect our particularized mode or condition of existence unless the "energy of the Self" is focalized — unless it passes through a sort of symbolical lens or fountainhead through which it reaches the sphere of our personal being.

The "real" world of science, as well as of psychology and of occult philosophy, is the world of forces or energy. With reference to a living organism, energy manifests as process. We cannot approach the study of human nature in a vital or effective manner until we are ready to interpret what we observe in terms of process, that is, of *structure-defined operations based on cyclic manifestations of energy.* Energy, however, must be focalized in order to be operative, in order to emerge from a condition of *universal potentiality* into one of *individualized (or particularized) activity.* Any organized system contains such points of emergence — or fountainheads — of energy.

In our geocentric universe, the Sun and the Moon constitute such sources of energy; but while the Sun is a "point of emanation" of energy, the Moon (and the planets) are "reflecting lenses"; they reflect a portion or aspect of the solar emanation. Analogically speaking, the energy which circulates through the ego-structure of the psyche is the reflected energy of the Self. We call it "lunar" energy. The Moon itself, however, does not symbolize the ego, but only the source from which flows the psychic energy circulating through the ego. This psychic energy (the *libido* as defined by C. G. Jung) is reflected energy: *that portion or aspect of the energy of the Self which the ego-structure is capable of containing and utilizing.* Its ebbs and flows are measured astrologically *by the periodical motions of the Moon.*

Thus, in studying the human personality, we have to carefully distinguish between two types of energy: (1) the *direct* (or "solar") energy of the Self pervading the whole of the personality (body and psyche), and

(2) the portion or aspect of this energy *reflected* (by the symbolic "Moon") into the ego-structure and the body — the psychic energy or libido. While the former is essentially steady and constant, the latter is subject to ebbs and flows. What this means in terms of body-functions is clear enough, for we can readily see that while the heart and the lungs (above the diaphragm) are in a continual and relatively constant state of functional activity, the other organic functions (metabolism, glandular secretions — including those of the sex glands — muscular activities, nerve responses, etc.) are subject to daily ups and downs, as well as to definite cyclic modifications throughout the entire life-span.

There is likewise a distinction between the "solar" and the "lunar" types of energy operating through the psyche. The former is steady, simple, "pure" — like a clear and all-pervasive *tone* vibrating through our inner being, yet unheard by all but a very few individuals whose spiritual "ears" (consciousness) have been opened. It is the tone of the spirit within, the direct emanation of the Self, the heartbeat of the Living God — or of the God-yet-unborn which may come to "breathe" within us *as a fully individualized Presence* (Solar Being). Then, there is the "lunar" energy which animates our ego-structured feelings, moods, desires, emotions — and our pride, which, when hindered or congested, becomes the substance of our complexes, fears, rebellions, loneliness, and anxieties.

This "lunar energy" is, I repeat, that portion or aspect of the energy of the Self which our ego-structure is able consciously to contain and to put to use. It provides us with *the power to make daily adjustments to our environment and to the requirements of our society, culture, religious tradition, etc.* It is therefore conditioned by collective factors; and yet, it also enables us to deal with our inner experiences, to develop an individual sense of values (Venus-symbol) and individual modes of thought (Mercury-symbol). This two-fold orientation of the psychic energy is symbolized by the fact that, half of the time, the Moon is *outside* of the Earth's orbit (our total being) — thus, related to the outer world and the planets of initiative (Mars) and social relatedness (Jupiter and Saturn) — while, the other half of the time, the Moon is *inside* of the Earth's orbit, and thus related to the inner planets, Venus and Mercury.

The average, so-called normal, human being lives almost exclusively in terms of his ego-structure and the ebbs and flows of psychic energy caused by the varying orientation of the "reflecting lens" which focuses the useable portion of the energy of the Self. The ego-structure determines the character of his "I"; the variously oriented psychic energy, his ever-changing "am-ness." "I am happy — I am angry — I am bad — I am sick" says the individual. The adjectives which qualify the "am" are expressions of changing moods and feelings, reactions to the environment, or to inner pressures. There is no stability in that realm of the ego because, while the essential structure of the ego (the individual character of Mr. So-and-So) may remain relatively unchanged as the sense of "I," the energy which *substantiates* this sense of "I" (its indispensable "am") flows in a constantly altered direction and always carries new stimulants to the instrumentalities of the consciousness – as the blood carries hormones and toxins, minerals and antibodies, in ever varying proportions to the brain.

The Moon, in astrological symbolism, thus represents the focus of the conscious attention. It is often connected with the mentality, in the sense that it indicates the direction of the process of relationship and adjustment to "objects" which constantly produces new consciousness, and consolidates or challenges old conscious data and types of adjustment or complexes. When the Moon is in close contact with Venus and Mercury (the two planets *inside* of the Earth's orbit – thus, representing mainly the individual's "inner functions"), it symbolizes a state of inward or introverted attention. The individual in this state has the possibility of reaching a consciousness of "solar" values. Mercury and Venus astrologically "rule" the breathing function and at least some aspects of the thyroid's activity – and these have a close relation to the heart's rhythm. Psychologically speaking, through his mind (Mercury) and his sense of value and sympathy or love (Venus), the individual in due time emerges from bondage to his particular ego-structure into the universalistic world of the Self. He breaks through Saturnian walls, and becomes aware of the light and power of the Self.

In order to describe this process, the old Chinese philosophers differentiated between the individual with a *closed centrum* and the one with an *open centrum*. The former would be an individual whose ego-structure is shut tight to the universal world of light. His consciousness is cramped, or entirely absorbed by the problem of maintaining its structure against every conceivable impact and encroachment; indeed, he is either insecure or in constant fear of losing his spiritual integrity. In the other case, we find an individual in a state of structural relaxation, or "openness to the world," breathing deeply and freely, in trust, faith, and inner mental-emotional security. The core of his ego is like the open diaphragm of a camera, letting light stream through.

In the first case, the consciousness is filled exclusively with "lunar" contents, determined solely by the ego-structure. The only "light" in the inner life of the individual is that of the "Moon" – the nexus of psychic energies from which the power of the Self is reflected. In the second case (the *open centrum* individual), the "diaphragm" of the psyche is wide open, letting the "solar" light (the energy of the Self) flood the consciousness. The individual is "illumined." This open diaphragm through which this light pours appears to the consciousness as an inner Sun. It becomes indeed, as Jung describes it, the effulgent center of a new and radiant personality. It is not really a "center," however, as much as an *opening* through which the various emanations of the Self — the Holy Spirit — pour into the ego-structure.

Before this diaphragm relaxes and opens, the ego-structure is dark, or Moon-lighted. As it opens, the ego-structure becomes filled with "solar" light and spirit. This is the Transfiguration. But as Jesus descended from the Mount of Transfiguration, his features were still those of the man born of Mary (the symbolic "sea" of human nature). Yet, now, they shone with light. He had surrendered only his darkness to God, his "lunar" self — his mother-complex, anima, and unconscious shadow. He had become "christed" with the vibrancy of his individualized "orbit" of Selfhood, and of a still vaster cosmic "orbit."

Thus, we find that the general structure of the solar system provides us with a most adequate symbolic representation of the totality of a human person — and this fact establishes a foundation for all astrological interpretations. As we seek to gain a vital and dynamic understanding of human nature and individual personality, the following points are of essential importance:

1. The "real" world is a world in which energies operate rhythmically within relatively permanent structural systems. It is a world of "processes" and of constant inter-relatedness of energies within definite spaces.

2. We have to distinguish two types of systems (or coordinates) in human beings, and two types of basic energies — which we can call "solar" and "lunar." The former refers to the Self; the latter, to the ego. Self is to be understood in terms of *space* (primarily the orbit of the Earth and later the space covered by the entire solar system); ego, in terms of *structure*. The energy circulating within the ego-structure is a reflected portion of the energy emanating from the Self.

3. The ego-structure is moulded by racial, ancestral, and cultural factors, and, in its individualized "upper level," by the child's reaction to his environment. It is thus conditioned by collective influences. The limited, particularized consciousness of the ego is sustained in an unsteady manner by the ceaselessly ebbing and flowing psychic energy reflected into

this structure by the Moon-factor. The Moon symbolizes the "focus of attention" of the consciousness, that upon which a portion of the energy of the Self reflects itself — becoming then modified and differentiated as psychic energy within the ego-structure.

4. The inner planets, Mercury and Venus, are focalizers of "solar" energy within the Earth's orbit. They establish vibratory paths or links between the ego-consciousness and the Self. The planets outside the Earth's orbit are external organic foci which link the individual psyche to the larger world of society. Uranus, Neptune, and Pluto represent the transcendent agencies through which the Saturn-bound ego-consciousness is transformed and repolarized under the inflow of direct "solar" energy. The individual Self (Earth-orbit space) is thus reoriented and finds itself (through a process of "psychosynthesis") a functional participant in a spiritual Group or "Communion" (the entire solar system). This is the "solar" We, itself a participant in a still vaster *pleroma*.

5. On these principles can be built a truly integral and harmonic psychology, in which the elements of psychic and bodily structure, energy and process, are seen related to a Self whose symbol is Space, the spiritual and creative fullness of vibrant being.

12   The Astro-Psychological Approach
to Self-Education:
The Way of Chela-ship

In preceding chapters, the term "personality" has been defined in the sense in which it is used in modern depth-psychology, especially since Jung clarified its meaning. The personality is the total human being — body and psyche, conscious and unconscious — considered as an organic whole capable of integrated response to its physical and psychical environment, and capable as well of creative self-determination and conscious, significant choice. The "individuality" of the personality is its character of indivisibility and unity, and at least relative uniqueness. It refers thus to the particular *structure* of the personality. The ego is the "name" of the personality, in so far as it is different from other personalities, that which expresses its individuality and its particular type of structural stability. The ego is a symbol of unity and the feeling-quality associated with all the conscious experiences which have gravitated around this realization of individual unity and "name-ability."

The child comes to know himself as an ego by referring all his ever-changing sensations, moods, and organic feelings to some inherent principle of stability and permanency which correlates into unity whatever is being consciously experienced. And — because any organism is animated by life-energy rhythmically circulating through it and maintaining the integrity of its structure in spite of the constant changes produced by growth and by the impact of the outside world — the sense of ego is not only based on a sense of inner structural stability, but also on a dynamic feeling of individualized power. The ego is not only "I"; it is also the "am" associated with the "I" — the "I am." The sense of ego, however, is constantly modified by inner and outer experiences, pulled by emotional responses and stirred by inner moods of desire, expansiveness, or fear. Thus in *normal* everyday actuality, the "I am" is always associated with a "this" or "that": I am angry — I am feeling good — I am ill — I am afraid — I am in love, etc. Indeed the realization of one's "I am-ness" unconditioned by any feeling or concept is difficult. It is the goal of many spiritual trainings, such as Hindu Yoga and modern New Thought.

When an experience reaching the consciousness produces an immediate response of repulsion, fear, alien-ness, and inacceptability, the memory of this experience is often not allowed to remain within the "field of consciousness" over which the ego rules. It sinks "below the threshold" of the consciousness, into the *personal* unconscious. The unconscious also contains many factors which the individual has not yet had the chance to experience — either subjectively or objectively. These *as yet unexperienced* unconscious factors are generic and collective. They are "generic" when they refer to "our common humanity" — that is, to any and all powers which are inherent and potential in every human being born, simply by virtue of his being "human." They are "collective" factors when they are the results of the racial, social, and cultural experience of long generations of ancestors. Thus the generic unconscious refers to those organic and spiritual characteristics which the child will experience as he grows into a mature personality through love and creativity, sickness and suffering, and in any way in which latent human powers become actual to him as a conscious individual. The contents of the collective unconscious — the social and cultural "archetypes" defined by Jung — will also be experienced by the individual as his personality develops in the midst of a social-cultural environment from which he learns to draw (and eventually to assimilate and digest) psychic and mental food. Not *all* these contents of the collective unconscious will, of course, be assimilated or even encountered in the conscious experience of any one individual. But the more such contents of the generic and collective unconscious are assimilated, the richer the mature personality will be.

The process of maturation and enrichment of the personality is a long one — a difficult one. It is also a dangerous one. "Personality" as an ultimate value and as a quality of radiation, creativity, and independent living is a goal to be reached only when the individual person attains a state of "definiteness, fullness and maturity" (C. G. Jung) — that is, as his bio-psychic organism becomes well integrated and resilient, capable of endurance and endowed with dynamic power — the power to protect and reproduce itself in and through society. When the psychologist speaks of "*the* personality" he means this bio-psychic organism structured by the ego (in the body, by the skeleton) and displaying functional unity. When referring to "personality" he means the quality that radiates from the relatively mature and dynamic individual person — in a sense, the famous "It" of movie and stage celebrities, the power of "projection" which makes for great performers, be it in show business or on the political scene.

Personality, in its fullest sense, is an ideal to strive toward. It is an ideal, just as sainthood in religion and "adeptship" in occultism are ideals. None of these can be attained in early youth (outside of the possibility of "divine" embodiment), though the potentiality of their attainment can be more or less strongly indicated since adolescence. Yet any individual showing tendencies toward self-assertion, independence of thought, and emotional intensity can be "educated into personality." But *how, by whom,* and *to what end?* In seeking to answer these most pertinent (and alas! often glossed over or superficially considered) questions, one encounters many difficulties. The answers are not obvious; their validity must be carefully weighed, not only in a general sense, but as well in terms of historical trends and the cultural needs of a society at a particular time, as well as in relation to the *readiness of the individual* who is to be educated into personality.

Presently, I will briefly indicate three basic types of answers proposed by the old Oriental "spiritual teacher," the modern depth-psychologist (like Carl Jung), and by the as yet unclassified and not clearly defined astro-psychologist who would seek to combine the potentiality for self-education contained in astrology with the attitude of the Jungian or Kunkel-ian psychologist. But, first of all, I will refer to the historical picture presented today by our modern, typically Western society in so far as the relation of society to personality is concerned.

The relationship of personality to society must always be considered as an essential background for any practical application of psychological ideals and techniques, because no individual exists in a vacuum and no man or woman is ever born as an individualized and mature personality. Every individual person must emerge from the collective womb of society — often, by violence! Throughout his career, the imprint of the conditioning received during this process of emergence will be felt, and will determine the further need of the person. Education to personality is both education *out of* the social-cultural collectivity of human beings in whose society the individual lives and seeks to reach his goal — and education *on the basis of* the historical attainments of that particular society. This may seem like a paradox; but in a sense all psychological development is based on paradox, on the reconciliation of opposites — a fact well known to the Ancients.

Our modern society, especially since the industrial and technological revolution which radically transformed the conditions of human existence, is characterized (psychologically speaking) by the constant pressure it exerts toward the "depersonalization" of the average human being. This is perhaps most characteristic (generally speaking) in the United States, in spite of the fact that individualism is the basis of our social system — or possibly *because* of this fact. Why? Because where people are so busy asserting their rights to their own opinion and their own choice, and "feeling" themselves different from others, they have neither the substantial foundation, nor the time and power of concentration necessary to build themselves as personalities — a slow and painstaking process of natural growth. And, where there is the peculiar optimism and ideological naiveté of the average American type, there is usually little understanding of the essentially "tragic" character of the process of "individuation" (*i.e.,* of personality development and integration) at the present transitional stage of human evolution.

This depersonalization of the human being in modern Western society does not mean that people do not seek to become individualized as separate and self-willed egos — which obviously they do! It means that these individual egos float like corks on the turbulent tides of modern society and modern production, and have practically *no roots* through which they can assimilate the real and concrete life-substance necessary to feed the growth of the bio-psychic organism of the personality. To cry out "I," "I," day in and night out, does not help the personality to become richer and more mature. It means an over-stressing of the *structural* factor in the total personality; but the structure may be both very strong and definite, and . . . empty.

What I call here depersonalization is produced by the lack of substance in the life of the personality. This substance necessary to feed the personality is not to be found by statements of self-will and gestures of ego-pride. It has to be gathered through *significant experiences.* Gathered from where? From the living of true and vital relationship — with one's fellow beings, with the deeply felt life of the group and culture to which one belongs, with the powers of nature (including the powers of generic human nature), with all that lives and moves on earth and in the vast universe of the sky. The significant experience of relationship — in an intimate, steady, lasting, and concentrated manner — is the *only way* to develop a rich and mature personality.

Indeed, the peasant who lives a warm communal life with a rich sense of contact with the soil, the seasons, and the other men and women surrounding him, has far greater chances to become such a rich and mature personality than the office-worker or factory-hand of a modern American city, *provided* this peasant remains in his limited environment. Because his scope of activity and consciousness are limited, and because he is individualized only in a most primitive way, the peasant's personality will not extend very far. Yet, within its narrow boundaries, it can be deep and full and warm, while the personality of the average city-worker is empty, superficial, and filled only with reflected thoughts (via radio, newspapers, magazines) and reflected emotions (via movies and cheap sentimental stories). He does not feed on a vitally experienced tradition, on the fruitful struggle of the man who lives on the land and mixes constantly with the tragic rhythm of birthing and decay. He is manipulated, tossed around by vast forces in an enormously complex social mechanism which he cannot vitally comprehend, and to which he is unable significantly to relate himself. Therefore, he can only gain bewilderment and surface-excitement from his experiences. Even if the modern city-dweller happens to be on top of society − as manager of some big organization − he finds his days so crowded, his mind so beset by competitive strife and anxiety, his nights so tense, that he has no time to grow as a human being, as a personality.

This does not mean that we should return to the peasant-status; far from it! There can be no vital meaning in a regression to primitive earth-bound roots − except for short periods of bio-psychic recuperation. What is meant is that *a new type of root* must be found and experienced. That root is what I have often called "man's common humanity" − not merely at the biological level of common organic human function, but at the spiritual level of our common "divine" origin and our common purpose: the full realization of "Man" through a global and harmonic society, through an all-inclusive and creative civilization. The way to such a group-realization in which all spirit-inspired and spiritually self-dedicated men and women should participate is the way of education to personality − and, after the mature and creative state of personality is reached, the way in which this wholesome and vibrant personality is *used* for a super-personal purpose − what I have called the "transpersonal way."* But first, there should be fullness of personality.

What is meant by this phrase "fullness of personality" has varied a great deal during the last six millenia of recorded history, and it will vary again, following new trends in the evolution of human consciousness and human society. In the India of some three or four thousand years ago, "Forest-Philosophers" began the tradition of transcendental thinking recorded later in the *Upanishads* (prototypes of the Platonic and Hermetic Discourses) and stressed the essential identity of the individual soul and the Universal Soul. The main emphasis was on the individual's "liberation" from bondage to the bio-psychic patterns of the instinctual and social

---

*   cf. *Occult Preparations for a New Age* (Quest Books, 1974), Part Three, "On Transpersonal Living."

existence of those days: bondage to sex, greed, anger – and bondage to the rigid rituals of a highly organized and planned society controlled by the Brahmin caste.

Yet, Occidentals and Orientalists trained in Christian thought fail, as a rule, to grasp the full meaning of Hindu transcendentalism as it existed before the perversions and the nearly insane devotionalism of the medieval era (mostly between 200 and 1400 A.D.). The Forest-Philosophers of 2000 or 1000 B.C. were men who had *fulfilled* all the duties of social living and who, in the last period of their life, sought to prepare themselves *to die significantly and in full consciousness,* and thus to bring a productive social life to a consciously individualized and spiritually valid consummation. This consummation was, according to their views, the "seed" determining the future re-embodiment on earth after a period of withdrawal in a purely subjective state of being. In this sense, personality was accomplished in death – in that "individual seed of consciousness" wherein the harvest of a life of earth-fulfillment blended with the spiritual essence of the immortal self, *atman* – immortal, because inherently one with the Universal Self, *Brahman.* Later on, however, the idea grew that this "great transition" could be made without the disintegration of the physical body. The seed-moment of life-consummation (normally at death) could occur at any time after a degree of personal maturity was reached. *To learn to die while remaining alive has been the essence of all spiritual teaching ever since.*

In India, the relationship of the spiritual Teacher (*guru*) to his few disciples (*chelas*) was a completely personal (or we should rather say "transpersonal") relationship. For the chela, the guru stood as a personalization of God – and conversely God was often called, in one of His aspects at least, *Mahaguru,* the Great Teacher. What the guru was essentially meant to do for his chela was:

1) To arouse to the fullest extent possible (under control and within the limits of physio-psychological safety) the *generic* and *collective* powers of the chela's organism, while the chela retained a clear, objective consciousness of them as well as of his own self; in other words, to arouse Man (the fullness of humanhood) in the particular individual man, without the latter exploding under the eruption of unconscious contents into his consciousness. This process is normally a very slow one. In the Hindu view, it takes many lives. But the special training of yoga, under a guru's supervision, was understood to be a short-cut – a dangerous one, even under the best conditions possible, but one which could lead to the greatest attainment a person could desire.

2) During such a process, a great deal of negative energy was bound to be released, and it was the guru's task to absorb, reorient, and control this energy, which, if let alone, would in most cases lead to personal disintegration, insanity, or death. As a result, the chela could reach a stage of "liberation" from his own past and his race's past (*karma*).

3) At the end of the process (or at least of one phase of it, for in a sense it is a cyclic and a very long process) the guru was to serve as a sort of spiritual "catalyst" enabling a basic psycho-spiritual reaction to occur in the chela's total personality. This was understood to imply a mysterious transfer of spiritual power, and was represented or focalized by the guru giving to his chela a "Mystery-Name" — his "passport" in the spiritual realm.

These seem to have been (underneath a complex veil of symbolism) the three basic phases of the process of human metamorphosis. During this process, the chela was led to experience what amounted to death, but also a consequent reintegration of energies on the basis of which a new spirit-polarized personality was constituted. The guru played an essential and indispensable role in this process. Not only did he make it relatively safe — provided all went well; but he alone could give to the chela a certain something — a spark or seed of divinity — which was necessary for the success of the transformation. He was also the link between the chela and the long "chain" of spiritual Teachers who had come before him, thus binding the chela to a timeless Company in which each person is as all, and all are focused into one. The concept of personality takes on a new dimension in terms of man's participation in such a Company. It includes all that has come before in one line of spiritual activity — paralleling at the level of the conscious spirit the mysterious synthesis that occurs in the fecundated ovum within the mother's womb when an embryo becomes one with the unending line of his physical ancestors, and they live once more in him.

The ancient concept of education to personality was expressed through a vast array of myths and symbols; and it definitely dealt with spiritual powers and bio-psychic energies. So-called "occultism," which inherited these mythological representations and alchemical allegories, essentially deals with the "realm of forces" — which is not exactly a physical realm, yet which operates *through* the bio-psychic organism of man — thus, through the personality in its dynamic nature. The yogi is not interested in his body as a mass of flesh and bones (at times, pursuing this lack of interest to a senseless extreme), but in the generic (also called "astral") powers inherent in humanhood and thus latent in every normal person.

For the modern psychotherapist of Jung's type, the human body is an integral part of the total personality, but of itself it does not carry the main focus of attention except as the organic foundation of "psychic energy" and as the common basis for the interactions between human individuals. Most psychotherapists do not take care of physical diseases except insofar as they are directly connected with psychical states, leaving all acute cases to the psychiatrist. There can hardly be any real process of education to personality where definite physical illness or acute malformation is an unsolved problem. In ancient times, perfect organic health was a prerequisite for any spiritual-occult training. Today, this emphasis does not have quite the same validity − the less so, the more the mind has become individualized and independent of physical-emotional pulls. Nevertheless, education to personality, even in the modern sense, is still so serious and relatively dangerous a process that basic ill-health in most cases accentuates the element of danger.

A typical series of statements made by C. G. Jung concerning the development of personality is to be found in the last chapter of his book *The Integration of the Personality;* as the book (which deals largely with the correspondence between alchemical and psychological ideas) does not make easy reading, I will quote a number of significant passages:

> No one can educate to personality who does not himself have it. And not the child, but only the adult can attain personality as the mature fruit of an accomplishment of life that is directed to this end. The achievement of personality means nothing less than the best possible development of all that lies in a particular, single being. It is impossible to foresee what an infinite number of conditions must be fulfilled to bring this about. A whole human life span in all its biological, social, and spiritual aspects is needed. Personality is the highest realization of the inborn distinctiveness of the particular living being. Personality is an act of the greatest courage in the face of life, and means unconditional affirmation of all that constitutes the individual, the most successful adaptation to the universal conditions of human existence, with the greatest possible freedom of personal decision. To educate someone to *this* seems to me to be no small matter. It is surely the heaviest task that the spiritual world of today has set itself. And, indeed, it is a dangerous task.
>
> No one develops his personality because someone told him it would be useful or advisable for him to do so. ... Nothing changes itself without need, and human personality least of all. It is immensely conservative, not to say inert. Only the sharpest need is able to rouse it. ... The development of personality

from its germinal state to full consciousness is at once a charism and a curse. Its first result is the conscious and unavoidable separation of the single being from the undifferentiated and unconscious herd. This means isolation, and there is no more comforting word for it. ... It also means fidelity to the law of one's being ... personality can never develop itself unless the individual chooses his own way consciously and with conscious, moral decision. ... True personality always has vocation and believes in it, has fidelity to it as to God, in spite of the fact that, as the ordinary man would say, it is only a feeling of individual vocation. But this vocation acts like a law of God from which there is no escape. That many go to ruin upon their own ways means nothing to him who has vocation.

To have vocation means in the original sense *to be addressed by a voice.* ... It happens to not a few, even in this unconscious social state, to be summoned by the individual voice, whereupon they are at once differentiated from the others and feel themselves confronted by a problem that the others do not know about. ... The inner voice is the voice of a fuller life, of a wider, more comprehensive consciousness. That is why, in mythology, the birth of the hero or the symbolic rebirth coincides with sunrise: the development of personality is synonymous with an increase of awareness.

In so far as every individual has his own inborn law of life, it is theoretically possible for every man to follow this law before all others and so to become a personality — that is, to achieve completeness. ... Only the man who is able *consciously* to affirm the power of the vocation confronting him from within becomes a personality; he who succumbs to it falls a prey to the blind flux of happenings and is destroyed.

In so far as a man is untrue to his own law and does not rise to personality, he has failed of the meaning of his life. Fortunately, in her kindness and patience, Nature has never put the fatal question as to the meaning of their lives into the mouths of most people. And where no one asks, no one needs to answer.

These brief excerpts, while they do not deal in detail with the "how" of the development of the personality, should at any rate help to situate the problem from the modern psychological point of view. The warnings given by Jung as to the seriousness of this problem are repeated by Kunkel. They echo similar admonitions, put in even stronger and more awesome terms by the occultist, theosophist, or even Mason, who also (in varied but related ways) deals with this central problem of all human life: the birth of an integral personality in which the individualized spirit (heralded by the "inner voice") meets and unites with the flowering of the bio-psychic and social-cultural life. Kunkel writes:

No one should be lured without urgent necessity to enter this turmoil of creativity and spirituality. If you are allowed to stay where you are, you had better stay. No curiosity, no scientific purpose, no moral duty gives you the right or even the possibility of going through the purgatory of depth-psychology . . . What are the minimum requirements for those who want to make this attempt? From the religious side two things are needed. First, the belief, or at least the suspicion, that there is or may be — as William James puts it — "an unseen order, and that our supreme good lies in harmoniously adjusting ourselves thereto." And secondly, a certain tolerance towards God, which means our readiness to allow God to be as he wants to be and not as we expect him to be according to our own conceptions, theologies and creeds (and our interpretation of the Bible which we think is the only right interpretation). We should give Him the chance to teach us something new about Himself. On the psychological side we need a certain amount of personal suffering, as we have pointed out; and a certain readiness to admit that something may be wrong in our own inner structure. If these four requirements have not yet been met we should wait. There is no hurry, for the inner situation will be better prepared when we begin some years later. And it is never too late. (*In Search of Maturity*, p. 234.)

Why these warnings? Because in the process of arousal which follows either contact with a true guru, the first consultation with a psychoanalyist, or the giving of oneself to the "inner voice," all the dark energies of the unconscious tend to be let loose. Everything — good or bad — is stimulated as we seek to reach a fuller consciousness. And, since we usually manage fairly well to ignore the memories of failures or perhaps evil thoughts or actions within our total personality (pushing them back into our unconscious), they are usually the first to be made apparent. This may lead to a sense of panic — even to the confrontation with the ghastly "Dweller on the Threshold" made graphic in Bulwer Lytton's *Zanoni*. But woe to him who recoils in horror and tries to reverse the process of growth! No man can safely "dis-educate" himself. Once the door of the unconscious is deliberately opened, once the call of the inner "vocation" is answered, the only way is ahead.

This is not a matter for the psychologists alone. It is indeed time for astrologers to realize that they too, consciously or not, deal with vital energies and unconscious powers *when each begins to face his own life in terms of the birth-chart;* and likewise when they assume the responsibility of giving psychological advice to other persons — clients or friends. From the Jungian point of view, the birth-chart can be considered an "archetype of the unconscious." It is a visible recording of the inner voice — of what God has wrought for us as a blueprint of what we could (thus, *should*) become. To earnestly consider this blueprint — this symbolic Name of our fulfilled personality — to give it a determining importance in our everyday living; to know ourselves as a concrete incorporation of its structural harmony — this indeed constitutes a most serious, most vital, and irreversible step.

By taking this step we precipitate upon ourselves as individuals shadows as well as light. Whatever is indicated in our birth-chart *becomes more strongly emphasized than before in our actual life.* We suffer more. We experience deeper strata of ourselves. We meet fear in a new way. We become more what we potentially are in all directions. No one who seeks to tread the astrological (or the psychological) way of education to personality should ever forget this. To do so without being ready or even conscious of what is at stake is to court the possibility of inner catastrophe as well as outer failure.

13

The Astro-Psychological Approach
to Self-Education:
Self-Education and Its Dangers

In both the ancient system of education to personality through *yoga,* and the modern practice of psychotherapy and psychosynthesis, great stress is placed upon the part played by the spiritual Teacher and Guide — or the psychologist — in the process of "liberation" from bondage to the past, "assimilation" of the contents of the generic and collective unconscious, and "union" with the spiritual Source or Self. There are several reasons, at different levels, why education to personality is believed to require an educator — one who "leads out" (*e-duco* means "to lead out"). On the other hand, it is also evident that if the number of individuals potentially able and ready to enter upon the path of *conscious and responsible* development of personality is very large, the problem of finding enough adequate "educators" becomes very great, because such a type of educator or personal Guide requires spiritual abilities, a profound sense of responsibility, and a power of understanding and compassion rare indeed in our age, or in any age. And, as Jung said: "No one can educate to personality who does not himself have it."

As a result, a number of psychologists — especially Dr. Fritz Kunkel — have sought to formulate principles and methods whereby self-education to personality becomes a possible, and not too dangerous, process. The value of astrology is particularly great in this field of self-education — even though the use of astrology toward the fulfillment of a mature and creative personality is never without danger and pitfalls. A better idea of potential obstacles in the way of self-education through astrology can be gained from Kunkel's discussion of these obstacles from the point of view of what he calls "religious self-education," provided we also realize that his point of view may overemphasize the dramatic element.

The first obstacle is the *egocentricity of the motive* leading one to undertake a conscious and self-determined process of education to personality. According to Kunkel, "The motive must be personal though not egocentric. The mature unegoistic personality should be the goal" for "God wants the person rather than the cause" (be the latter social, moral, or religious). "The ideal motive" is "God's own command, the voice which told Jonah to go to Nineveh and Jesus to go to the desert in order to be tempted. But we are rather deaf, nowadays, or we mistake the stirring of some unconscious egocentric desire for the voice of the Lord. . . . Fortunately God uses many languages. . . .   The language which we understand best is suffering. . . . Suffering should make us aware of the fact that there is a higher goal, and that more suffering is in store if we fail to reach this goal. . . . The decisive point is that the goal of our self-education must not be an arbitrary idea about what we want to be like. It has to be the very goal of human history, the will of God."

In other words, the goal of self-education is to become fully and consciously as an individual person what we are potentially as an idea or plan in the divine Mind. It is to fulfill the law of our individual being, our vocation; to find our individual place in the universe and in humanity. Or as the mystic injunctions of old had it: "Know thyself" and "Become what you are." The essential means to reach this goal are to "cooperate with life" (Kunkel) by "finding out what may be the desirable step, the creative reaction, in every given situation." If this be so, then obviously the value of astrology is incalculably great; for the birth-chart symbolically expresses the individual law of being — thus, what we inherently "are." By studying it we can "know ourselves." By carefully ascertaining and meditating upon our astrological progressions and transits, by erecting horary charts to discover "the desirable step in every given situation," we should succeed in cooperating with life, consciously and in deep understanding of the meaning of every life-confrontation.

Kunkel does not refer to astrology in his book, but the "serious obstacles" he mentions in the way of such a cooperation apply just as well to whoever uses astrology as a technique of self-education.

> By analyzing ourselves, it is said, we shall grow even more egocentric. Introspection leads us into all kinds of vanity, until finally our main occupation will consist in writing a diary, and our chief interest will lie in becoming a more exceptional case. This is true, if the original motive was too egocentric. But if sleeplessness or marital troubles gave the incentive, be sure your pains and sorrows will prevent your becoming an interesting case. Therefore it would be better to wait until the situation is disagreeable enough.

In other words, unless there is a driving urge, born of an intolerable life-situation or inner discontent, to face oneself unaided and to win or die, there *is* indeed a danger that a prolonged study of one's reactions and psychological problems might lead to a worse "cramp in the conscious" — to use Jung's splendid phrase — than ever before. I would add that it is not only egocentricity (in the usual sense) that is to be guarded against; but a tightening of the structures of consciousness, an "ego-itis" (inflammation of the ego!) due to an over-subjective and rigid focusing of the problems of life.

This danger is somewhat lessened by contact with a good psychologist and especially a true *guru* because through this contact, the individual partakes in a broader life than his own even while concentrating on his own. His problems and dreams become amplified and universalized and given a far larger frame of reference through the interpretation of the Teacher and Guide. Eventually, the student learns to see himself through the Teacher's eyes; and this extraordinarily valuable objectification of one's ego by means of a temporary identification with a wise and compassionate Teacher is lacking where there is only self-education.

The only alternatives to a living Teacher with whom one can exchange thoughts and currents of feeling are either an ideal spiritual Personage (Christ or a Master) who becomes like an objective touchstone of value, so real is the belief in what he represents in the student; or the astrological Sky — *also an ideal personification (more abstract in character) of universal order and divine intelligence.* The danger here is to build an "idol" *and to substitute it for the living reality.* This is a serious danger for the over-zealous student of astrology who increasingly refers his experiences and his smallest problems to his birth-chart and progressions — or constantly erects horary charts before doing anything at all. To so behave is to substitute an external *image* of value to one's own inner *experience* of value. It is to become utterly dependent upon a symbol for living reality.

Just as no true psychotherapist or spiritual Teacher will countenance or encourage such an attitude of dependence upon himself in his client or pupil, so too should astrological charts be used in the process of self-education to personality: primarily or solely as a "court of appeal" asked to solve an especially confused issue without reliable or known precedents. No human should ask God a question he himself can sincerely answer. What he should do, however, is to establish in himself a frame of reference to which, almost automatically, he can refer the problem for objective elucidation and amplification, so that it may be seen *sub specie aeternitatis* — that is, in terms of the pattern of all life-cycles, small or large (an "eternity" being, in concrete terms, nothing but a *complete* cycle).

Dr. Kunkel listed a still more serious obstacle to the successful attainment of the goal of psychological self-education: the integration of the total personality. And here we approach the rather confusing concept of what Jung called the Shadow. The concept seems at first quite obvious, but it is somewhat thrown out of focus by being related, if not identified (at least by Kunkel and a number of Jungian psychologists), with the controversial and ambiguous concept of "evil." As Dr. Kunkel saw it, the integration of the personality

> ... means the acceptance and assimilation of unconscious
> contents, such as repressed desires and undeveloped capacities,
> into our conscious mind. How can we do this? Our ego does not
> want to see the things which would destroy it. Its resistance
> against conquest of the unconscious is a struggle for survival.
> Only an objective helper, a psychologist, a modern father-
> confessor, can overcome this resistance.
>
> Answer: This would be true if there were only one evil, one
> Shadow, one darkness. But evil is always manifold; and its
> different forms are contradictory and antagonistic. In time the
> Shadow, for instance irritability, will increase to the point where
> you identify yourself with its tendencies: "I am furious!" and
> then you will disown and condemn your former ego, the softness
> and smugness of the pseudo-Christian. The ego and its Shadow
> are equally evil; blaming each other they bring to light hidden
> hideousness. All our unconscious deviations and possibilities will
> become conscious if we go on raging against ourselves — which is
> the very meaning of the word "crisis." All we need, in addition to
> suffering, courage and patience, is a good, simple and clear
> psychology of the unconscious; a zoology, as it were, which
> teaches us how to deal with the beasts of our unconscious Zoo.
> Then our courage will grow into faith, and finally we will be able
> to face the lions in Daniel's den. Your unconscious resistance is
> the stronger the less faith you have; and vice versa.

This answer — based as it is on Dr. Kunkel's somewhat questionable
definition of the ego — leaves many points unsolved. Above all, it does not
tell what the seeker after completeness of personality will do when
confronted with the aroused energies of his generic and collective
unconscious, the revengeful monsters his repressions and fears have
engendered in his psychic depths, all the blackness his search for light has
evoked by inevitable compensatory reaction. In many cases, this reaction
of the dark roots of the psyche may not be so strenuous that it cannot be
handled more or less sensibly by the lone traveler on the path of
self-education. But in many other cases, the confrontations may be rather
terrifying. A spiritual counter-action is necessary from a person who not
only symbolizes light and wisdom for the distracted seeker, but who can
actually wield the *power* of light, and is able to channel and focus "divine
Grace" — and we shall presently discuss the meaning of "Grace" in the
occult-mystical (as in Sufism) sense as well as in the religious traditions.

The main problem we encounter refers thus to the nature of the
Shadow — a Jungian version of the occultist's "dark Forces." Jung states
that "the meeting with oneself is the meeting with one's Shadow." Frances
Wickes in *The Inner World of Man* adds:

The personal Shadow is the negative side of the ego-consciousness. It turns toward the dark unknown ... darkens and confuses our ego-choices. It contains also the strength of the dark forces needed for our life. It holds the negative intuition.

The nature of the Shadow can be understood abstractly by realizing that the ego is a structure, and that any structure (or form) divides the world into what is inside and what is outside of that structure. Consciousness is the inside content of the ego-structure; the unconsciousness, the outside darkness. The Shadow is the result of crossing the threshold from the lighted room of the ego to the dark outside. As one turns one's back to the lighted realm, one finds that the outer darkness is like a "black mirror" (such as painters have used in order to get a sense of plastic and light and shade values without the glamour of colored surfaces). This black mirror reflects the shape of the ego, minus the light and the glamour of the usual conscious feelings about oneself. This shape is the Shadow — a harsh, coldly objective, unfriendly and pitiless image of what makes one "different" from the whole world, what isolates and compels one to follow a particular and lonely road as the Karmic result of past frustrations, fears, and evil deeds. As we clearly and coldly see what our ego has become as a result of becoming imprisoned within walls built by our insecurity and fear, we become aware of it having turned into "the Shadow"; and it can be a sobering and, in some cases, a frightening experience.

It is an almost inevitable experience in the process of education to personality because there can be no integration and fulfillment of the personality without the eventual assimilation of the powers which are outside of our walled-in ego-structure, inasmuch as they belong to humanity and to universal life. How then can the experience be made bearable and relatively safe? By "projecting" this Shadow upon someone, who absorbs it without reacting to it in a still more intense and destructively dark way. This someone can only be a true psychologist and spiritual Teacher. In other words, if, as the would-be mature personality opens the door that leads to the outer darkness of the unconscious, instead of seeing nothing but a black mirror showing him his Shadow, he sees the image of his Teacher, he then "projects" the Shadow upon the Teacher — he gets angry with him, blames him for whatever happens, perhaps even sees him as a betrayer. This may be a tragic experience, often referred to as psychological "transference," yet it is not as awesome as would be the experience of meeting "evil" personified as the reflection of one's ego. The experience would be disastrous if the Teacher, unaware of what was occurring, reacted in anger to the projection and projected the evil image back upon his disciple — and this is exactly what happens whenever one projects one's Shadow upon any less spiritual, less compassionate, and easily aroused person (friend, or marriage partner, for instance). But, the true Teacher understands; and, by returning love (or even impatience) instead of evil, he makes it possible for his disciple to *gradually* become accustomed to, and unafraid of the ancient (in terms of reincarnation) evil, or, more normally, of the selfishness that has shaped the disciple's ego. The disciple comes to accept what he is as an ego, without too great a despondency or fright; then – in time – he is able to see beyond this Shadow the countenance of his true Self in whom (according to Jung's concept of the Self) unconscious and conscious complement one another, as the outside of any form complements the inside of it.

This mysterious drama between disciple and spiritual Teacher was symbolized in some ancient religious rituals by a "sacrifice." The Teacher gave the disciple a consecrated knife with which the disciple was to symbolically stab him to death; and the magic "power" of the Teacher entered the soul of the disciple, who became thus "initiated." This sacrifice motif is not only found in old religions (particularly the Hebrew), but it is indeed the very substance of the concept of Christ's Atonement through the Crucifixion. What this means, psychologically speaking, is that Christ came to focus, in His person, all the powers of the unconscious of a humanity bound by the racial-personal exclusivism inherent in the old tribal state of culture and religion, at the time when this humanity had become *collectively ready* to begin its "education to personality." Thus Christ descended to "hell" and "redeemed" the ancient collective evil of humankind – that is, enabled people to face more safely the image of their ancestral sins of separateness and pride, and (eventually) to assimilate them in clear consciousness. Christ is, in that sense, the spiritual Teacher of collective Man. In His name, the *collective* "Dweller on the Threshold" of humanity is potentially vanquished. It belongs, however, to the *individual* seeker after completeness and maturity of personality to emulate Christ; to take His cross and follow Him to "hell" and be resurrected; to overcome the Shadow by absorbing it in the name of Christ – through the power of divine Grace, the Holy Spirit of Truth and Understanding that, according to the Christian tradition, came down upon the Apostles at the Pentecost.

In ordinary cases the experience of the Shadow is not as terrifying as some occult novels have described it, for the simple reason that most people open the door to their unconscious very hesitantly and close it back at their first peep into the darkness beyond. This is both self-protection and lack of courage or faith. Then the Shadow is, as a rule, strictly "personal"; that is, it is limited to the realm of what Jung calls the "personal unconscious," distinguished from the collective unconscious. The former deals only with whatever negativity an individual has accumulated (through fear, frustration, anger, etc.), since his birth; but the latter is made up of the negativity of an entire people or race, of a whole family, or of a long series of "lives" (if one believes in the reincarnation of the "divine spark" within a series of personalities). When the evil the disciple meets at the threshold is rooted in ancient collective failure, then indeed the confrontation may be tragic. But it can hardly happen in an individualized manner except to strong and daring souls, who at the same time find themselves linked with transcendent powers of light. Then the individual person becomes a battlefield, and his main task is to remain steady and with clear faith, letting the God within him be the warrior — as it is said in the *Bhagavat Gita.*

It may also happen, of course, that a person is forced to face the embodied Shadow, not as an individual but rather as a member of a nation, social class, or religious group. He may be a Jew tortured in a Nazi concentration camp merely because he is a Jew, or a French Underground worker whose sense of collective spiritual value compelled him to face the massed evil of an invading nation that had given itself up collectively to the Shadow. In these cases, the individual is confronted with the challenge of developing his own power of resistance and endurance against a frightening collective pressure, of finding his own light through an intense arousal of the will to victory. Wherever such confrontations with more than personal evil are experienced, it is usual to find that, astrologically speaking, Neptune and Pluto are strongly active. The whole of this century, called the twentieth, is an outstanding case in point, for when the 1900 series of years began (midnight January 1, 1900) Neptune and Pluto (still broadly conjunct in Gemini) were opposing in the 9th house a massing of planets in Sagittarius (Jupiter, Uranus, Mercury, Saturn), Capricorn (Sun, Moon, Mars), and early Aquarius (Venus).* And as Pluto was then yet unknown, the *conscious* emphasis, at least up to 1930, was set on the Neptunian power of dissolution — the dissolution of the obsolete framework of European feudalism and imperialism within the intellectual mind (Gemini) of Occidental man. When in 1942 Uranus came to activate the 1900 positions of Neptune and Pluto, the time struck for

---

* Historically speaking, the 20th century may be said to have begun only January 1, 1901; but with the numerical change from the 1800 to 1900 years, the new vibration 19 was really set into operation in the mass consciousness of humanity — which is what really matters.

the release of new powers in humanity (atomic power) and of a new vision in individuals who had met the challenge of Neptune and Pluto in Gemini *in their own birth-charts* (those born approximately from 1888 to 1902).

The ordinary meeting with the Shadow in the average individual seeking to become a mature personality should, however, be understood most significantly, not in terms of striking Neptunian and Plutonian confrontations *which may not necessarily be connected with such experiences of darkness,* but in relation to the individual's approach to his own birth-chart, transits, and progressions. The particular *quality* of this approach characterizes what the individual *actually is* as an evolving and maturing personality, because it expresses how the individual is able to orient himself in relation to his own growth and to the process of self-discovery. And, as we already saw, "the meeting with the Shadow is the meeting with oneself" – *i.e.,* with oneself, *minus* the lovely trappings, the flatteries, the pomp, and the sweet illusions which have been built around the ego. Thus one meets the Shadow whenever one is forced to face the harsh challenge of pride or happiness-destroying circumstances, or severe inner pressures compelling one to question what had comfortably been taken for granted. And this means particularly in astrology: facing "bad" aspects.

With this, we are dealing with a basic factor in astrology which, as a rule, has been consistently ignored. We are dealing with the fact that the concentrated and eager study of one's chart – and particularly of soon maturing planetary configurations, by transits or progressions – is bound *to force the potentialities of the individual life into more complete actualization; thus, to intensify the so-called "evil" as well as the so-called "good" in the individual personality.* And, as human beings are usually more struck by and respond more crucially to the "bad" than to the "good," if a person strives after self-knowledge by studying his birth-chart with an intense belief in the validity of astrology, this study very often leads to an intensification of Karmic confrontations. This is as it should be; for this intensification of pain and tragedy through the focusing of Karma is an inevitable part of the process of purification and purgation (*catharsis*) of the ego. And this process is the first manifestation of the fact that the "education to personality" is gaining momentum and becoming effective.

As Jung pertinently wrote:

> The fear that the majority of natural human beings feel before the inner voice [that which establishes one's "vocation" and leads to the process of psychological education] is not so

childish as one might suppose. . . . What the inner voice brings close to us is generally something that is not good, but evil. This must be so, first of all, for the reason that we are generally not as unconscious of our virtues as of our vices, and then because we suffer less from the good than from the bad.

The character of the inner voice is "Luciferian" in the most proper and unequivocal sense of the word, and that is why it places a man face to face with final moral decisions, without which he could never attain consciousness and become a personality. In a most unaccountable way the lowest and the highest, the best and the most atrocious, the truest and the falsest are mingled together in the inner voice, which thus opens up an abyss of confusion, deception, and despair. —*The Integration of the Personality;* pages 302-3.

We can see in our birth-chart the astrological equivalent of our "inner voice," for the chart constitutes a symbolic record (a "signature") of our individual law of being as the Great Architect of the Universe blueprinted it in the sky of our birth as an independent living organism. The birth-chart represents the state of the universal Whole in an individualized form. The individual is that form. His birth-chart is the hieroglyph of his individuality. His task (*dharma*) is to embody this abstract form in a concrete and wholesome organism of personality. As Jung used this term, personality means "fulfillment, wholeness, a vocation performed, beginning and end and complete realization of the meaning of existence innate in things." And, to realize this innate "meaning of existence" requires our being objective to it.

To be objective toward the things one likes and to one's ego implies a process of *severance* which, in turn, necessitates (almost inevitably) suffering and the experience of evil or contradiction. Evil, as understood in the European tradition, is God's adversary. It is God inverted or negated. Evil perpetually stands against all established and therefore static values — against what we normally consider as peace, law and order, health and happiness. But just because it denies what is, evil can be necessary to force us to give up the "good" for the "better."

Something good is unfortunately not eternally good, for otherwise there would be nothing better. If the better is to come, then the good must stand aside. This is why Meister Eckhart said, "God is not good, or else he could be better." —(*The Integration of the Personality*, page 304).

In its very first manifestations, the "better" often takes on the appearance of evil, because it is thrown out of correct perspective and deviated by its occurring within an irrelevant frame of reference. This produces fear in the minds and souls still bound to this now obsolete frame of reference; they react violently and senselessly, thus giving to the first unsteady and inchoate manifestations of the new the character of evil. Indeed, the evil nature of any new life-development *consistent with human growth* is an expression of the resistance and the fears of those forces (in society or the individual) whose privileged position depends on the preservation of the old order.

In astrology, this resistance and the fight necessary to overcome it are represented by planetary squares. A square between two planets occurs midway between the conjunction and opposition of these same planets. By generalizing the names associated with the phases of the Moon (i.e., the aspects between the Sun and the Moon), one can say that the "first quarter" type of square (from conjunction to opposition) represents a refusal of the ego and the will to adjust themselves to the inevitable results of the new evolutionary start which occurred when the two planets were in conjunction. On the other hand, the "last quarter" type of square (after the opposition) represents the refusal by the conscious mind to let itself be fecundated by the new vision which occurred during the opposition (the "full Moon" type of illumination). These refusals come to a climax at the time of the square aspects, and this climax releases a Shadow, as the by then crystallized past stubbornly blocks the new will or the new light, gesticulating against the inevitable (though alas! often tragically delayed) triumph of the creative Power in the individual or in society. The only way to dissipate this Shadow and the fear it inspires is to absorb and assimilate the creative Power which is Light. This is "theosynthesis" − a process which is the vital core of any real self-education to personality; which transmutes fear into faith, the blasts of tragedy into the blessings of Grace that flows from the heart of divine beings in whom compassion and all-inclusiveness have become the irrevocable Law of their nature.

14

The Astro-Psychological Approach
to Self-Education:
From the Greater to the Lesser Whole

Of all the great enemies of man, the greatest is fear. We have seen how fear arises in the process of development of the personality when the maturing individual finds himself confronted by the shadow cast by his refusal to constructively face the challenges of a new order of life and consciousness. When such refusals have accumulated through a long series of cycles, in a particular civilization or in an individual of high spiritual development, the confrontation with the Shadow can indeed become cataclysmic; but in the vast majority of individual cases, the meeting with the Shadow is experienced less dramatically as a somewhat uncontrollable fear of the unknown, making us shrink from taking the bold step across the threshold which, through the vast darkness of the unconscious, would lead into the realm of the mysterious generic and collective powers (or "Archetypes") which Goethe named in *Faust* the "realm of the Mothers." These un-individualized, universally "human," or even cosmic powers are indeed the "Mothers" of the eventually mature individual personality; they provide the latter with substance and energy, with psychic-mental life. But before these powers can truly operate as "Mothers" of any individual personality, they must have become "impregnated" by the divine spirit; for, without such an impregnation, their creation must remain spiritually unformed and without evolutionary meaning – the mere proliferation of psychic substance multiplying itself senselessly toward inevitable disintegration. The spiritual impregnation – the descent of the creative Spirit into the consecrated soul ("Mary") – can be blocked by fear. The ego can recoil before the Visitation, and tightly close the gates of its psychic and mental structures. The "unhappened" is then bound to turn destructive. "Evil" is the shadow of the good that was not allowed to happen – the shape of our unlived life.

The devoted and eager (perhaps over-eager!) practice of astrology in relation to one's own life often tends to give rise to an insistent, even if elusive, fear: the fear of "bad" aspects. As already stated, the fervent and concentrated study of one's own birth-chart and progressions must of necessity *intensify* whatever the chart contains. The personality's attention being consciously focused upon the potentialities which the chart reveals, these potentialities are thereby impelled to actually manifest with greater vigor. Anyone put in the spotlight reveals himself at his best or at his worst! Light is energy; consciousness releases power. To be conscious of a possibility ahead is to activate its coming to a focus of manifestation. The essential point is, however, that no such possibility includes as a predetermined and set factor the human meaning of what it will be when actualized. Any possibility can become either a positive or a negative actuality. *Fear* tends to make of it a negative manifestation; *faith* turns it into a positive fact. Fear, as a first reaction or impression, may not be avoidable; yet, if fear can be transmuted into faith *before* the potentiality becomes an actuality, no harm need be done. Indeed, it is by means of the repeated transmutations of fear of impending changes into faith in the creative spirit of renewal that personality reaches individual maturity and power; for to reach maturity is to have *won* over the fear of responsibility and of losing oneself into a greater Self. An individual's power is the power he has *won* over the inchoate energies of nature forever running fatefully downward toward a dead level ("entropy"). The true life of personality is a life of ever-renewed victory; there are no *final* victories.

The central problem of the education to personality is therefore the transmutation of fear into faith. Astrologically speaking, this means acquiring a constructive attitude to one's "bad" aspects, and to any so-called evil or unfortunate feature in one's birth-chart. Whoever develops or stresses a negative attitude of fear with regard to any and all such astrological factors rouses, consolidates, and gives added power to the Shadow. "The meeting with the Shadow" is the meeting with oneself – but, if one faces oneself with courage and with faith in the Self, the Shadow vanishes. It vanishes when *caught between two lights: the light of one's courage and the radiance of God's Grace.*

This principle is fundamental in any valid self-education. The only way to absorb a shadow is – as every photographer knows – to catch it between *two* sources of light. Not to increase the intensity of one source, however spiritual or divine – note well! If God – or any great "Master of compassion" – appeared among us, the light He would emanate would generate the darkest kind of shadows, unless all people could match, at least to some extent, His light with theirs. This is why whenever Avatars (or Manifestations) of God occur on earth (because of an irrepressible evolutionary *need*), they arouse at once powerful enmity in at least a few; they drive unyielding egos to irrational hatred and insanity. Martyrs fall to ghastly tormentors as, confronted with the divine Light, those who cling desperately to their old privileges and their cultural idols are compelled by the very terror this Light causes in them to enact the blackest deeds. For these deeds, according to old Gnostic teachings, any Christ-being must suffer and atone (as well as for the failures of His accepted disciples), because the blackness of the deeds is in direct proportion to the glaring intensity of the Light. For this reason, no God-like personage will reveal his light to those with rigid egos unless he must do so for an evolutionary all-human purpose, knowing fully the tragic effects of such a revelation, and the sacrifice it would require of him.

If, on the other hand, a person contains a strong light in his own soul, then that light should burn brighter in response to the divine radiance, and, as a result, the very structure of his psyche becomes translucent and transfigured. This capacity for translucency and transfiguration is the ability in an individual to assimilate divine Grace (in Greek, *Charis,* whence Charity), what the Sufi mystic calls the *baraka* of the Teacher, or what Sri Aurobindo defines as the Mother-force. The process of assimilation of this downflow of Grace out of the great compassionate heart can also be called a process of *theosynthesis* — analogous to the life-process in the vegetable kingdom known as "photosynthesis." Photosynthesis is the process by which the green leaves of a plant under the impact of light-rays chemically transform the carbon dioxide and water of the atmosphere into the sugar or starch-like compounds (carbohydrates) necessary for the plant's growth — and indirectly, for the growth of all animals who feed on plants. Through this chemical transformation (and through it alone!), the energy of the Sun is "fixed" into the plant, assimilated and made available for the sustenance of all life on earth. This is the essential function of the vegetable kingdom in the economy of earth-life.

Similarly, there is some element in human nature which is able to "fix" and assimilate the energy of spirit emanating from "divine" Beings. The diffused energy of the universal spirit is absorbed by the human organism *through the breath;* and we may speak here of "pneuma-synthesis" (from *pneuma* which means both breath and spirit), a process of assimilation in which the red corpuscles of human blood play a part analogous to that which the green chlorophyll of the leaves performs. But besides this process of spiritual absorption, which has been considered by some occultists as the basic factor making possible (in due time) ego-differentiation and individualization, one should also speak of the process of "theo-synthesis" which operates at a higher level in terms of pure consciousness and of "mind-substance." The Greek word *theos* means "god," but it does not have to refer to the Christian concept of a personal God. In the Gospels, the terms "Kingdom of Heaven" (Heaven being a translation of the Greek, *makarios,* which means "the Sky") and "Kingdom of God" appear to be interchangeable. *Theos* is *cosmos* considered a unity. This unity can be microcosmic as well as macrocosmic. Thus, at a high stage of spiritual development, a person can radiate a "divine" energy — the *baraka* of the Sufi Master — as well as God, whose

"Grace" manifests as the Holy Spirit. A human being immured within his ego-walls, shuts himself off from these "gift-waves" of divine Love and Mercy. He is then like a plant growing in a dark cave.

By this process of theosynthesis, the human mind, in the spiritual organism of the individualized and conscious Self, "fixes" the energy of divine Grace, as the leaf fixes the energy of sunrays in its chlorophyll granules. It is this energy which feeds the "Body of Christ" (or in Buddhistic and Taoist philosophy, the "Diamond Body") within every human being who is spiritually ready to give it birth "in his heart." This readiness is measured by the *quality* as well as the intensity of the person's faith. Faith in what? Not in a personal God who dispenses salvation to the sinful soul; but *faith in the "spiritual fullness" of the universal Whole within which the individual comes to experience himself as a participant.* A person's birth-chart, when significantly understood, is a localized and individualized expression of this all-encompassing spiritual fullness – the *pleroma* (spiritual fullness) of the whole sky focused upon the point of birth at the exact time of the "first breath." The process of theosynthesis is the assimilation of the *Idea of God* (archetype) which the birth-chart formulates in geometrical patterns in the sky, and of the *Energy of God* which was released through this birth-sky – and is released through it at all times – and all its progressive modifications, if we turn our minds to God in faith, as the green leaf turns itself toward the physical Sun.

The word God may be replaced here by many others. What I am discussing is purely factual psychology. It is also astrology, once astrology is seen as a method of self-education and as a path toward the fulfillment of the *essential harmony* (rather than the "law") of our individual being. The core of this fulfillment is the process of theosynthesis, the action of the greater Whole upon the lesser whole, man as an individual, and the response of this individual person to the downflow of cosmic forces consciously focused through the lens of a clear and open mind. But this process of fulfillment would be meaningless if the astrologer did not have a holistic approach to the birth-chart. The absence of such an approach can totally vitiate whatever traditional knowledge of a psychological character has been transmitted to us from the archaic ages – before it became personalized in Greece and Alexandria.

The first and basic principle of this holistic approach can be stated as follows: The only true and valid "I" is that which includes the whole of the personality; thus, the whole of the birth-chart. Anyone who, looking *at one single factor* in his birth-chart, says "I *am* this or that" commits a basic sin against wholeness – which means also "holiness," wholesomeness, and health. It is very much the same as when the ruler or executive of a nation identifies his rule with the interests and prejudices of only one class or group of people in the nation. Every planet in a birth-chart is a potential "pressure group" trying not only to attract the attention of the ego (the government), but to control its judgments and decisions. Every function of the personality seeks to be the dominant function around which every other function and feeling revolves. By identifying itself with such a dominant function, the ego throws the whole organism of personality out of balance and harmony. This is the cause of much, if not all, personal misery and in a sense, the source of evil — the result of mistaking the part for the whole.

In the average psychologically undeveloped person, one function after another usurps the prerogative of the "I" and forces this "I" to become identified with itself. The "I" is thus like a cork floating helplessly on the surface of a pool churned by winds blowing from all directions. There is no stability, no possibility for the divine purpose of the personality to be visible to the ego — whose only task is to keep from splitting into many fragments. If, however, the ego manages to get a firm grasp of the psychological situation, it may find itself driven to act as a dynamic ruler; but, in such a case, what actually happens is that it rules under the driving power of some particular motive which excludes other motives basically essential to the wholeness and health of the personality. For instance, the ego's rule may be given its direction and special character by a dominant passion, such as greed or the fanaticism of puritan morality. In either case, the ego rules by *suppressing* some vital parts or functions of the total organism of personality. The result may be a spectacular life driven by a one-pointed energy toward a set goal. Yet it is not a "wholesome" life. It is a fanatic life, in which "God" cannot normally manifest, because God is absolute Harmony. The process of theosynthesis cannot operate adequately or completely in that life, because the substance of divinity is, above all, characterized by its harmonic quality, its balanced rhythm. Even if such a substance could be assimilated by the soul, it would at once deteriorate, poisoned by the discordant emphasis of the fanatic life. Any type of fanaticism makes it impossible to reach the condition of a fulfilled and spiritually mature personality. However, I must add that in the process of differentiating and individualizing the ego-structure, one-pointed devotion to one particular goal, however limited and narrow, is often a *temporary* necessity. It is perhaps a necessity; yet, it must be regarded as a tragic necessity, for it inevitably leads to the formation of a deep shadow, which in turn will have to be absorbed and neutralized by a play of lights when the soul is recovered enough from its fanaticism to absorb light by theosynthesis and gradually match the illumination that comes from the divine Source with its own radiance.

What I am discussing here is the process of development toward harmony and wholeness, a process which must take into consideration everything the chart contains and which is oriented toward an intuitional perception of the chart as a whole. The chart is a "chord" of energies and functions. What counts in it are not the component tones considered as isolated factors, but the harmony of the whole. Thus, the astrologer on the path to personality integration should first of all establish in his consciousness a "harmonic" realization of the wholeness of his birth-chart. In this realization nothing is to be left out; nothing is to be seen as evil, or unfortunate, or particularly hard. Likewise, no birth-chart is to be considered as unique. It is a formula for integration; it is not "unique." By *using* this chart as a principle of harmonization, the individual can become an integral whole; but so can other people born at the same time or close to it. There is nothing "spectacular" in any birth-chart. None is inherently "better" or "more fortunate" than any other. Some depict a relatively smoother path than others, but every person has latent within him the power necessary to harmonize his personality and make of it a chalice for the reception of the power that ceaselessly flows from the cosmic Whole to the open consciousness of man. If the task is harder, the power is commensurably greater: the proportion between the difficulty and the power necessary to overcome it is basically *the same* in all individuals. It is, in the field of personality-development, what the speed of light (C) is in the Einsteinian formula, $E=MC^2$, which measures the relationship of energy (E) to mass (M). It is a "constant" of the spiritual world, the world of divine Grace — which means, *of light*.

In his previously mentioned book, Dr. Kunkel analyzes some of the main difficulties to be overcome in the process of self-education: How can we "get rid of the ego or the idol" and "find our real center"; how to transcend either rebellion against or passive obedience to moral laws or God's commandments; how to navigate between the dangerous rocks of "unrestricted self-expression" and "repression." Kunkel offers as basic methods what he calls "confessional meditation" (accompanied with "conscious sacrifice") plus its complementary pole, "positive training." And he adds these characteristic words: "What does God want you to discover, or to understand, or to do? This question is the first beginning of your spiritual reaction." Astrologically speaking, this means: What does this birth-chart want me (who is the wholeness of it) to discover, to understand, to do? Why these squares? To what refusal to act or refusal to understand and be illumined do they refer? And as this progressed Sun of mine meets my natal Neptune, what mysterious alchemy of consciousness must I learn to perform; with what metamorphosis of ego must "I" cooperate — "I" that am ego, yet far more than ego; "I" that am the potentiality of total, all-inclusive Selfhood.

The natal Sun is not the Self. It is only the celestial symbol of the source of the energy of the Self, which means, of spirit. The Self is the whole birth-sky localized and focused by the place and time of our first breath. This Self is God-in-us — the universal Whole focused into the core of our total being as an individual person. As we study any event (past, present, or adumbrated in the future), any trait of our character or any recurrent failure, misfortune, or dream, our study must always be referred to this Self, to this wholeness which we potentially are, yet which we have to concretely become and express. Whether a so-called benefic or malefic, every planet and every configuration of planets is a *path to our Self*, and as we consciously and deliberately tread these paths, we should never lose sight of the wholeness of our chart — and never lose faith in our ability to reach that goal and become the harmonic totality of our being, the Self in us.

The Christian mystic spoke of the "practice of the presence of God." The astrologer in his quest for psychological and spiritual wholeness could well try to never lose sight of the Presence of the Cosmos, of which the whole sky is the potent Image and symbol. We can not (except at a Planetarium) actually and visibly experience our birth-sky; but we can visualize our two-dimensional birth-chart, and evoke that which in us is the Archetype of the Self. We can live in the presence of the Sky. This is, etymologically speaking, what is meant by the word "consideration" (from *sidera*, stars). "To consider" literally means to *commune with the stars.* It is to feel, think, and act in terms of the vibrant wholeness of any moment, of any situation, and of our individual nature. It is to place ourselves and all that is ours within the frame of reference of the total Sky. And by the total Sky, I mean not only the visible heaven, but *also* those parts of the whole universe which can only be seen from the antipodes; thus, the "inner world" of depth that forever complements the "outer world" of height — the inner world which is also we, for we are eternally the Whole, experienced from one particular point. To realize this is to open one's total being to the downflow of a transfiguring Light, to assimilate that Light through the spiritual process of theosynthesis. As we do so, we too, like green plants, can change the atmosphere of the Earth. We can provide "food" for the multitude of still un-whole and discordant egos yearning for peace and harmony.

Part III

Astro-Psychological Vistas

Anyone even slightly acquainted with psychoanalysis or the "analytical psychology" of Carl Jung knows that in these approaches to the understanding of human nature much is made of the Mother Image and Father Image. However, it is relatively rare to find a non-professional person who has a very clear idea of what these images actually and basically mean. Indeed, many psychologists with official degrees lack a vital grasp of these matters. Astrology can throw a great deal of light on this most important subject. Conversely, when one understands what these images signify in terms of a person's attitude toward everyday life, the psychological value and meaning of astrology itself and the reason for the long-sustained and eager human interest in it stand revealed in a new light.

Psychologists use the term *image* in various ways and with different shades of meaning. To me, a psychological image is the form which some basic function in human nature takes in a particular person, and also, collectively speaking, in a particular society and culture. Thus, what I call the Mother Image is an expression of the fundamental function of adaptation to the pressure and challenges of everyday living in a particular environment. Every living organism must adapt itself to its environment while it acts in such a way as to satisfy the basic needs of its organs. Everyone must eat some kind of sustaining food, evacuate waste materials, find means to maintain his body temperature through clothing (in most climates) and to protect himself within some kind of enclosure. Sooner or later, he must satisfy the reproductive urge. People are driven from within (by life itself, we might say) to satisfy such primary functional needs. Satisfaction produces a sense of well-being; frustration leads to discomfort, pain, and deterioration. Everyday living, in the most basic sense, is occupied with the business of gaining this organic well-being and avoiding discomfort, pain, and eventually death. This business is what I have called adaptation. While every human being inherently has the capacity for such an adaptation, the newborn baby does not have this capacity developed at birth. He is indeed totally helpless and must depend entirely upon his mother to provide him with the satisfaction of his immediate needs.

As the baby gradually gains the conscious awareness of his organic needs and the agency which satisfies them, an image of that agency begins to form in his brain-mind. Very likely, this image is at first hardly separate from the baby's sense of living. That which needs, has pain and is satisfied, and that which provides the satisfaction are probably felt by the newborn as two parts of one whole. Gradually, however, the sense of distinction between the body that needs and the mother who attends to the need must grow sharper. A definite image of the mother as need-satisfier builds in the baby's consciousness. Its character obviously depends on the particular way in which the mother succeeds or fails in making life comfortable for the baby. The image is affected by the mother's incomprehensible (to the baby) changes of mood, her sudden disappearances, the way she responds to intrusions in the baby-mother relationship (i.e., her attitude toward other persons), and so forth. The larger the family and the more other persons share with the mother the ability to make the baby satisfied and comfortable, the less the Mother Image tends to exclusively fill the field of the slowly developing consciousness of the baby. Yet, if the other persons are upsetting, unreliable, or hurtful and the mother saves the situation repeatedly, then the Mother Image takes on the character of the savior or the intermediary between the baby and strange or frightening forces – people or animals, elements, dangers of all kinds. As the child grows up, understands words and learns to talk, remembers and expects repetitive acts, and is faced by at first unexplainable and seemingly arbitrary *don'ts*, the Mother Image becomes ever more definite. The child acquires a more clear-cut and mentally formulated sense of how his needs are being taken care of by the mother – or left frustrated if the mother is not capable of making a successful adaptation for him.

Gradually, by imitation, then explanation, the child normally learns to develop the capacity for adaptation which at first was totally vested in the mother. This can be a long and painful process. The mother may overprotect the child; or she may be ineffectual, preoccupied, and moody, too full of her ego and too busy with things and people. The mother-child relationship may be too binding or broken too early by a variety of factors (a new brother or sister, unjust punishment, anger, etc.). All of these factors affect the development of the child's and adolescent's capacity for adaptation to everyday living and give the resulting Mother Image (in the youth's consciousness) a particular quality, form, and emotional flavor.

The hackneyed phrase "Mom knows best" simply shows that if the youngster finds himself faced by special difficulties and conflicts in the satisfaction of his basic organic urges (and their emotional-intellectual by-products or overtones), he normally goes to his mother for advice as to how to gain pleasure or success and avoid pain or defeat and frustration. If the actual mother has failed him or has gone away, the child, still unable to satisfactorily use his capacity for adaptation, tends to transfer his dependence to another woman. This woman becomes a substitute mother and the child projects his Mother Image upon her. However, it does not need to be another woman! For instance, the Mother Image is transferred to a church if the advice of the Church and its more or less impersonal officials is felt to provide all the answers to whatever baffling problems arise in everyday life. The Mother Image can also be transferred very effectively to astrology! It is so transferred whenever a person will not take an important (or even unimportant) step without consulting an astrologer, without looking at the ephermeris or casting a horary chart for the problem.

Any such transference is by no means necessarily bad! If we had been traveling to Tibet some centuries ago, we should have greatly welcomed the guidance of a lama who could speak our language and was familiar with our customs so that we might successfully adapt ourselves to the ways of Tibet. At each step leading to completely unfamiliar conditions, everyone needs guidance of some sort if the adaptation is to be successful and relatively smooth. But such guidance should be temporary only. Another kind of guidance is available once one is familiar with the new conditions: the guidance of a "map." A reliance on maps, principles of organization (physical, social, cosmic), a sense of structure, and a recognition of one's place in structures of various kinds – these can be substituted for a Mother-Image dependence. This type of reliance is at first normally associated by the child with his relationship with his father.

In astrology, the Moon traditionally stands for the mother and Saturn for the father. The reason for this symbolism is clear. The Moon is our only satellite, and as such, it constantly turns around us; likewise, the mother unceasingly attends to and surrounds the little baby. In the old geocentric astrology and in alchemy, what we now call the orbit of the Moon was named the sub-lunar sphere. This sphere was conceived to be like a cosmic womb, the life-giving placentum of our planet Earth, often thought to be as yet in the embryonic state (the Earth is not a sacred planet, occultists say even now). In modern astrological charts, the essential function of the Moon should be defined as that of adaptation to the business of everyday living. From that central character, all other secondary meanings follow. For instance, the type of mentality associated with the Moon in natal charts is the kind of mind which is utterly dedicated to the business of making a success and a pleasure of living in one's environment. It is the mind that is cunning, opportunistic, and flexible; the chameleon mind always ready to adjust, temporize, and compromise for the sake of practical success. The Moon also represents personal moods, the feelings, etc., for all these are more or less passive ways of fitting in, of responding to inner or outer situations as they unfold every day.

Saturn, on the other hand, was known until recently as the outermost planet. Even today, with the symbolism of its rings, it can still be considered to mark the real confines of the solar system as a limited and well-defined organic whole. The more distant planets (Uranus, Neptune, Pluto) refer to the less tangible zone surrounding the well-defined body — to the aura, to those functions which relate the strictly physical organism to the larger cosmic whole — say, the galaxy. Saturn represents not only the actual father, but more generally whatever defines our permanent structure of being and our place within a larger scheme of existence. Physically, Saturn refers to the skeleton which establishes the basic form of our organism; intellectually, to logic; psychologically, to our ego with its set patterns of response to social impacts; and in general, to our potential "place" within any "greater whole." Indeed, in older societies, the status of the father almost irrevocably established the social "place" of his children — their caste, class, profession, or potential mate. Today, the father gives his name to the child, even if socially nothing more.

Saturn means structure and where anything fits in a structure — thus, a thing's place in a man or a definite, rhythmic, schedule and process. Because of this, all astrology is actually based on the Saturn function, for what the natal chart does is simply to establish your place in the space-time unfoldment of the solar system. It shows where you fit and your fitness for whatever happens to you. But it does not tell you what to do! It does not guide you, except by showing you a map of what is possible according to the structure of things at the place and the time you live.

These last sentences have a very basic importance for anyone concerned with psychology and astrology. They imply the existence of two essential approaches to the practical use of astrology: the Mother Image and the Father Image type. If you go to an astrologer (or to your ephemeris) expecting an answer to "What should I do?" this simply means that you rush to a supernal mother for factual guidance in the belief that "Mom knows best." I repeat that this is not "bad," for if you were invited to visit the Dalai Lama or the Pope, you would have excellent reason for asking guidance as to exactly how to behave. Similarly, if you are confronted with an unfamiliar problem involving a choice of alternatives, the nature and end results of which you have (to your knowledge) no way of ascertaining by yourself, then astrological guidance of a concrete type may be most valuable. However, such external guidance can be valuable only if it is understood to be temporary. By its very nature, you must grow out of it or you will remain in a state of dependence upon a Mother Image — thus, forever a child. The true mother will, however, lead her child to the father, for what the father (theoretically, at least!) has to offer is a knowledge of structural principles, laws, and regulations. Mom may exclaim to the inquiring teen-ager: "Oh, don't do that!"; but the true father will unfold a map (symbolically speaking, of course) to the child and show him where the action would lead, what laws he might be breaking, and how it might affect his character and destiny.

A true father will never give a definite solution to a half-grown child who has gained something of the power to understand the structure and place of at least some things. He shows the way, the essential place of things, the quality of living expected if certain results are to be obtained. He leaves the child free to accept or reject. His one function is to throw light, to be clear, honest, true — on the basis of whatever he has himself learned and applied. Of course, that is not the common picture our American society has of a father — witness our comics! Nor is it even the picture of the autocratic and rigid father of past eras, or even of our Puritanical tradition. When either of these two pictures prevails, the child tends to develop a negative Father Image. If the father is the caricatured modern American variety, the child is easily caught in the web of "Mom-ism." If the father is the autocratic type, the youth develops a rebellion against all authority — i.e., against any structural pattern where he would fit, against fitting anywhere.

There are approaches to astrology which correspond to these negative Father Images. In the first case, the astrologer is constantly bossed by his supposed intuition or hunches — also perhaps inventing new systems as escapes from a real structural grasp of cycles and planetary patterns. In the second case, the astrologer is a rigid believer in Fate, making for his clients or himself pictures of fateful happenings, inevitable illnesses and tragedies, or wonderful happenings in the future — money, love, etc. On the other hand, I see the positive Father Image approach to astrology as being based on a thorough grasp of cyclic patterns and their complex interrelationships. It deals with the structure of processes, with the form or gestalt of the chart as a whole, with planets as correlated functions in the whole solar system. It studies the *fittingness* of everything. It places events and opportunities in maps of structural destiny. But it does not predict precise events as such — only crises and turning points. It shows what is possible within the framework of your space-time individuality — which is as well your destiny, for the real you and the particular destiny defined by your space-time data of birth are one and the same.

When you want to go from Los Angeles to San Francisco, or New York to Chicago, there are many possible ways to travel. Yet there is only one map. But the map does not force you to take any particular road — unless you have to make an important appointment at a certain time, and this seems to limit your choice to the quickest way. Still, what is the quickest way? You might get drowsy on the speedway and have an accident — or find some less frequented road the faster possibility, even if longer by mileage. Structure does not compel. It defines. It is there to be used, not as a tyrant to enslave you. True fatherhood is clarity of form, illumination. It does not bind; it shows the way as it is. It does not offer any particular dogma to believe in worshipfully; it induces the fire in you that will provide for your light on the way — any way.

This lighting of the way cannot be directly linked with Saturn; yet, in an indirect sense, it is so linked by the principle of complementary opposites. Saturn and the Sun are complementary opposites because one inevitably arouses the activity of the other if the activity of the first is essential, thorough, and true. The Sun is constantly emanating radiation; but without the structural power of Saturn, this would actually mean at best a random state of explosiveness. It is only because there is a polar interplay between the Sun and Saturn that there is a rhythmic to-and-fro tide of solar energy — which we know as the sun-spot cycle. From center to circumference, from circumference back to center, Saturn times the solar tides. The great message of Christianity has been: "The Father is within you." Destiny is individuality. If you trust father Saturn implicitly, you become Sun. If you have absolutely no fear of destiny, all that is possible in terms of that destiny can indeed take place — at the proper time, in the right place. To be like the Sun is to be your own potential, in full process of gradual actualization.

Then there is no more Mother Image or Father Image. The two ancestral symbols of the past — Moon and Saturn — are absorbed within a solar present. You are what it is necessary for you to be at any moment, without fear of the future or regret of the past. This is a very difficult state to attain! Yet it is difficult not because it means performing some spectacular act, but on the contrary because it requires that we become free from effort, tense activity, and precise expectation. What is needed is that we surrender our dependence upon any image, be it Father or Mother Image.

What does this mean in terms of our attitude toward astrology? Simply this: we see astrology as a means to an end, as a highly valuable technique to develop certain capacities in us — just as the examples of, and our relationship to, our mother and father (or their later substitutes) are but the means of developing our own capacity of adaptation to life and our own sense of fitting a superior order establishing our place of destiny and our fundamental individuality. Each generation renders that service to the coming one. Yet what each generation receives from its parents is only training, and it should never produce a sense of bondage or identification. Likewise, what astrology can do for us is to train both our capacity for feeling out the best way of responding to the new challenges and problems of ever-new situations, and our ability to perceive cosmic order and the structural unfoldment of all natural processes, even where life seems most chaotic.

A Mother Image approach to astrology may develop our sense of expediency and give-and-take in the timing of our activities so that we do not crudely force our self-will upon any circumstance and irrelevant environment. Through it, we may learn to accept guidance for our egocentric and restless impulses. Yet, if this guidance means dependence, we are thereby condemned to a kind of perpetual childhood. Astrological guidance of the maternal sort serves its real purpose when we realize we no longer need it — and prefer our own mistakes to uncertain advice. An old proverb says: "When the Son leaves the Mother, he becomes the Father." When we are willing to not ask "Mom," even if she should know best, then we can enter the realm of the "father knowledge," the knowledge of cycles, form, and harmony through apparent disorder and conflicts — the knowledge of what we are there and then. Our true father is he who can lead us to, or give us the foundation for, that knowledge. He may not be our father in a biological-social sense. He may be our "guru" or Initiator. But this father-exemplar and teacher, once a person has reached a certain level of maturity, provides essentially the training — and perhaps the illumination. It is ours to do the walking on the path that has been lighted and to imprint our own realization of order upon whatever we touch and impregnate. We must become fathers in our own right; and what is pulsing within us is not actually, if we are true and free, the father as a being — but the power of the fatherhood!

You may look at your birth-chart and say: This is what I am — my seed possibilities — what I should make actual, concrete fact. But the essential purpose of this study of your chart is to be able to forget the chart while retaining the realization that you are, in fact, a solar system ordered in an individual manner! The Father Image approach to astrology should train you and discipline your mind so that your awareness of being an individual person may be transferred from the level of a merely Saturnian ego to that of a self that is, analogically, the entire field of a solar system powered by a flaming Sun. If astrology does that, it has been a good and true substitute father.

In the end, however, it is what is beyond the training and the precedents that really counts. It is the great symphony which the composer creates out of the dynamic truth and rhythm of his original nature without any concern over the rules he once studied. It is the great painting which makes people gasp, startled — yet they may perhaps "see," henceforth, in a different manner. It is the life which is lived, not by moral rules or social laws or astrological progressions, but by the inherent, conscious power of the creative self that freely sees this entire life, from birth to death, as one great statement, one creative word, one world--transforming destiny.

Wherever there is life, there also the principle of polarity operates. This may be because, as biologists are now realizing, life essentially implies positive and negative electrical phenomena. All cells are electrically charged, and the nerves operate on the basis of electrical currents. In the total nervous system of a human being, two great subsystems oppose each other in their action; health results from their dynamic equilibrium. Indeed, all activities require the release of electrical charges, and electricity has a bi-polar character — a positive and a negative aspect. In the human organism, many functions are at work. Health is present when these functions operate harmoniously and in rhythmic interdependence.

Ancient Chinese philosophers expressed this rhythmic, self-regulated character of all life processes in the Tao symbol in which two forces of opposite polarities, *Yin* and *Yang,* are shown to be interrelated within a circle. The picture is not static; it represents a bi-polar process. It illustrates the yearly rhythm of the seasons, and the astrological zodiac is a symbolic expression of this bi-polar process.* What I call the Day Force refers to the "masculine" polarity, *Yang*; it has the least strength at the winter solstice (the symbolic Christ birth). The Night Force, *Yin,* is at the apex of its power then. Through the winter months, the Day Force increases (and the days become longer); the Night Force decreases. The two forces have equal strength at the spring equinox; at the summer solstice, the Day Force reaches its maximum power, the Night Force its lowest ebb. Afterward, the Night Force waxes in strength while the Day Force wanes, once more to become equal at the fall equinox, and so on.

The principle of polarity also operates in the realm of life as what we call sex. The earliest forms of life were not classified according to sex. The uni-cellular organism divided itself into two, each half becoming an independent unit which also divided, and so on *ad infinitum.* A human being is born male or female; but until about the third month of gestation, the embryo in the mother's womb has in itself the germs of both the male and the female organs; the structural differentiation which occurs afterward is not absolute. The male body retains something of the potential female organs, and the female body displays structures related to the male set of characters. Indeed, the full bodily expression of sex comes

---

*   cf. *The Pulse of Life* (Shambhala Publications, 1970).

only at puberty, even though the actualization of such a fullness of sexual manifestation has been going on since birth. As Freud has stressed (and overstressed!), the dynamism of this process conditions important aspects of the infantile consciousness, especially before the age of seven (the traditional "age of responsibility"), when something else theoretically happens. In a very real sense, one cay say that the sex forces build, or power the building of, the child's body. But the body represents only the *outer aspect of personality.* To this outer aspect, one must add an *inner* aspect, which is usually called the "psyche." A human being is composed of both a body and a psyche; every individual person has an inner life as well as an outer life. The forces which have brought forth the male or female character of the body are not the only ones. In and through the male *body,* a *female psyche* also is active. It can be said to be derived from the primordial female characteristics existing during the pre-sexual phase of embryonic growth.

In other words, the fecundated ovum in the womb is *both* male and female in potentiality; and when the "germ" of the male functions becomes dominant and the embryo gradually develops rudimentary masculine organs, the female germ does *not* disappear. We might say it does not entirely lose its strength, but it grows in a direction opposed to that of the sex-building male germ. It develops along "countersexual" lines – i.e., psychically.

In the male embryonic body nearing birth, the sex glands produce hormones which not only affect the growth of the physical body, but also build what we might call a masculine type of neuro-intellectual adaptation to the outer environment of the future child. In the case of a female infant, the female hormones likewise build a feminine type of adaptation to the conditions of the future girl's existence. For instance, in the male infant, the countersexual feminine energies also operate. They operate within the *subconscious* as a potentially compensating factor in the inner life. They may *seem* non-existent in the boisterous all-American boy of 9 or 16, but this is largely because of the special nature of the American society; in France and in numerous Oriental countries, a boy *before* reaching puberty often has an almost feminine charm and his eyes may seem strangely open to psychic vistas.

If some physical or organic shock occurs in childhood or adolescence, the sexual character of the youth may be affected, blocked, or deviated; then the countersexual factors (feminine in the boy, masculine in the girl) have a chance to manifest more clearly. They then influence the psychic or mental fields of the personality. This may even produce "psychosomatic" results, or at least condition the development of a somewhat unusual personality – perhaps imaginative and artistic in the boy; intellectual, scientific, or actional in the girl.

Any experience which decreases the tone of, or gives a negative emotional value to, the sexual factors in the growing personality of the youth tends thereby to increase the influence and actual effects of the countersexual life principle. It is almost as if, during the summer months which should be an outdoor period of life, a long stretch of very bad, cold weather forces one to pass the days indoors and to focus one's mind upon occupations best performed inside the house. For this reason, many religious disciplines have stressed ascetic practices to shock the sexual part of the nature into near collapse, allowing the countersexual energies of the psychic life to emerge powerfully from their subconscious abode into the field of consciousness.

Astrology offers a very revealing picture of the processes which have just been outlined, for in the Sun and the Moon, we find symbols of the sexual aspect of human nature, respectively, in the male and female bodies; while Jupiter and Saturn give us significant clues to the activity of the countersexual forces in the masculine and the feminine psyches, respectively. The Sun (male) and the Moon (female) are the "Lights" of life on the earth's surface. The Sun is the primary source of all energy on the planet; it is the active releasing principle, the fecundator and dynamizer of all life processes. As to the Moon, I believe that we can never fully understand its astrological and occult significance unless we realize that it does not refer only to the earth's satellite as a material globe but, rather, that it symbolizes what ancient astrologers called "the sublunar realm" – that is, the entire space around the earth outlined by the monthly revolutions of the visible Moon. This sublunar realm is, as it were, the matrix (or, if one prefers, the aura or electromagnetic field) inside of which our planet – and, therefore, humankind as a whole – exists. In this sense, our astronauts will not have fully left the earth's sphere until they are able to go beyond the Moon and (symbolically, at least) to rise from the "hidden side" of the Moon which is always turned toward outer space and away from the Sun.

The Moon, therefore, symbolizes the traditionally "mysterious" aspect of sex in the woman; and the changes of appearance of the Moon represent the female cycle of ovulation and menstruation and the *bioglandular* moods of women. Likewise, the Sun in astrology stands for the sexual body-building power of sex in the male person. With the Sun and Moon, we are essentially dealing with the outer biological and sexual aspects of man and woman. Moreover, the sexual power operates through organic structures which are "ruled" by Venus and Mars in both sexes: Venus referring to the testicles and ovaries, Mars to the mechanisms of release of the sexual energies.

When we come to the countersexual aspects of the total human individual, we enter a realm in which a great deal of elucidation is needed, at both the psychological and the astrological levels. I relate such a countersexual aspect to Jupiter and Saturn. Marc Edmund Jones long ago spoke of these two planets as the "social planets" — and, in another context, as the "planets of soul." In the most basic sense, they refer to whatever emerges from the living together of human beings; they deal with the organization and maintenance of communities, social and religious institutions, and nations. Jupiter refers to the social sense — thus, to the rhythms of group feelings, the companionship between people who share common interests. Saturn is specifically concerned with the place that any member of a group or community rightfully occupies and the social function he can perform efficiently when at his proper place and under his legal, socially guaranteed name. Saturn thus refers to the problems of defining, stabilizing, and keeping secure this place and mode of operation in the group.

Saturn and Jupiter deal with collective factors in the human being; the Sun, Moon, Mars, and Venus (the organic instrumentalities-building planets) with *individual* factors. I have shown in my books that these two principles — individual and collective — are the two most basic polarities in all forms of existence. The Day Force in the cycle of the year (the Chinese *Yang*) actually manifests in life as the drive toward *individualization;* it builds limited, clearly defined organic systems and outwardly operating personalities. The Night Force (*Yin*) operates as the drive toward socialization and the building of more or less large *collectivities* of individual units.

The emergence of an infant human body out of the womb — and, in larger evolutionary terms, of the first living organism out of the sea — is the outcome of the drive toward individualization; and sex (i.e., the process of self-reproduction and self-multiplication) is a force acting at the very core of such a drive. But the new-born — and, later on, the self-sufficient mature individual — is not alone in the world. He could not exist and unfold his human birth potential alone. He is born within a group, a collectivity of human beings; and it is this collectivity and its tradition which provide this individual human organism with what he needs, at both the biological and the mental level — i.e., food and the knowledge, language, and social institutions absolutely required for the fulfillment of any individual personality.

What we call the "inner life" of a person is conditioned *mentally* by the language, symbols, and collective thinking attitudes of his or her society and culture; it is conditioned *emotionally* by at first taken-for-granted patterns of interpersonal relationship, the parental example, the contagion of group feelings. Even if the individual rebels against the ways of thinking and the ethical, religious, and social ways of living of his family, group, or nation, this rebellion itself is conditioned by and starts from the primordial sense of "belonging" to the group.

You cannot escape from the pressures of your collectivity and your culture; your very revolt must use words and gestures inherited from the cultural-social past in order to take a form and become effective. Carl Jung has spoken of the collective unconscious, not only as the repository of the harvest of experience of perhaps millions of generations, but even more as the sea out of which arise the many small islands that we know as individual persons. Thus, when the biological soli-lunar forces whose work it is to produce an individual human organism succeed in completing their outward-oriented drive in the development of the sexual aspect of a human personality, male or female, they do so by pushing the counter-sexual forces back into the unconscious. These may not seem active in a personal, conscious, and wilful manner, but they are there, conditioning the *psychological climate* of the individual, somewhat as the sea, its currents and the fog it produces, conditions the climate of the small island which has risen out of the water — and sometimes a tidal wave may submerge the island of consciousness!

When Jupiter and Saturn are spoken of as "planets of soul," the term "soul" refers to the part of the total person which ever seeks to *complement* the outward-oriented, self-conscious and conscious parts of the personality. Carl Jung spoke of this part as the *anima* in the man and the *animus* in the woman; he spoke of them as undifferentiated and often archaic psychic functions. They may manifest in dreams, creative fantasies, sudden intuitions, and super-normal faculties — some of them now being called "parapsychological." They constitute the less obvious or "hidden" aspect of what the planets Jupiter and Saturn represent.

The individual person functioning outwardly as a male organism would find, if able to look into his psychic depths, a countersexual feminine power (the "anima"). It is this power which, unknown to the individual consciousness, urges him to seek not only social fellowship with other men, but also perhaps a dedicated participation in the collective activities of a group — church, nation, or even humanity as a whole. The "soul" of a man is collectively oriented; that of a woman is individual-istically oriented — because, as the childbearer, her *outer* nature and sex functions have to be pervaded (in all normal cases) with a dedication to the human species, the existence of which she has to perpetuate.

Thus, the feminine type of intellect (also a part of her outer nature) is normally wide open to collectivizing social currents. A woman tends to conform to institutionalized religion and ethics as well as to fashion. But within the unconscious part of her psyche, the basic drive is toward individualization. If she eagerly accepts a state of dependence upon her husband (so glorified in Hindu culture), or upon Jesus as Divine Beloved (if she has transcendentalized her need for a love which will reveal to her her true essential self), or upon some Oriental Teacher, Swami, or yogi (who supposedly can provide a technique of self-revelation), it is because her unconscious nature is forever seeking to reach a condition of individualistic integration. It seeks this through a process of identification with some exemplar, with a catalyzing personality or life situation. Saturn, the individualizer and stabilizer, is thus the symbol of a woman's inner drive; while Jupiter, the socializer, is the symbol of a man's semi-conscious or totally unconscious psychic yearnings.

This drive within the psyche may actually manifest as a deep, unclear compulsion seizing the man or woman and dominating his or her outer existence; but, in any case, it has as its foundations the countersexual forces. Very often what *seems* to a man or a woman to be the motive for actions, or the cause of feelings for a person or a situation, is not at all the real motive or cause. A man may join a fraternal organization — he thinks — because this would serve his outer social or business interests, his power of self-expression; but the real cause may be that his "soul" is yearning for deep social fellowship and group belonging — and this, in a sense, represents a kind of psychological "transference" of the infantile relationship of the boy to the mother in early childhood.

On the other hand, a woman may *consciously* believe that she is seeking the love of a man as an outlet for her sexual feelings while, in reality (unconsciously or semi-consciously), she is yearning for a transcendent power that would reveal to her what she essentially is as a spiritual being. Sex play may be more often than not a pretext, a means to an unconscious or dimly conscious end. The love act for a woman may actually be symbolic; the reality, deep beyond the symbol, is the catalytic process which, in some mysterious manner, will reveal her true self to her. It is, thus, truly an "initiation" occurring in her *inner* life — an activity in which the unconscious countersexual part of the woman is the active factor. For the man, the act of love is normally a conscious expression of sex power, one of many events (or incidents) in his *outer* life.

For the woman, the planet Saturn symbolizes the figure of the solemn Hierophant who celebrates the mysterious rite of purification *from* or *through* — whichever may be the case — her sexual nature. Saturn is astrologically the father image because the father is (or should be, in natural conditions of life) the symbol of authority and mind power; and — as the little girl feels in her psychic depths — he has been her mother's "initiator." The girl, identifying her collective biological-social role with her mother, projects her unconscious yearning for individualization (which implies mental development) on her father. If the father is an unworthy or ineffectual screen for the projection, she feels frustrated and will subsequently tend to seek someone able to live up to her ideal image. She may develop a deep confusion in her quest because of mixing up the sexual and countersexual drives — and this brings many an American marriage to divorce. The "inner" and "outer" shortcircuit each other.

A man's inner longing for fellowship and sharing — of which the Christian Communion and earlier forms of "sacred meals" taken in common in a mystic brotherhood are the religious expressions — may also become confused and materialized when mixed up with the outer drive for power and wealth. These constitute a "socialized" kind of sexual and ego-building activity. Religious movements and secret brotherhoods (such as original Free Masonry) become easily perverted or, at least, materialized as the "outer" invades the "inner" and the body draws the soul into its vicious circle of desire.

The difficulty in making use of the foregoing psychological facts and astrological concepts in the study of an individual's birth-chart is that several other factors may enter into the picture and affect the person's character and life. Above all, pressures from the environment, particularly the nature of the actual everyday relationship between child and parents at an early age and at the time of adolescence (the latter especially for the girl), can considerably alter the natural development of the personality.

This relationship operates at both the inner and outer levels — and differently at each level.

For a boy, the mother is *outwardly* represented in the birth-chart as the Moon. The mother normally envelops the child with attention, care, and love. He depends upon her for his well-being and for his meeting as successfully and happily as possible the everyday difficulties of existence. This outer dependence may tenaciously persist after adolescence, and the young man may transfer it to his wife. But there is also a subtler form of relationship affecting the boy's *inner* life, for he normally *identifies* himself with his mother in a communion of love participation. He and she constitute a "we"; they belong together — until perhaps this we-feeling is shattered by the mother's carelessness or lack of real love. If the we-feeling is shattered, the boy will carry through his life a psychic sense of being wounded or a feeling of inner emptiness. He will then seek to fill this emptiness by developing a social and Jupiterian yearning for fellowship, for being loved by his equals, for belonging to a group.

Thus, in a man's chart, the position of both the Moon and Jupiter have to be considered, in addition to that of the Sun, which is always an indicator of the basic drive for outer self-expression and self-aggrandizement, sexually or socially. The instrumentality of this drive is the Mars function (which rules all muscles and organs of action), and also the Mercury function (which deals with the intellect and its associative memory). The mutual relationships (aspects, Parts, etc.) existing between these planets should enable one to make a relevant picture of the sexual and countersexual forces at work in the total personality of the man.

In a woman's chart, the Moon represents her female nature and also, during childhood and adolescence, her relationship to her mother, whom she normally wants to *imitate*. Even if she dislikes and rebels against the mother's behavior, she may eventually see herself repeating some of her mother's life patterns. Since the countersexual aspect of a girl's personality is represented by Saturn, the aspect between the Moon and Saturn is quite revealing. When these two planets are in opposition, it is quite possible for the girl to completely overcome, sooner or later, the outer bodily pressures of her sexual drives upon her inner soul consciousness and mind. Yet a negative result can also occur in some cases — some kind of disassociation of the inner and outer life.

A conjunction of the Moon and Saturn may indicate the beginning of a new cycle of life (if one believes in reincarnation) or a confused sense of insecurity, as if one were functioning in a new and unfamiliar spiritual environment. It may mean emotional involvement with the father; his presence and influence may so strongly polarize the girl's nature that ambivalent feelings of quasi-incestuous attraction and guilt are aroused. Whether this complex reaction remains in a hazy subconscious background or, on the contrary, haunts the conscious personality, depends theoretically on the planetary contacts between the father's and the daughter's charts.

A close contact between a man's Jupiter and a woman's Saturn can be an indication of a karmic relationship whose roots reach deep into the past; a typical symbol would be a Romeo and Juliet situation. When a man's natal Sun is conjunct Jupiter, his personality tends to become a forceful expression of a deep inner compulsion to fulfill a superpersonal purpose. President Johnson was almost a representative of this situation; but the presence of Mars rising between Jupiter in Leo and the Sun in Virgo confuses the meaning of a conjunction which is neither close nor in one zodiacal sign. The best example is the great prophet, poet, and yogi, Sri Aurobindo, whom his disciples consider an "avatar," i.e., the embodied expression of a divine destiny and purpose. He was born with the Sun near Jupiter just rising in Leo.

A retrograde Jupiter in a man's chart and a retrograde Saturn in a woman's chart tend to more sharply differentiate the inner from the outer life, the countersexual from the sexual aspects of the personality. But, I repeat, all such indications are subtly psychological and should hardly be considered in a superficial and quick chart analysis. They belong to a new type of psychological astrology which goes hand in hand with a psychology oriented toward a realization of the total meaning of the individual person.

17 *The Mysteries of Sleep and Dreams*

If I were to select one astrological teaching as the most fundamental, it would assuredly be the principle of polarity. Every factor used in astrology has its polar opposite. Every sign in the zodiac has as its polarity the opposite sign. The winter solstice balances the summer solstice — the spring equinox, the fall equinox. Every planet is paired with another planet (Sun and Moon, Mars and Venus, Jupiter and Saturn, or Jupiter and Mercury). Each section of the natal chart (each house) above the horizon is the complement of the one facing it below the horizon. The eastern ascendant balances the western descendant.

Astrology is primarily a method for gaining a full understanding of living organisms; these may be bodies or personalities, even social organizations (like nations and business firms) which somehow operate as more or less permanent wholes, organizing the productive activities of human beings. Life, in any form, operates according to a bi-polar rhythm — just as does electricity which, when active, always has a positive and a negative pole. So the understanding of polarity is essential to the study of astrology. The most striking of these polar oppositions in human life is that of waking consciousness and sleep. In some civilizations and religions, this alternation of conscious activity and unconscious slumber has been extended to embrace the idea of a similar alternation of incarnated existence on Earth and "discarnated" absorption into a transcendent state of being beyond the portals of death.

This last-mentioned area — the doctrine of reincarnation, as it is usually called — is rarely well understood; it can be significantly understood in a simple manner only when related to what we call sleep. Unfortunately, we have only a vague notion of what sleep means! We do not bother to ask *why* we sleep — though we pass a third of our existence sleeping — except for the fact that we know we must go to sleep when we are too tired. But why does sleep rest us, why must we lose our usual consciousness (our day sense of identity, of being "I"), and why do we experience these peculiar phenomena called dreams? We take these things for granted, just as we take death and sickness as inevitable events which we must accept, even though we do not understand them.

Religions and philosophies are supposed to enlighten us on such basic matters. But their explanations often shed very little light and are cloaked in superstition and fancy. As for science and modern psychology, they have many theories about sleep and dreams; but what they say explains very little and merely replaces one unknown with another. Is there no way of reaching a simple explanation which presents, at least in outline form, a picture of the relation between the state of waking, conscious activity and the condition of unconscious sleep? Obviously, such a picture would have to include the phenomenon of dreams, for somehow dreams occur at the borderline between waking consciousness and sleep, partaking in some peculiar manner of both states. I believe that the tools and symbols provided by astrology can serve to elucidate (in a general way) this problem; and I shall suggest a simple key which, if we use it well, could bring much light upon matters usually shrouded in mystery.

We know now that some of the Greek philosophers understood that the Earth revolves around the Sun, but it was only after Galileo, Kepler, and Newton, some five hundred years ago, that the modern picture of the solar system became clearly outlined. It was only after Uranus and Neptune, then Pluto, were discovered within the last two hundred years that astrologers could use this new "heliocentric" (i.e., Sun-centered) picture of the solar system in its true meaning. I do not refer here to the heliocentric position of the planets in the zodiac. These positions can be studied with very valid results; but this requires a special ephemeris, as the tables astrologers ordinarily use today give the geocentric positions of the planets — that is, their movements as seen from our Earth. But even if we use the geocentric positions of the planets in erecting birth-charts, we can keep in mind the modern heliocentric picture of the solar system and think of the planets as representing dynamic functions within the solar system as a whole.

The solar system, with the Sun at its core, is a cosmic unit and, in a symbolic sense at least, a "living organism." It is for this reason that, by studying the related cyclic motions of the planets, the astrologer can understand better, and to some extent foresee, the periodic ebbs and flows of life and consciousness within a human being — or the course which emotions, urges, and trends of thought may take during the life span of an individual. The whole solar system is thus seen to represent the individual personality as a whole.

It has become clear to the psychologically informed astrologer that the complexities of a modern human personality require all the planets we now know to describe and represent them. The ancients stopped at Saturn when casting their charts; but actually, the orbit of Saturn is only the dividing line between two types of planets. The planets between the central Sun and Saturn (included) refer to one aspect of the human personality as a whole; the planets beyond Saturn (Uranus, Neptune, Pluto — and there may be more!) represent another aspect, one which balances and complements the first. A definite polar relationship exists between these two groups (or series) of planets. It is this relationship which we must try to understand. The majority of astrologers speak of Uranus, Neptune, and Pluto as if they were planets in the same sense as the others. Others have conceived the idea that the three "trans-Saturnian" planets are "higher octaves" of Mercury, Venus, and Mars — though their opinions differ as to which of the latter series correspond to the former. In my opinion, the higher octave idea, even if partly valid, does not go to the root of the differences between the two groups of planets.

What is the real difference? What makes one series the polar opposite of the other? Any organic system or cosmic unit is subjected to two contrary forces. There is the pull which draws every part of the system to the center (for instance, the pull of gravitation); but there is also the pull exerted by outer space, which actually means by the larger system within which the first system operates. In the case of the solar system, this larger system is called the galaxy. Our Sun is but one of millions of stars composing this immense spiral nebula, the galaxy (or Milky Way); this in turn is part of a finite Universe composed of millions of nebulae of various types. Every planet of our solar system and every living being on Earth is to some degree affected by the pressures and pulls which reach us from the galaxy; we are also affected in an opposite direction by the gravitational power of the Sun, the center of our system.

Saturn, however, represents a basic line of demarcation between these two opposite forces, galactic and solar. The planets inside of Saturn's orbit are mainly creatures and vassals of the Sun; while the planets beyond Saturn are what I have called, many years ago, "ambassadors of the galaxy." They focus upon the solar system the power of this vast community of stars, the galaxy. They do not completely belong to the solar system. They are within its sphere of influence to do a particular work, to link our small system (of which the Sun is the center and Saturn's orbit the circumference) to the larger system, the galaxy.

This may at first sound quite fanciful; but if we apply the idea to the facts of human existence, we will at once see what it actually means. An individual person — everyone will agree — does not live an isolated existence. He is part of a family group, a community. He is thus a small unit active within a larger whole. He is an individual having some part to play within a collectivity. Here then is the polarity of which I spoke when

I mentioned the solar system and the whole galaxy — the individual star and the vast galactic community of stars. Truly, the individual acts upon the collective life of the community within which he is born and he lives; but the collective thinking and behavior of the community — its traditions, religion, culture, ethics — have molded this individual and constantly exert a pressure, an influence (constructive or destructive), upon him. If he rebels against this influence, he still remains conditioned by what he rebels against.

There is an even deeper kind of polarity, in which the conscious and self-determined individual with a purpose of his own stands in contrast to the vast ocean of universal life — the life which animates his body and all human bodies, which gives power to, yet controls as long as it can, the individual's basic urges, emotions, and instinctive thinking. It is to this most basic polarity that we must primarily refer the alternation of waking consciousness and sleep — and ultimately of individual bodily existence and death. The principle of such an alternation is very simple. The life of a human personality is the result of a relationship between two polar forces: one seeks to make of this person a conscious, self-sufficient, self-determined, purposefully acting individual; the other tries to draw him back into the vast undifferentiated, unconscious, unindividualized ocean of life. When the individualizing force is positive and dominant, a human being is awake and busy with conscious endeavors and planned activities of some sort. But when the power of universal life gains control and the individualizing force turns negative (what we call fatigue and its psychic equivalent), then the person falls asleep.

In a psychological sense, this is also the case in the less basic polar opposition between individual and society. When the individual is strongly and positively self-determined, he is mentally and spiritually fully awake — he creates new values or rebels against obsolete ones; he stands out as a power in society. But whenever society ruthlessly compels its would-be individuals to conform to its norms and collective standards, then the human beings in that society exist in a somewhat somnolent mental and spiritual state — as happens in all totalitarian societies.

When we deal with the polar opposition between individual and society, we still find ourselves within the realm of conscious, wakeful activity. The contrast, astrologically speaking, is one between such personal planets as Mars, Venus, and Mercury, and the social pair of planets, Jupiter and Saturn. But when we come to the polar opposition between waking consciousness and sleep, between the conscious and the unconscious (to use modern psychological terms), then we deal astrologically with the contrast between all planets within and including the orbit of Saturn, and the trans-Saturnian planets — Uranus, Neptune, and Pluto.

When we speak of the unconscious, we consider sleep and all manifestations of life which transcend consciousness as being simply the negation or absence of consciousness. Likewise, for a long period, scientists and philosophers thought of space beyond the limits of our solar system as completely empty — thus, in a negative sense. But now we begin to realize (as the ancients well knew!) that space outside the solar system is not mere emptiness. Rather, it is the field of active existence of the vast cosmic organism of the galaxy. We "live, move, and have our being" in the immense body of the galaxy. We cannot think of this galactic space in a negative sense; it is a fullness of forces, a *plenum,* a field of electro-magnetic energies — and perhaps of many other kinds of transcendent energies unknown to us.

Likewise, what modern psychologists call (quite unfortunately) the unconscious is not a realm of emptiness. When we sleep, we do not go into nothingness. We change polarity. The conscious, individual pole of our total being turns negative to the life-pole which now becomes strongly positive and active. Life takes over the controls. A time comes, however, for waking up; the "waters" of all-powerful life partly withdraw from the mind of the sleeper, from his nervous system, and from the fringes of his cells' activities. Saturated for a period with this undifferentiated life-flow, his brain and nerves, every cell and organ of his body, now respond to a new surge of conscious self-directed activity, thinking, and feeling. Individual problems are faced again in the sunlight of consciousness. But what of dreams?

Sometimes when the tide withdraws from the beach, small pools of water remain, especially where rocks jut out and contain the water. It may help the reader to think for a moment of the little shrimps, fishes, or even small octopi often trapped in these tide-pools as representing some of our dreams. At times, a huge whale may be left on the sand, dying or dead. All kinds of flotsam and jetsam are left on the beach by the receding tides — and often we can hardly recognize what they were. They are washed upon the shores of the conscious out of the depths and currents of the unconscious.

There are many kinds of dreams, and this illustration applies at best to only a few of them; thus, it must not be taken literally or as covering all instances of dreams. It would, indeed, be best to think of dreams generally as the reactions of the unconscious to what has happened during, and what results from, the individual person's conscious activity during waking time. Just as society reacts to the productive or distinctive deeds of an individual by bestowing wealth or fame upon him — or by sending him to jail — so the unconscious pole of our total being reacts to our conscious feelings, thoughts, and behavior as soon as the polarities reverse themselves. Life, being in control during sleep, has its say. It takes the conscious part of our total being to task, even as it tries to somehow repair the damages done by our willful, individualistic conscious ego.

If the ego is particularly determined and successful in challenging the traditional and moral ways of the collectivity, the culture and religion — or deeper still, in opposing or blocking the natural instincts and emotions of human nature (as in asceticism, for instance) — then at night, while the individual sleeps, the collective pole of his being raises strong protests, warns of danger, and seeks to impress upon the ego-polarity pictures of disastrous consequences or a sense of inevitable failure and futility. When this happens, some impressions of the protests of the collective pole are left upon certain sensitized areas of the brain, even on some of the big nerve plexi in the body. When the polarities once more reverse themselves and the individual pole (the ego) comes back to conscious control (i.e., we wake up), these impressions are caught by the consciousness as dreams.

The reason dreams are so puzzling is a manifold one. First, the collective pole of our being (society and life or human nature) cannot communicate its upsets or protests in intellectual language; it can only fumblingly capture from the storehouse of past images which the brain or memory contains, a few which are linked analogically, or in some way attuned to, what the unconscious tries to convey to the conscious. These images are therefore primarily significant in terms of analogies and symbols; and they are presented in a sequence which has little to do with the principles of conscious logic. The dream represents a spatial sequence of pictures impressed upon the brain or other nerve centers. The sense of sequence in time arises only when the awakening ego, as yet barely recovered from its negative or passive sleep condition, tries to quickly scan these impressions made upon the portions of the human organism with which this ego is most closely associated (i.e., the nerve centers). It is as if a busy executive rushing into his office in the morning would see a mass of papers spread over his desk; phone calls are already reaching him, and all he can do is to hurriedly scan the spread-out papers, in most cases not in the order in which his several secretaries had placed them before his arrival. Occasionally, some important information stands out. The executive is roused while at home by someone who gives him a crucial message:

the president is very ill, the stock market is likely to collapse early in the morning; there is a fire in the warehouse, etc. Yet, even though the message may reach the executive (the ego) with a bang, it may be all jumbled up; it may come to him through a servant or his wife, who may not have gotten it accurately over the phone, etc.

All such illustrations are, of course, quite inadequate; they can only hint at the character of a process which cannot be accurately translated in terms of conscious experiences alone. Astrology may add another dimension to our analysis of the dream processes by making us differentiate dreams into three basic categories: Uranian, Neptunian, and Plutonian.

The Uranian type of dream is a direct challenge to the narrowness, self-satisfied inertia, selfishness, or ruthlessness of the Saturnian ego. The ego is essentially of a Saturnian character because Saturn represents the structure and boundaries of the individual pole of our being. When we become overindividualized in a separate, exclusive, narrow, and rigid way, then this overemphasis upon the Saturn function calls forth a complementary polar reaction from society, life, or the God within our total being. It is as if the galaxy were sending a stream of powerful rays into a solar system whose electromagnetic field had become overinsulated and might, thus, become a "cancerous system" in the galactic community. Galactic power reaches the solar system by way of Uranus. The Uranian type of dream is, in its highest sense, prophetic and illuminating. It may even be an apparition, a flash of inspiration or illumination that comes during the wakeful phase of conscious ego activity — as, for instance, Christ's image and words violently impressed upon Paul on the road to Damascus in answer to his blindly traditional and fanatic ego decision to destroy the believers in the new Divine Revelation.

Uranian dreams are usually highly disturbing. They come as a challenge, and not one that the ego readily accepts. Solemn words may be part of the dream; often light, or one definite color, stands out as a strong element of the dream picture. What C. G. Jung called "archetypes of the unconscious" usually appear in such dreams; they refer to one of the deepest and most universal experiences of humankind. They are related to a basic aspect or function of universal life as it operates in human nature. Thus, they often have a religious character; and the dream may have the power to transform the dreamer quite basically (conversion) or to thoroughly disturb his or her self-sufficiency, egocentricity, or pet ideas.

Neptunian dreams are perhaps the most frequent, however. They are reactions to anything that disturbs the normal, average balance of the individual's relationship to his society, his health, his digestion, or the basic instincts of his body. Neptune, in this sense, answers by dreams to any disturbance in or danger to the complex functions performed by Jupiter, in both the body and the psyche. Any challenge to a social or moral principle of conduct, any encroachment upon a safe "diet" (of body or mind) tends to arouse Neptunian dreams, and they are usually very fanciful! If the body becomes cold at night because of a sudden drop of temperature, one may awaken remembering a long and dramatic dream of walking in a snowstorm, falling into icy water, etc. If one is led by a powerful urge to break moral or social rules of conduct, it is likely that, sooner or later, one may dream of dramatic scenes in which the participants in the situation will appear in strange but symbolic surroundings, perhaps under disguises which make the deep truth of the situation less unpalatable at first shock to the individual.

The Freudian system of dream analysis has accustomed the modern mind to think of what Freud called the "censor." This censor is said to represent, as it were, a kind of private guardian of the ego's personal safety, protecting it against any unpleasant upsets or attempts at revolution in its realm. The disturbing impressions left by the collective pole of our being are thus censored, changed, garbled, or altogether obliterated before the conscious individual can become aware of them. Whether such a censor actually exists is very doubtful. What it refers to is simply a particular stage of the relationship between the two polarities of our being — individual and collective, conscious and unconscious, day activity and sleep — a stage at which the individual is particularly rebellious against the collective and the insecure ego feels constantly in need of protection from society.

Plutonian dreams are rarer than Neptunian dreams. They can be quite destructive of the integration of the total personality — strange nightmares leaving a ghastly feeling of fear, foreboding, death. In more spiritual individuals, they may be the projections and symbols of profound experiences of self-renewal and of expansion of the very essence of the self. Uranian dreams are heralds of what might be; they show the way ahead, they inspire to go on, they rouse the ego-bound soul to new possibilities. Plutonian dreams may be the reflection upon the waking consciousness of real steps taken in inner unfoldment and soul growth — or, negatively, they reveal the pain or despair of the soul who has (at least temporarily) failed, and perhaps they show the abyss ahead and the dark presences that fill those abysmal depths. If, as is probable, there is at least one more planet beyond Pluto, such a planet should refer to even more real and definite inner experiences in the souls who have become, at least to some extent, integral parts of the vast community of godlike souls — of which the galaxy is the astrological symbol.

Jung said that there are levels upon levels of the collective unconscious. It is so, inasmuch as there is a vast hierarchy of levels upon which individuals can act consciously and creatively. The galaxy, too, I repeat, is but one among the myriads of spiral nebulae which constitute a universe; and universes may be parts of a far vaster cosmos. There is no conceivable end to the possibility of becoming a conscious individual at ever more inclusive, more cosmic, levels. Yet any individual — unless he be the all-inclusive Godhead — is but an active center within a larger whole, a collectivity. There must always be a relationship operating in alternating phases between this individual and this collectivity. As human beings, we know such alternating phases as waking consciousness and sleep, embodied existence and death. But these terms have meaning only in terms of our human experience.

The Hindu philosophers spoke of the Days and Nights of Brahma — the Creator of universes in which consciousness unfolds and of conditions of absolute non-being in which nothing exists. Yet, to the sage, beyond those cosmic days and nights, beyond consciousness and unconsciousness, there is that which contains both. The Hindus symbolically named that the "Great Breath," exhaling the world into being, inhaling it into immense peace. Thus, we experience our conscious ego being exhaled into the world of day activity as we wake up and inhaled into sleep as we lie down for rest. In a sense, we are both conditions, conscious and unconscious; we are also that which includes both. The planets from the Sun to Saturn drive us to conscious activity; but the planets beyond Saturn — when the day is over — lead us to the vast spaces of the galaxy, where we know our greater self, the stars that we are. When the alternative rhythm brings us back to day consciousness, then Uranus, Neptune, and Pluto ever seek to make us remember that we are not only a Saturn-bound, Sun-centered, individual self, but that we belong as well to the greater community of the stars.

We all know that a human body goes through a pattern of changes during its life span; it grows up, matures, and gradually loses its resilience and vital energy. Its organs — particularly its endocrine glands, which produce all-important hormones — at times undergo processes of readjustment; the harmonious and delicate balance of their activities becomes disturbed, then re-established (if all goes well) in a different way. What we call adolescence and the "change of life" are the most frequently mentioned of these periods of organic and glandular readjustments, for they quite obviously have a repercussion upon the emotional life and behavior of persons passing through them. There are other turning points in the development of an individual which, though related to less-notice-able body changes, are nevertheless of profound importance in the unfoldment of *character*. One can define "character" in several ways. For the purpose of this article, I shall say that the word refers to a person's attitude toward his (or her) self (or individuality) in relation to the world at large, particularly in relation to the people with whom he (or she) is closely associated, either in kinship, friendship, or business comradeship.

Let me explain: what establishes your character is what, in the deepest part of yourself, you feel *you are* as a person, as a self. You may feel inferior or superior, frustrated or self-assured, depressed by your own inability to act successfully or buoyant and ready to conquer the world. You may feel that you are an individual, unique and filled with a sense of mission or destiny; you may by instinct, and perhaps out of fear or deep-down insecurity, seek the comfort of a conformist's attitude. You may love to single yourself out by what you do, what you wear, what your unusual feeling-responses are to ordinary or extraordinary life situations; or you may fear being conspicuous, feel shy, hate the spotlight, rely heavily on tradition.

I mention only the most obvious opposites of character attitudes, but there are endless varieties. Each type of character represents not only a particular inner feeling of what you are *as a self*, but also a way of meeting all human *relationships* and the small or big challenges of everyday life. "Self" and "relationship" are the two poles of every human action; and in an astrological birth-chart, these two always interconnected and comple-mentary poles of character are represented by the ascendant and the descendant — the cusps of the first and seventh houses, which are the actual eastern and western sections of the horizon at the time of birth. The signs and degrees of the zodiac found there and whatever planet or planets may "rise" and "set" are the main astrological indicators, respectively, of what self means to you, the native, and of how you most characteristically approach all human relationships.

The two above mentioned periods of organic changes, adolescence and the "change of life," have a profound effect upon the development of character. However, what I consider the most fundamental turning points in this development do not come at these times, but years later. More accurately, what is noticeable is a kind of wave pattern of development which is based upon a 7-year and a 14-year rhythm. The 7-year cycle in human life has been known to ancient civilizations; we find references to it in our Christian-European society as well. The Jesuit educators used to say that if they took care of a child during the first seven years of his life, it would not matter what would happen later. Seven was considered to be the "age of reason," after which the child was supposed to be "responsible." Some European occultists have claimed that at that age, the "soul" for the first time enters into, and can act from inside of, the personality of the child. Fourteen is usually considered — depending on social heredity and climate — as the time of puberty. At twenty-one, a boy or girl definitely "comes of age," is accepted as a voting citizen, can sign business contracts, etc.

Then comes the twenty-eighth birthday; and it is to this period that I want to pay special attention. It used to be said that the normal or theoretical length of a human life was "three score and ten" years; but now the life expectancy in America is reaching beyond 70. Significantly, since Uranus was discovered at the dawn of the industrial and democratic era, we have now a new archetype — a theoretical pattern — for a human life, as Uranus' cycle of revolution around the zodiac is almost exactly 84 years. Fourteen years have been added to the old-type of human life pattern. Eighty-four is 12x7; thus, we have a complete twelvefold "zodiac" of 7-year periods.

This twelvefold zodiac subdivides itself very significantly into three 28-year periods. It is, we might say, as if, from this Uranian point of view, a person was born in Aries, became 28 in Leo, 56 in Sagittarius. Many years ago, in my book "New Mansions for New Men," I spoke of these three periods as the first, second, and third births — i.e., birth as a physical organism determined by parental heredity and developing biologically, then psychically, within a particular social and cultural environment which from the very beginning moulds its emotional and intellectual attitudes; then, rebirth as an individual, asserting (if all goes well) his or her self in an individualized manner in order to fulfill a more or less unique destiny; lastly, a possible final readjustment of this individuality by means of which a more mature, more mellowed, wiser participation in social affairs is made possible.

This means that there are two fundamental turning points in this 84-year theoretical pattern of development – around 28 and around 56. Whatever you have been born as, whatever your birth environment and your body started to be, there are two great turning points in your more or less mature life as an adult when you can *reorient and transform* your character and the nature of your capacity for human relationships. You can "see" yourself inherently; as a result, you can also meet others in a new way. You can do that between the ages of 27 and 30; you can do it once more between the ages of 56 and 60. Of course, the change is likely to be gradual throughout your life, particularly every seventh year. Yet during the two age periods just mentioned, the possibility of a very basic transformation of your character and your most essential response to people and to society is usually very strongly emphasized. It can often be emphasized to the point of a radical crisis – and "crisis," etymologically speaking, means a period of *decision.*

The reason I speak of periods of years (27 to 30 and 56 to 60) is because during these periods, *several* important astrological cycles come to an end and a new beginning. By considering the nature and significance of these cycles, one should be able to understand better the meaning of these two great turning points. The main cycles to consider are:

1. the about-27½-year cycle of the progressed Moon, at the end of which the latter returns to its natal position;

2. the cycle of Saturn, which takes nearly 30 years to bring the planet to its natal position;

3. the progressed lunation cycle of about 30 years, at the end of which the Sun and Moon are in the same relative position to each other (i.e., aspect) as they were at birth.

One should also realize that Jupiter and Saturn at 30 are in an aspect opposed to (thus, complementary toward) their natal aspect. If, for instance, they were conjunct at birth, at around 30, they must be in opposition. This is significant because in the second great turning point of individual development, they will be, at about 59, in the same relative position as at birth – and, what is more, at about the same zodiacal places.

The great Jupiter-Saturn cycle is actually a 59- to 60-year cycle, even though the two planets meet every 20 years.

A similar but less well-known situation exists with regard to the Moon's nodes, which constitute a very important axis in a birth-chart, nearly as significant, psychologically speaking, as the natal horizon or meridian. The north and south nodes are, of course, always in opposition to each other, as the nodes are the two ends of a line which cuts the zodiac — a line produced by the intersection of the plane of the ecliptic (actually, the orbit of the earth) and of the plane of the Moon's revolution around our globe. This nodal axis symbolically relates the entire yearly path of the apparently moving Sun and the monthly path of the Moon — thus, the solar and lunar components of a person's total personality. The north node is essentially a point of reception of energy, of ingestion and assimilation; the south node, a point of release and letting go — whether it be the excretion of unassimilated and unwanted material or the projection of seed — and there can be a psycho-mental seed (as in the works of a great artist or prophetic figure) as well as a biological seed.

The nodes take between 18 and 19 years to make a complete cycle of the zodiac. It is closer to 19 years, and this 19-year cycle was much venerated in antiquity, particularly in Persia. It is still the basis of the calendar of the religious movement started by Persian prophets a century ago and now spreading widely, as it seeks to establish a new "World Order" — the Bahai faith. Three of these nodal cycles make almost exactly 56 years on an average — a very interesting fact. Thus, when a person is about 28, the positions of the Moon's nodes in the zodiac are inverted in comparison to their natal positions — a cycle and one-half have taken place. The north node is at the place occupied at birth by the south node, and *vice versa*. This means that around 28 to 30, a definite inversion occurs in the relationship between Jupiter and Saturn and similarly with regard to the Moon's nodal positions. On the other hand, the progressed Moon ends its first complete cycle. The Sun-Moon relationship, by progression, is similar to what it was at birth; and Saturn also has returned to its natal place. If we interpret these cyclic indications together, we can see how they fit what, at least theoretically — or potentially — is occurring to a human being from the age of 28 to 30. The Moon and Saturn essentially represent the two parents — or, in a more general and psychological sense, the kind of "images" a young person builds up within his or her consciousness of *mother* and *father*. The actual parent may be quite different from these images; but the images constitute the effective reality of the relationship which has been built through the years between the child and adolescent and his or her parents. This relationship usually goes even farther than the parents themselves; it expands and generalizes itself into a relationship between the youth and his religion or his community (an extended "mother image") and between the youth and all symbols of authority and legality ("father image").

From 28 to 30, a cycle ends with regard to all these relationships. The first period of growth of character and individuality closes; a new one begins — or at least can and normally *should* begin. The first period, which began with physical birth, has been obviously dominated by the development of the physical body and the need to gradually assimilate something of the culture and social-religious heritage of the child's environment. The youth may have readily fitted into this environment and the traditions of his people; or he may have, to a greater or lesser extent, rebelled against what was presented to or forced upon his growing personality. In either case, he is bound by this biological, social, and cultural set of influences, for we are bound by what we rebel against, or hate, as much as by what we follow passively or love.

The first period of 28-30 years is a kind of *thesis;* and it is quite naturally followed by an *antithesis.* That is to say, the youth who for these nearly 30 years has actually lived, whether he liked it or not, dominated by *collective* influences has now come to the great turning point when he can really begin to assert *his true individuality* – his unique destiny, his particular function in the universe, his (to some degree) creative "vocation." However, it is not at all certain that he will make such an assertion of individual selfhood. He may live merely as one of the many who passively follow the ancestral ways, undistinguished as well as indistinct. But if he does assert his individuality, it is because he has gained a new perspective upon his tradition; and, in astrology, this gaining of perspective is represented by the opposition aspect.

The Jupiter-Saturn relationship of his birth-chart is reversed. Jupiter and Saturn are the planets symbolizing all social processes and the person's relationship to the institutions of his society, his culture, and his religion. This reversal gives the maturing youth a more *objective* view of the traditions of his people. There was a similar reversal when he was 14-15 – thus, during or immediately after the crisis of adolescence. But at 30, the adolescent rebelliousness should have become more stabilized because transiting Saturn is now located *where it was at birth.* The 30-year-old person touches bottom; he can once more tap his roots – but now this Saturnine strengthening can operate at a new level. I should add also that there is a Jupiter-Uranus cycle of 14-years' duration which can be related to the changes of social consciousness *potentially* occurring every 14 years — thus, at 28.

At age 28, the Moon's nodes have also become inverted. One might almost say that the solar and lunar forces have exchanged places. The solar vitality received throughout the years can be released through the lunar agencies — i.e., through the personality creatively facing the everyday problems of life adjustment. A similar situation exists during the tenth year and the thirty-eighth year. These often witness important turns in the pattern of destiny — though, of course, they may not do so in lives which become quite set at an early age and are, therefore, less sensitive to *potentialities* of transformation. Potentialities, rather than fated events, are what a birth-chart reveals.

The nodal cycle of 9-10 and 18-19 years also establishes the pattern of eclipses. Thus, if there were eclipses around the birth-time affecting sensitive natal planets or angles, these will recur at the ages above mentioned; and eclipses can be highly stimulating factors, even if they often cause problems and dilemmas — particularly the lunar ones, which occur when the Sun and Moon are in *opposition* (Full Moon time).

Nowadays, a person is often considered still "middle-aged" at 56. What happens, theoretically at least, is that between 56 and 60, one decides (unconsciously or consciously) whether the years ahead will be years of creative fulfillment and harvesting, or of gradual settling down to the inevitable sclerosis of body and to the mind's loss of organic intensity and the power of self-renewal. Just as what occurred at the time of puberty, around 14, gave rise to organic and psychological factors which set the stage for the character crisis of self-expression from 28 to 30, so what took place during the midforties (normally, the beginning of the "change of life," at least at the psychological level) largely conditions the manner in which the individual (if he is *really* an "individual"!) will meet the challenge from age 56 to 60. Around 59, both Jupiter and Saturn return to their natal places — Saturn for the second time, Jupiter for the fifth.

At 56, the cycle of Jupiter to Uranus comes to an end for the fourth time; and a fifth cycle begins, with the possibility of change of social-religious attitude. At the same time, the third Moon's nodes cycle is completed; and a fourth one opens, indicating a potential renewal of the pattern of destiny and personality integration at a fourth level (from 56 to 74½). The progressed Moon has completed its second cycle around the birth-chart during the 55th year, but the natal Sun-Moon relationship repeats itself by progression (progressed lunation cycle) around 59. This age of 59 seems to actually be the turning point in the majority of cases; but what reaches a climax then has often begun to unfold around the age of 56. By the time the sixties begin, the new trend should have become clearly defined. A keynote has been set for the remaining years of the life — or, at least, for the 14-year period ending around 70 to 72, after which what can be normally considered today as "old age" begins. It may, of course, actually begin at 60 if the individual does not take a *positive* attitude toward the change of life vibration and of opportunities.

Such a positive attitude may have a great variety of meanings and results, the more so the more the person reaching age 56 to 60 has lived a truly *individualized* life — that is, a life unpatterned by the regular routine associated with the social average, the altogether collective and undistinctive norm. In Greece, 60 was considered the "age of philosophy" because philosophy implies, in a deeper sense, a search for essential meaning and fundamental values. If the first 30 years can be seen as a "thesis," the second thirty years as the "antithesis," the years after 60 should witness an effort at "synthesis." Then the full meaning of the relationship of the *collective* life of his people (thesis) to his own *self-asserted individuality* (antithesis) should become clear. On the basis of this meaning, an individual may act more wisely, he may help others to see the way which he may have missed, or he may help them to be more efficient and productive — and serene while being efficient and productive. He may become indeed "philosopher" or "elder statesman," able to realize the meaning of confusing events on the background of both his approaching death (Saturn perspective) and the continuing life of his community, nation, and humanity (Jupiter perspective).

The various cycles of transiting and progressed planets beginning between 56 and 60 open to the individual the *possibility* of a "third birth." I repeat, the first birth is the beginning of biological existence — birth as a body and a personality based on the exercise of body functions and their overtones in the psyche. The "second birth," at 28 to 30, is the theoretical beginning of maturity as an individual person — birth of true individuality. The "third birth," if it happens at all, is a birth in "light," in wisdom, at the level of the superindividual soul in which collective and individual values — the race and the individual person — find their adjustment of destiny. The individual brings the spiritual or cultural-social harvest of his experience to his community. He may receive for it honor and relative fame — or, at least, some degree of social security. In other cases, his people or the intellectual leaders of his society may not appreciate the value of this harvest, and the later years of life may be years of increasing Saturnian isolation.

A study of the planetary transits and progressions at the beginning of each of these cycles, starting at 28-30 and 56-60, should tell the astrologer — able to "feel" the pulse of such cycles — what might be expected of the over-all development of the individual during the 28-year or 30-year periods which follow — that is, what this development is more likely to be, in what direction it will proceed, how easy or rugged the path.

For instance, Franklin D. Roosevelt was elected to the New York Senate as he came close to his 29th birthday. Saturn was then moving back and forth, by transit, over its natal position at 6° 5' Taurus. At that time, Pluto was passing over his natal Mars, retrograde at 27° 1' Gemini in his tenth house. Gemini rules the nervous system; the tenth house, the public life. Within eleven years, he was stricken by polio, which paralyzes sets of nerves. His public life centered around the vast crisis of a deep economic depression and later on World War II, quite accurately symbolized by Pluto conjunct a particularly crucial and elevated Mars. In 1941, when he was 59 years old, Saturn and Jupiter came to the same relative positions they had in F.D.R.'s birth-chart, after repeated conjunctions in Taurus. At birth, F.D.R. had Saturn, Neptune, Jupiter, and Pluto in Taurus; in 1940-41-42, there were not only conjunctions of Jupiter and Saturn, but also of Saturn and Uranus. The former occurred around his natal Neptune; the latter, almost exactly on his natal Pluto, some six months after Pearl Harbor — ominous indications, yet promises of world-wide responsibilities.

Before this, in 1930, as World War II started — he was in his 48th year — Neptune was crossing Roosevelt's probable ascendant. Uranus crossed his natal Neptune and his Jupiter through 1938, as the Moon's nodes were returning to their natal places, just before his 56th birthday (1938). Jupiter was vitalizing, in his natal fifth house, his Aquarian Venus-Sun conjunction; the transiting Venus was also there, once more in conjunction with the Sun — and the Moon and Jupiter. Thus, this entire period was marked by significant and powerful transits. These could well evoke something of the world destiny which became his after his 56th birthday — and the possibility of a tragic, yet glorious, end.

What reached a climax at 56-57 with World War II had begun at 28-29, when F.D.R. entered the political arena as New York Senator. In his case, the crisis of the mid-forties took a particularly tragic character: his fight against paralysis. But on the basis of that fight, he gained true strength of character, which made possible his forceful carrying out of vast responsibilities. Saturn had been conjunct F.D.R.'s ascendant as he contracted polio. Saturn moved over his natal Venus and Sun just as he was about to assume the Presidency in 1933.

Meeting Crises Successfully:
          Life in the "Psychological Century"

One of the most characteristic features of the personal and social life of men and women at the present time is the emphasis being placed upon psychology. This new focus of interest extends to nearly all fields of human activity, from medical psychiatry and psychoanalysis to advertising and psychological warfare or "peace fare." There are many types and schools of psychology and psychotherapy for mentally disturbed or completely sick individuals; and there is practically no field of business, social institution, or branch of government in which the preoccupation with and the use of some sort of psychological technique are not to be found.

When we think of the European Middle Ages, at the time of the Crusades and when the great cathedrals were built, we think at once of the tremendous role which religion played in everyday affairs. Today, this role is increasingly being taken by psychology. Modern life is ever more completely conditioned and influenced by psychological ideas and preoccupations. Our twentieth century may come to be known as "the psychological century," even more than as that of the discovery of atomic energy. Actually, both the new emphasis on psychology and the discovery of atomic energy are related to a basic historical fact: our Western civilization, which our ancestors took for granted and relied unquestioningly upon, is in a state of complete *crisis*. Not only do individuals live from personal crisis to personal crisis and in a state of psychological as well as economic insecurity; nations and groups are facing a seemingly unending series of crises and conflicts, "cold" or "hot." The basic root of this nearly universal state of crisis is the enormous social and economic changes which have been brought about by modern science and modern technology.

All of this is well known; but what is usually not clearly enough understood is that the increasingly more widespread emphasis upon the practical use of psychological techniques is the direct result of the need to meet this universal state of crisis. Psychology, in all its modern forms, is an attempt to deal with crises — no crisis, no need for psychology!

There are many kinds of psychology; but all of these can be broadly divided into two categories according to the basic attitude they take toward any and all crises. What *is* a crisis, whether in the life of an individual or in the life of a nation and society? What *meaning* has a crisis? Obviously, the problem of how to find a "solution" for a crisis must depend upon what the psychologist (or the social-political reformer) thinks the crisis not only was *caused* by, but was *intended* to produce.

With these words "intended to," we come to the very crux of the problem. Some psychologists accept the idea that *all* crises are, basically if not superficially, purposeful. According to them, a crisis is *a phase of the process of growth* of either an individual or society. It has a definite aim and meaning with reference to the overall development of the personality or the collectivity passing through it. It is necessary for this development – as, for instance, the usual crisis of adolescence is necessary for the full development of a human body and personality. The crisis is necessary, but the *form it takes* is not inevitable. The state of change and transition, the fact that there is disturbance, are necessities of human experience; but social change does not *need* to mean violent revolution, any more than a personal crisis of growth needs to produce illness, neurosis, or insanity. However, if there is acute neurosis and a more or less prolonged state of definite bio-physical crisis, the question naturally arises: What should be the final aim of the treatment? What are the results to be sought by the psychoanalyst, the healer of body and soul? This is where the schools of psychology basically differ, their difference being the outcome of two essential approaches to human nature and to the meaning and purpose of the relationship of individuals to society and to the universe or to God.

According to one type of psychology, the goal of the cure is to re-establish the state of normality which had been disturbed by one cause or another. According to the other type, no cure is real and significant unless the patient emerges from the crisis a greater human being than he was before *and thereby fulfills the implicit "spiritual" purpose of the crisis.* In the field of psychology which Freud opened, these two attitudes are clearly seen, though sometimes the two are somewhat combined; this should be of very great interest to the astrologer who sees himself essentially as a psychologist and helper of human beings, for he too has to define his approach to and interpretation of past or future crises which he may see in his clients' charts.

There are various kinds of crises clearly foreseeable by means of astrological techniques, and the interpretation the astrologer will give to them must necessarily depend upon what he himself thinks of crises in general. He may think of crises as deviations, tragedies pure and simple, as things to cure and quickly forget about; or, he may regard them as necessary phases of a process of growth, as experiences from which a rich harvest can and must be gathered, experiences without which no "maturity" is possible – however dark, tragic, or seemingly destructive the crisis may be.

The first type of psychology may be called *normative:* the goal of the treatment and cure is to make the disturbed person "normal again." Normality is, obviously, a relative matter and can be defined only with reference to the general standards of a particular culture and society. Thus, most "social psychologists" are normative psychologists. Freud also belongs to this category because his approach is essentially pessimistic and without a real sense of spiritual purpose for the individual as an individual.

The second type of psychology may be called *metamorphic* because it considers *all* crises as – at least potentially – means to induce and produce some kind of inner metamorphosis. Human life is seen, moreover, as absolutely requiring recurring and periodical processes of metamorphoses – thus, crises – because without them, the person remains merely "one of the mass," normal perhaps, but patterned after a collective type or culturally accepted mould. To be truly an "individual" is to have emerged from, and risen out of, the collective norm of the society of the day; this emergence can take place only by passing through crises of some sort, through real and basic experiences of metamorphosis. These experiences are usually stressful and painful, and always disturbing; yet *they must be welcomed, understood, and assimilated* if there is to be real individual maturity . . . and perhaps, to some degree, "genius" or the spiritual attainment of a true "disciple of Christ," who is *"in* the world but not *of* the world."

In astrology, these two approaches to personal or social crises are to be referred to the pair of "social" planets (Jupiter and Saturn), and to the transcendental or "metamorphic" planets (Uranus and Neptune), respectively. Each of these pairs operates at a special level of activity and consciousness. At the Jupiter-Saturn level, the crises of emergent individuals and potential geniuses, saints, or apostles appear as *deviations from the social norm.* At the Uranus-Neptune level, they are to be regarded as more or less tragic, but necessary, *processes of rebirth and self-discovery.*

The same distinction applies to crises like wars, revolutions, or economic collapses in the case of nations. From the second point of view, the greatest tragedy is not that there should be war or revolution, but that after the conclusion of these crises, the government and the people might have only one basic thought – to *return* to normalcy and the "good old days," to *go back* to the same old home and the same familiar and "normal" behavior *as if nothing had happened!* Indeed, we in America know only too well what this attitude means, for we have held it, as a people, after each of two World Wars; as a result, while we won the wars, we have, in a very real sense, lost the after-war, the peace that was to be. We — and most other nations as well! — lost it so far because we have not been able to give to the war tragedies the meaning of a great process of inner, spiritual growth for the whole of humankind.

No war is ever really won that ends with the idea of re-establishing the "status quo" and the pre-war level of normality. It is necessary to "maintain" the general structure of a way of life which has proven valid; but there would have been no crisis, no challenge to growth if something had only to be "maintained." Growth comes from the new creative acts, the transformations required to meet the challenge of the crisis; if there is challenge, purposeful challenge by life or God, it is because a new creative impulse has become necessary or because the old impulse has bogged down and there is need for some kind of purgation or catharsis.

With the planets Uranus and Neptune, we reach the level of catharsis and metamorphosis, of purgation and rebirth. If we are hypnotized by Jupiter and Saturn, we are bound to see Uranus's and Neptune's activity as destructive; yet the two remote planets are actually our liberators. They challenge us to be greater individuals, to grow by creating our own future greatness as individuals. These challenges bring crises. Thanks be to God for these crises! Yet we must be victorious — or else defeat is costly and tears us down. *How* can we be victorious? In what does the victory consist? The answers to these questions differ with every individual case, and particularly with the age of the individuals confronted by these Uranian and Neptunian crises. Here, astrology can be of very great assistance to the psychologist, in that it can *time* the occurrence and the probable length of crises. It can point out the purpose of the crises, *what they are meant to transform in the life and temperament of the individual.* Knowing this, even if only in general terms, we can *consciously work with* the crisis-producing process of metamorphosis, instead of rebelling against it and its intended end results.

In geology, "metamorphic" rocks are rocks transformed by intense volcanic heat and pressure. In psychology, a metamorphic Uranian crisis is also a release of intense spiritual and psychic heat and pressure which can melt and recrystallize the most basic elements of the personality. It *can* do it, but it need not do it. The aroused energies, the utterly disturbed life conditions and emotions may well settle down after the crisis and leave only scars, weariness, or the resigned readjustment of social normality along the ways of the past. Yes, everything is "as before": peace is restored, the old routines are re-established, the patient is "cured" — but God *has been defeated.*

There is often no worse defeat than a meaningless "victory"; and the greatest of tragedies is a crisis that has been in vain. We endure suffering, catastrophe, insanity of a sort perhaps, the personality ploughed under, the structures of the ego shaken loose and the net result *nothing:* no growth, no rebirth, only a panicky or self-satisfied reorganization of this same ego along the same old lines, yet with the ghastly feeling — unacknowledged and subconscious as it may be! — that *it all happened in vain.* Humanity is today sickened by such a collective feeling, a mixture of guilt, hopelessness, and deep soul fatigue. Our insane asylums are overflowing. The only solution is a new type of psychotherapy — and astrology — centered around the deliberate arousal of the creative factor in every individual.

Astrologically, the problem revolves first around a deeper understanding of what Uranus and Neptune represent in a birth-chart — of what they *can* mean — and then of the cycles of transit of these two planets. I say transits only because the planets move too slowly for secondary progressions to mean anything, save in a relatively few cases when Uranus and Neptune make close aspects to other planets. Only such aspects may become exact, during the lifetime, by direct or "converse" progressions. A number of astrological textbooks list completely negative meanings for so-called "bad" aspects of Uranus and Neptune; even the presence of these planets in natal houses is often given a mainly destructive interpretation. As already stated, such an interpretation is, at best, valid only where the life and purpose of an individual are seen solely from the point of view of a Jupiter-Saturn type of social and personal "normality"; where ease, static happiness, comfort, and social-economic success are considered the ultimate values for human beings. But we are not living in a static society. Ours is an intensely dynamic age — an age of upheavals, constant change, and of spiritual as well as social metamorphosis.

The twentieth century may be the Plutonian century. But before Pluto can be approached and experienced in a positive, constructive manner, humans must have learned to successfully pass through the upheavals and the crises of growth represented by Uranus and Neptune. If Pluto is to establish the foundations of a rebirth into a wider sphere of life, the individual must have been renewed by Uranus and cleansed by Neptune. These last two planets are symbols of "the threshold." One can stumble over a threshold and land in a hospital; or one can enter through it, into a new life. It is only as the latter alternative *is realized not only as a possibility, but indeed as the only desirable goal,* that one may successfully meet the challenges presented by Uranus and Neptune with a minimum of disturbance. It is Uranus's function to reveal this goal to the individual with a downpour of new light — blinding as it may seem at first. Once the new vision, the new goal, is accepted, then Neptune can constructively proceed to change the chemistry, the very substance of an individual's personality. If the person refuses to change or even admit the possibility of change, then life will either break him down or will leave him stranded in his small egocentric world with his gradually emptier successes and virtues or his "average" follies and sins.

Where Uranus is in the birth-chart, look for the place and the field of experience in which deep personal change, self-transformation, or tragic revolutions are most likely to come; try to learn to understand and welcome *the purpose* of the metamorphosis — to work consciously with it. Where Neptune is in the natal chart, look for that biological and psychological function and that realm of experience or field of personal development which should become reoriented, renewed, and "transsubstantiated" ("chemically" changed or repolarized) during your life. Here, however, it must be made very clear to anyone interested in astrology and in his own (or his friends') charts that Uranus remains for seven years and Neptune for about thirteen years in one zodiacal sign. Thus, *any* interpretation of these planets' natal positions in a zodiacal sign refers to *any person* born within a seven-year and a thirteen-year period, respectively. This means that the interpretation must be very general indeed and that it simply *cannot* apply to specific illnesses or traits of character, for these are obviously not shared by *everyone* born during such periods.

Take, for instance, the case of Uranus in Scorpio. Uranus passed through this sign from 1891 to 1898. Every person born during this period, therefore, had in his makeup the presumed characteristics of "Uranus in Scorpio." Some kind of Uranian "common denominator" in all these persons must be found if "having Uranus in Scorpio at birth" means anything at all. What can it be? It must be something as elusive as the traits which make an Englishman appear and act "English," a Frenchman "French," etc. These types of *collective traits* are not easily defined, especially in a few concrete terms. However, the generation born in the "nineties" of last century, in most cases with Uranus in Scorpio (and always with Neptune and Pluto in Gemini), is the one which was in its twenties at the close of World War I and lived through the "Jazz Age." It experienced a generalized rebellion against sexual taboos. Not every individual did, and it would be senseless to state that all sought to break sexual conventions, but it can be said that the Uranian challenges to self-transformation for these people took the form of crises related to the use of the type of vital energies associated astrologically with Scorpio – sex being only one among the several aspects of the bio-psychological functions to which Scorpio refers.

Every generation (using the word to mean, really, an "age-group") has a basic approach to the solution of a basic problem of personal growth. This approach is conditioned by past cultural and social influences, by the parents' behavior, by social-economic and political pressures. The presence, for a few years, of one of the most remote planets in a particular sign of the zodiac symbolizes this approach. It establishes an accent in consciousness which works in two ways: in the way of unconscious or irrational root energies (the zodiacal signs in which these planets are at birth), then in the way of conscious behavior and attention (the sign through which the planets pass at the time of the crises).

Thus, the Jazz-age and its Uranian crises of restless rebellion, self-transformation, and release from Victorian age standards were based most typically on a Uranus-in-Scorpio foundation; but they carried the outer, conscious, accentuation represented by Uranus in Pisces (1920-27), some of the most symbolic features of which were the wholesale disregard of the Prohibition Act, the search for excitement, intoxication, dramatic self-expression, etc. In its late teens and twenties, this Uranus-in-Pisces age-group experienced World War II's heaviest military holocausts, and it has had to carry on the world's business through the salvation or disintegration of our "Piscean Age" culture – perhaps leaving to the Uranus-in-Aries group the challenge of releasing (Aries) a new creative impulse whence may be born a new society.

As far as the individual person is concerned, the presence of Uranus in one or the other house of the actual birth-chart is usually the most revealing factor. It establishes *the field of personal experience* in which Uranian crises of self-transformation are essentially to be met – or, one might say, the focus of the crises. The natal house in which Neptune is found indicates the type of confrontations in which an individual can most typically renew the very substance (or "chemistry") of his nature and his character or ego. Through such a type of confrontation (and each natal house represents one type), the personal ego's limitations can be dissolved and the individual may realize his spiritual freedom – the next problem, thereafter, being what this freedom is *for,* the purpose of it. These indications coupled with those given by the symbols associated with the exact zodiacal *degree* on which the planets were located at birth are, in nearly all instances, most revealing.

Wherever transits of Uranus and Neptune are studied, both planets should be considered together. Serious crises tend to occur more particularly when both form aspects to important natal planets at the same time. In some cases, Uranus or Neptune will transit the natal Sun, Moon, or "ruling planet," while the *progressed* Sun or Moon will be in square or opposition to the natal Uranus and Neptune. These are usually decisive cases in which the challenge will come, as it were, from both inside and outside. The inner life is ready to change; and under the pressure of this interior, spiritual, and perhaps biological necessity to change ("progressions"), a chain of striking events will bring matters to a very sharp focus, profoundly disturbing the individual's social or family life ("transits"). In any case, the important thing for the individual is to understand, accept, and work with the process of metamorphosis and not to rebel against or shrink from it in fear or emotional dismay. This, however, usually requires much spiritual courage and a steady, objective mind or an intense faith in God. Where these are lacking, the stunned ego either collapses and opens itself to the invasion of irrational or destructive forces or shuts its gates so tightly that it will be very difficult to open them again. At best, another crisis will be tragically necessary to shatter them and, thus, make the delayed process of growth operative.

The condition of the social and family environment deeply affects our ability to successfully meet personal crises of self-transformation. Where this environment is itself chaotic, as during wars and revolutions, the tendency for individual breakdown becomes much stronger. Yet there are souls who, *just because* the world is in chaos, succeed in summoning from their own spiritual core the power to stand steady and strong in contrast to this outer chaos. Whether or not a personality can summon such power is a matter that no one can ever determine on astrological grounds alone, for *any* astrological indication can be either constructive or destructive *in its ultimate results.*

The combined cycle of Uranus and Neptune lasts about 171 years. There was a conjunction of these two planets in 1821, in early Capricorn; the next one will occur in 1992, in mid-Capricorn. The conjunction of 1650 in mid-Sagittarius has often been associated with well-known upheavals in England. The year 1821 marked the time of Napoleon I's death and the early beginnings of the Industrial Revolution and the generalized Romantic Era. The opposition of Uranus and Neptune was the world-wide symbol of the first decade of our present century. The process of global metamorphosis begun by humanity around 1821 reached its point of potential fulfillment then. However, because humanity had been so unsuccessful in wisely, ethically, and spiritually managing the tremendous new energies released after the 1821 conjunction, the opposition of the two "metamorphic" planets brought the beginnings of a vast process of world-wide cleavage and destruction. The rise of Japan, following that of Imperial Germany, and the first (unsuccessful) phase of the Russian Revolution after Russia's defeat in Manchuria, started this destructive process. Our "World Wars" are actually phases in the global "civil war" of a humanity which has clung to the social-political ghosts of "imperialism" and "absolute national sovereignty," allowing these ghosts to poison the minds of those who are slaves of greed and lust for wealth and power, those who are also bound to obsolete institutions, ideologies, and social-religious biases.

The last square aspect of the present Uranus-Neptune cycle (1821-1992) became exact in October, 1953 (with Saturn, moreover, in conjunction to Neptune), and repeated in 1954 and 1955 (with Jupiter then in conjunction to Uranus). Quite obviously, a phase of catharsis (a "purging" of crystallized, dead materials in the social-political body of humankind) is inevitable. Such is the world-wide crisis which our ancestors' and our own follies and "sins" against the Creative Human Spirit have made necessary; and it can take a variety of forms. Humankind will obviously be, and now is being, "tested"; but while the "last quarter" phase of a cycle can be a time of breakdown of old structures no longer useful to life, it is also the time when the *seed* which will be the foundation of the future cycle is taking definite form. Within the period from 1955 to 1992, this "seed" can be expected to grow.

Actually, it is the seed which, as it grows within the fruit, kills the plant which bore it. The future, when ready to be born, makes the past obsolete. This is the meaning of all crises. Those who win are those who go fearlessly toward the future and, while retaining in their own substance and memory the spiritual values produced by the past, do not hesitate to relinquish the outer forms of this past. Every crisis is a death to the "has-been." It is the gestation of what "must be" if the individual, the nation, and the human race are to be consummated. Those who stand in the way of this consummation must suffer and experience tragedy or death — until they accept, welcome, and clearly understand the divine purpose. The individuals who do accept, welcome, and understandingly assimilate the new goals of evolution, for themselves and for humanity, become the "seeds" of the new cycle. They are the "parents" of greater tomorrows, the fountainheads of more abundant living.

20 *The Astrologer's Role as a Consultant*

I remember glancing through a magazine about public relations a few years ago and being attracted by a statement to the effect that, "Ours is the Age of the Consultant." The article went on to say that in a society having become extraordinarily complex and stressing specialization, people confronted with the many problems of business and social organization have found it necessary to periodically turn to trained specialists and advisers in order to get a clearer picture of these problems, to sharpen their skills, or merely to feel reassured that they are taking the right approach.

What is a fact in the business world, or in that infinitely hazardous business which is government and diplomacy, is also true where the private lives of modern men and women are concerned. Everywhere, confused and harassed individuals are wending their ways to the offices of "consultants" — be they psychologists, health food specialists, marriage counselors, mediums or clairvoyants, or astrologers. People need advice now more acutely than when they were led to the confessional, the pastor, or the family doctor of olden days. They ask for this advice in a much more precise, more "scientific" way than ever before — that is to say, not on the basis of general ethical, religious, hygienic principles, but in terms of clear-cut indications as to how they can acquire a reliable technique for the solution of their problems. The huge success of the "how to" books is another aspect of this craving for technical information; but book knowledge rarely seems to completely take the place of the consultant, for people begin to realize that the basic problem behind all other problems is *themselves;* and no one can truly and objectively know oneself except in the mirror of someone else's eyes and mind. Books are too full of ink to reflect the image of the reader to his anxious gaze!

There are evidently all sorts of consultants; and there is a great difference between the business specialist being consulted by an executive, the eminent scientist asked to advise on the building of a complex physics apparatus, and the professional astrologer or the renowned clairvoyant to whom a person unable to successfully meet special problems of inter-personal relationship comes for advice, in the hope that some pleasurable prognostication may be made. Nevertheless, there are basic factors in any form of consultation which should be considered if the work of the consultant is to be truly successful — not only at the superficial level of precise advice, but at the deeper psychological level of the *effect of the consultation upon the person seeking advice*. That person presumably needs, in most cases, more precise information; but he or she very often needs more; that is, he or she needs to be reassured and — after leaving the consultant — to feel better able to handle problems in general. In other words, the consultant should be able to give not only information — a book or machine can do that — but self-confidence as well. Not all consultants do that; and many do just the opposite.

Some years ago, a Red Cross planning committee came up with eight qualifications defining the consultant and the essential character of his function. The consultant is a person: (1) who is sought after for help; (2) who helps others to help themselves; (3) who has a broad knowledge and an objective point of view; (4) who has specialized training and skill; (5) who is adept at creating a climate for desiring help; (6) whose advice may be either accepted or rejected; (7) who is neither a doer nor an operator; (8) who must have adequate time to do an educational job. These specifications apply remarkably well to the person who is being consulted on the basis of his astrological knowledge and interpretive skill.

As I have pointed out for many years, natal astrology is a technique which enables human beings to obtain a specific kind of help in the solution of problems which they cannot, unaided and by rational methods, *both* fully understand and solve. But the word "problem" can have an ambiguous meaning. As I am using it here, it refers to any situation in which the elements are unclear, confusing, and conflict-generating — a situation which seems to require a decision, yet which does not provide adequate knowledge upon which this decision could logically be based. A sound decision demands that we objectively understand the causes of the situation facing us; and we can only make a significant and "free" choice if we have adequate grounds for judgment and evaluation. Yet in life we very often have to take a new step without having any rational way of knowing what other people involved in it will or can do, what may occur in the near future in our environment, or even how we ourselves will react when confronted with the results generated directly or indirectly by our actions. This is, of course, what makes the concept of "free choice" quite ambiguous.

Are you "free" to decide when there is no normal way of knowing the causes of the situation requiring a choice, or the results of the possible choices? The animal in the natural state usually chooses the right way to react on the basis of compulsive instincts. Humans have developed intelligence at the expense of at least some of our instincts. But intelligence needs to have conscious grounds for its judgments, and so many times there are no such grounds; and the famous "voice of intuition" is not reliable, for it may be the voice of something else – a psychological complex, a fear, laziness, or even a real "spook" (a pressure exerted by some psychic entity, or "hidden persuader"). Where intelligence cannot provide us with the logical grounds which we need for a deliberate decision, astrology can come to our help – and we indeed need help! But there is help and *help!* We can become irrationally and compulsively bound to the helper, or we can be helped to help ourselves. In the first instance, we have passively accepted the dictates of an authoritative source of information which has usurped our sacred human prerogative of decision making; in the second case, we have been given a new perspective, a new way of looking at our problems, and some grounds upon which we can now make a decision – an objective, conscious, and informed decision.

There are astrologers – many of them – who, together with various types of "inspired" mediums and "miracle workers," are only too willing to announce what is going to happen, what course of action to take, whether this is good or bad for you, etc. People run to them, for most human beings are glad to accept "authority" and "to know the Truth" (with a capital "T"). Other astrologers are real *consultants;* they have "a broad knowledge and objective point of view" as well as "specialized training and skill"; but they do not intend to be "doer" or "operator." They establish a truly consultative relationship with their clients so that whatever advice is given "may be either accepted or rejected." The only thing they insist upon – or *should* insist upon if it is feasible (which is not often the case) – is that they "must have adequate time to do an educational job," for an astrological consultation should be a form of education and, therefore, should be a repeated experience, for there is no education without repetition. What kind of education can it be? One in which a person learns to be objective toward his own total lifespan and becomes aware of the basic rhythms of his or her existence as an individual person. These rhythms can be seen operating through the years of life which have gone by; they should be carefully studied. It is only on the basis of *a vivid understanding of the past* that one can orient the activities immediately ahead toward a constructive future in which the individual's innate potential can be more fully and harmoniously *actualized.*

The astrologer cannot predict the *precise* future events of an individual's life; if he could, astrology would be baneful and destructive of the person's integrity. No one can precisely predict such *individual* events, not even God; and whenever there are stories of such predictions, very basic factors are not mentioned. For instance, in the case of the famous ancient astrological books of India in which the exact destinies of many people, even some born today, were apparently written down many centuries ago, only a person passing rigid and selective tests was allowed to hear the prophecies for his day of birth. In other words, he, out of thousands of persons born on that day, had to prove himself to be the one fitting this specific archetypal pattern of soul experience in terms of particular events. Astrology can usually reveal the structuring pattern of the life of an individual, the basic rhythm (or "form") of the process of existence from birth to death; but if a *structure* is determined, this does not mean that the actual existential *events* which fill in this basic structure are also predetermined. A glass can contain delicious wine or poison; both substances are shaped by the form of the glass. Everyone has a basic structure of being; it is the pattern of his individual selfhood. It is also his "destiny" — if by destiny we mean the schedule according to which what was potential at birth may become actualized during the lifetime; and I said "may" because many people during their lifetime actualize only a fraction of their innate potentialities.

Astrology tells you what "may" be actualized, not what "will" happen, but because it can reveal the inherent *structural order* of an individual's selfhood, it can "educate" this individual in meeting the confrontations of his everyday life with orderliness and objectivity — that is, in terms of his whole potential of being, in terms of what Zen calls his "fundamental nature." The true astrologer is a specialist in structural values concerning personality unfoldment, a specialist in human destiny. He can be consulted on all matters affecting the actualization of an individual's potential — that is, on all matters referring to the question: "How can I *become* what I innately *am* as an organic whole of human existence?" He can, theoretically at least, answer such a question and its many ramifications *as a consultant.* But as a consultant, he cannot be expected to tell his client what will happen next month or next year or what he must do; this would be the province of a soothsayer or an oracle. The distinction is most important and should be made very clear in order to avoid deception and illusions.

An astrological consultant, I repeat, should have a broad knowledge of human nature, of the social conditions in his client's environment; he should have an objective point of view — i.e., an approach not biased by his own subjective attitude and his personal biases. Of course, he should also have training and skill. He ought to realize a number of basic facts which are inherent in his role as a consultant. The first of these facts is that, even if the client trusts his competence, he may still feel that the consultant cannot put himself in his (the client's) place. An objective approach always appears somewhat suspicious and beside the point to someone subjectively and emotionally involved in a deeply upsetting situation. The astrological consultant may have to go back to somewhat similar issues in his client's past, and, as a keen psychologist, to show him what were the inner or outer results of the unsuccessfully met past crises. He must prove to his client that he has "empathy" with him, that he can "feel with" the client's deepest emotions, thereby creating an atmosphere of confidence at a more than technical level — that is, at a human level.

The consultant also has to realize that his client will tend to resist any suggestion implying a basic change of attitude on the client's part. It is very human indeed to want situations changed, provided *we* do not have to change. This is where a broad picture of the client's life as a whole, with its basic rhythms of development and its cycles (planetary transits, progressed lunation cycle, and numerological cycles like the fundamental 7-year and 28-year cycles), should be of the greatest importance. A "person" does not want to change because he is hypnotized by the present moment. But this *"now situation"* has no deep meaning in terms of the individual self of the client until it is referred to the structure and rhythmic development of his whole life. A young girl's first menstruation would be a devastating experience if she were not told that it is a phase of the total development of her body and of her life as a woman-mother-to-be. The "present" is but a fleeting phase of cyclic time; it acquires meaning only when it is placed within the cyclic process of a whole life, from birth to death — and, theoretically, even beyond birth and death if reincarnation is a fact one can live by intelligently and knowingly.

"Why does this happen *to me?*" questions the harassed client. What can the consultant tell him that will mean anything unless he can point to the place and function this harrowing experience occupies and fulfills within the total life scheme of actualization of the birth potential? To say, "Oh yes, Saturn is now moving over your Venus square Mars," is no consolation. Rather, it gives a more objective, inescapable, and frightening character to the situation. If Saturn is involved, let the consultant study with his client the entire cycle of this planet, all the aspects the planet makes, the motion through one house after another; above all, let the consultant picture the *total* transit and progression situation of the chart and not emphasize only one apparently disturbing aspect. All planets are always active, whether there are exact aspects or not. What matters is the *total interplay of their cyclic motions* at any time in relation to the character of the natal chart.

Another point which needs to be emphasized in the client-consultant relationship is the usual eagerness of the client to discover a solution to his problem or problems *at once.* The desire for quick results and easy solutions is the bane of modern life. The factor of time is rarely considered by anyone in trouble in our society, which has lost touch with the basic rhythms of seasonal life and slow biological unfoldment through the years. Because we all feel that we live through a period of enormously accelerated change and in a crisis of transition between two eras, we have become impatient with delays and unaware of the need for a process of healing and "redemption" which, if it is healthy, must begin at the deepest layer of the substance of the mind of humanity as a whole and only slowly reach the surface. The mind of humanity has suffered grievous wounds during the last two millennia – the period during which humanity has been growing up from the old tribal stage of bondage to the soil, traditions, and ideals of exclusivism – up to a still dimly understood state of planetwide organization and harmonious cooperation. Likewise, the psyches of grown-up clients are usually twisted or scarred by old complexes, memories, and fears when the astrological consultant or the psychologist is asked for a solution to an especially poignant, more recent problem.

Modern persons have become accustomed to consider psychoanalysis or psychiatric healing a long and costly process; but they still expect astrological consultants to bring them solace, hope, and faith in themselves in an hour or two. The consultants are under pressure to immediately discover magical factors which will free the mind from anxiety and cause everything to turn out well – *very soon.* This is, of course, an impossible situation; it arises from the fact that most people still consider astrology a mysterious art able to cure all kinds of anxieties and uncertainties. It is useless to ask this of astrology. Astrology is a technique of understanding and a discipline of thought, thanks to which a person can get a new outlook on his entire life and a more objective and structured understanding of the place and function of his most important life experiences and crises. Astrology can transform a seemingly meaningless crisis into a process of catharsis, a prelude to rebirth at a higher, more inclusive level of existence. It can tell whether a client is at the beginning, middle, or end of certain cycles – and whether or not it is wise to push ahead at once or to wait for a more opportune and significant time.

It is not the task of the astrological consultant, or any other type of consultant, to make decisions for his client. The consultant is essentially an educator and adviser; he should assist his client – perhaps even train him – in acquiring a new approach to life problems and especially to the problem that the client himself presents in his contacts with other people and social traditions. Of course, such assistance requires that the astrologer and the client truly communicate with each other; and for the astrologer to communicate what he sees in the relevant astrological charts is often very difficult. It is difficult because astrology is a special language, whose inclusive symbols cannot easily be translated into the ordinary language of words which have a more or less precise and concrete meaning familiar to the client. The astrological language is even more difficult to understand for academically trained scientists because it is a language whose words (planets, signs, houses, nodes, etc.) can refer to many different levels of significance and may have, in many cases, either a positive or negative meaning. Thus, what the astrological consultant may "feel" about his client's situation, as pictured by the charts in front of him, can often not be stated in terms of definite and concrete actions. In this respect, the astrologer's position is similar to that of the genuine clairvoyant who, when consulted about some matter, "sees" a symbol (or a symbolical scene) which he or she knows represents the solution of the real problem. But the real problem is not always the problem which the client tells about, and the solution expressed in the symbol may not be easy to put into words which would *communicate to the client* what the real meaning of the situation is.

This, however, is what can occur in any consultation – medical, psychological, astrological, sociological – where questions are raised referring to individual persons and interpersonal relationships; in such areas of human experience, levels of reality interpenetrate and conscious factors are rarely entirely separate from unconscious or semi-conscious drives, hopes, and fears. This is what makes these professions fascinating and, at the same time, dangerous. They require that the consultant have not only a broad scope of knowledge of human nature and technical skill, but also the capacity to *resonate* in sympathetic vibration with the client so that the deeper advice he can give will be conveyed without words – i.e., by the sheer contagion of his presence and of what he stands for. This is a big order. Very few consultants can fill it; but these few are not always the most sought after because what the great majority of people want are clear-cut solutions and easily worked out recipies formulated in simple terms which their ego-minds can quickly grasp – and usually forget or fail to act upon because of sheer laziness or indifference! There is a time for everything. A consultant should have an accurate sense of timing. Some things can be said at the end of an interview which would be detrimental at the beginning. Here again, the astrological consultant is usually most seriously handicapped by the traditional form of the relationship between astrologer and client — one fairly brief interview during which the client expects everything to be said.

A new type of relationship is badly needed today — indeed, a new approach to astrology. The present-day astrologer's concern about "raising" astrology to the acceptable level of a "science" by means of statistics and other analytical tools worshiped in our official "factories of knowledge" (universities) will not produce a more constructive approach to the problems faced by the astrological consultant in relation to clients. It is more likely to make such a relationship less effectual because, in order to be really effectual, it must be a relationship of person to person — and science does not deal with *individual cases*, but with *statistical averages*. Science does not deal with human values, but a person comes to an astrological consultant asking for help. He always unconsciously asks for help even if he is *consciously* motivated by curiosity. He comes for help with his sense of unique individual selfhood, even if his stated problem seems a common one; and it is with this sense of self that the consultant must deal. For we are all our own most basic problem; and astrology should help us meet it objectively and serenely, without evasion and without the sense of insecurity that our intellectual ego can generate.

★   ★   ★   ★   ★